Immersion Education

BILINGUAL EDUCATION & BILINGUALISM
Series Editors: Nancy H. Hornberger *(University of Pennsylvania, USA)* and **Wayne E. Wright** *(Purdue University, USA)*

Bilingual Education and Bilingualism is an international, multidisciplinary series publishing research on the philosophy, politics, policy, provision and practice of language planning, Indigenous and minority language education, multilingualism, multiculturalism, biliteracy, bilingualism and bilingual education. The series aims to mirror current debates and discussions. New proposals for single-authored, multiple-authored, or edited books in the series are warmly welcomed, in any of the following categories or others authors may propose: overview or introductory texts; course readers or general reference texts; focus books on particular multilingual education program types; school-based case studies; national case studies; collected cases with a clear programmatic or conceptual theme; and professional education manuals.

All books in this series are externally peer-reviewed.

Full details of all the books in this series and of all our other publications can be found on http://www.multilingual-matters.com, or by writing to Multilingual Matters, St Nicholas House, 31-34 High Street, Bristol BS1 2AW, UK.

BILINGUAL EDUCATION & BILINGUALISM: 111

Immersion Education

Lessons from a Minority Language Context

Pádraig Ó Duibhir

MULTILINGUAL MATTERS
Bristol • Blue Ridge Summit

DOI https://doi.org/10.21832/ODUIBH9832
Library of Congress Cataloging in Publication Data
A catalog record for this book is available from the Library of Congress.
Names: Ó Duibhir, Pádraig, author.
Title: Immersion Education: Lessons from a Minority Language Context/ Pádraig Ó Duibhir.
Description: Bristol; Blue Ridge Summit: Multilingual Matters, [2018] | Series: Bilingual Education & Bilingualism: 111 | Includes bibliographical references and index.
Identifiers: LCCN 2017061007 | ISBN 9781783099832 (hbk : alk. paper) | ISBN 9781783099856 (epub) | ISBN 9781783099863 (kindle)
Subjects: LCSH: Immersion method (Language teaching) | Concentrated study. | Irish language—Study and teaching—English speakers. | Language and education—Ireland. | Language policy—Ireland. | Education, Bilingual—Ireland.
Classification: LCC P53.44 .O4 2018 | DDC 491.6/282421—dc23 LC record available at https://lccn.loc.gov/2017061007

British Library Cataloguing in Publication Data
A catalogue entry for this book is available from the British Library.

ISBN-13: 978-1-78309-983-2 (hbk)

Multilingual Matters
UK: St Nicholas House, 31-34 High Street, Bristol BS1 2AW, UK.
USA: NBN, Blue Ridge Summit, PA, USA.

Website: www.multilingual-matters.com
Twitter: Multi_Ling_Mat
Facebook: https://www.facebook.com/multilingualmatters
Blog: www.channelviewpublications.wordpress.com

Copyright © 2018 Pádraig Ó Duibhir.

All rights reserved. No part of this work may be reproduced in any form or by any means without permission in writing from the publisher.

The policy of Multilingual Matters/Channel View Publications is to use papers that are natural, renewable and recyclable products, made from wood grown in sustainable forests. In the manufacturing process of our books, and to further support our policy, preference is given to printers that have FSC and PEFC Chain of Custody certification. The FSC and/or PEFC logos will appear on those books where full certification has been granted to the printer concerned.

Typeset by Deanta Global Publishing Services Limited.
Printed and bound in the UK by the CPI Books Group Ltd.
Printed and bound in the US by Edwards Brothers Malloy, Inc.

Contents

Preface		vii
1	Introduction	1
	Setting the Context	1
	Aims of this Volume	4
	Structure of this Volume	6
2	Immersion Education in Ireland: Origins and Current Context	9
	Introduction	9
	Geographical and Political Context	9
	The Irish Language in Education	11
	Irish-Medium Schools Since the 1970s	15
	The Sociolinguistic Context of Irish Immersion Education	20
3	Language Learning in Immersion Education in Ireland and Internationally	26
	Second Language Learning	26
	Sociocultural Theory and Second Language Learning	33
	Research and Pedagogy in Immersion Education	46
	Research on the Acquisition of Irish as a Second Language	56
	Summary	65
4	Design of Studies	67
	Introduction	67
	Corpus-Based Studies	67
	Other Studies	73
	Conclusion	76
5	An Analysis of a Corpus of the Spoken Irish of All-Irish Pupils	77
	Corpus Analysis	77
	Analysis of Corpus for the Presence of Errors	80
	Code-Mixing and Code-Switching	82
	General Use of English Words	84

	Layout of Glosses	84
	Pupil–Pupil Exchanges: Language-Related Episodes	85
	Syntactic and Morphological Features of Irish	86
	Syntactic and Lexical Features of All-Irish Pupils' Irish	90
	Use of Interrogative Pronouns *Cad*, *Cad é* and *Céard*	105
	Pupils' Use of the Pronoun *é* 'it'	107
	Discussion	110
6	Pupils' Reflections on Their Communicative Performance in Irish	115
	Introduction	115
	Stimulated Recall Activity	115
	Phase 1: Pupils' Perceptions of the Quality of Their Irish	116
	Phase 2: Correction of Mistakes Following Reflection on Output	118
	Phase 3: Pupils' Insights into the Inaccurate Features of Their Irish Output	126
	Discussion and Conclusions	135
7	Use of Irish Outside the Classroom	139
	Introduction	139
	Study Design	142
	Results	143
	Discussion	150
8	Principal and Class Teacher Interviews to Explore Pupils' Proficiency in Spoken Irish or French	153
	Introduction	153
	Design	154
	Results	156
	Discussion	168
9	Discussion	171
	Conclusions	173
	Pedagogical Practice	174
	Further Research	176
References		178
Appendix A: Pupil Questionnaire – Attitude/Motivation Test Battery (AMTB)		194
Appendix B: Interview Schedule for Irish/French Immersion Teachers		199
Index		201

Preface

When I reached the age of four and it was time for me to start school, my parents discovered to their dismay that places in the local school were oversubscribed and there was no room for me. Fortunately, there were places available in an all-Irish school close by and I attended that school for just three years before transferring to an English-medium school. This proved to be a formative experience for me that gave me not only an excellent basic competence in Irish but also an interest in and enthusiasm for the language that I have carried throughout my personal and professional life.

Having gained a qualification as a primary school teacher and taught for a number of years in a school where Irish was a core subject, I got the opportunity in 1985 to teach in a newly established all-Irish school. *Scoil Chaitlín Maude* was established as part of a relatively new vibrant movement where parents were leading the demand for education through the medium of Irish. During 14 exciting years as a teacher and principal I faced many challenges with excellent colleagues in meeting the educational needs of the pupils. There was a dearth of policies, guidelines, materials and resources that we now take for granted to guide us and aid us in our work in immersion education. As teachers, we created all of these things incrementally, drawing encouragement from colleagues in other all-Irish schools. It would be fair to say that our pedagogy was very much practice driven rather than research driven.

The all-Irish school movement has continued to grow from strength to strength since that time. Part of the strengthening of the sector has been the greater body of research that now informs practice. One of the frustrations for me and my colleagues as teachers was the non-target-like output of our pupils' Irish despite up to 6000 hours contact with the language in primary school. This output manifested itself in particular in deviations in terms of sentence structure and idiomatic phrases. We tried many strategies to address these issues, such as focus on form lessons, corrective feedback and incentives. Our interventions appeared to have only limited success. Among my motivations in subsequently becoming a teacher educator was the desire to better prepare teachers for teaching through the medium of Irish and to provide a greater evidence base for this work. If teaching is to be successful it should align as far as possible with the way that children learn. One of the aims of this volume is to help immersion educators to gain a greater understanding of how young immersion learners learn and acquire the target language taking account of in-class and out-of-class factors.

As a parent in an Irish-speaking home, I was grateful for the support we received from the all-Irish schools that my children attended in enriching their language acquisition. I observed that many of their friends who visited our home were happy to converse in Irish with me but not with one another. As my children have left school and grown into adulthood, the only domain in which they generally have opportunities to speak Irish is at home. Despite the fact that many of their friends received all their primary and post-primary education through Irish, they seldom communicate with one another through Irish. It appears that the speaking of Irish has not been normalised as their language of socialisation.

Scoil Chaitlín Maude has reached the stage in its development where former pupils now send their children as pupils. Very few of these former pupils speak Irish as their main language in conversations with their children at home. Nonetheless, they are content for their children to receive an Irish-medium education which will ensure that the children will have at least a basic or adequate ability to speak Irish.

These observations have prompted me to ask the following questions: Are all-Irish schools successful in educating pupils to become competent Irish speakers? If so, how might this language competence be converted to active bilingualism in the wider community beyond the school gates? There seems to be an assumption in the discourse on language revitalisation in Ireland that if only the teachers had better competency in Irish and if the schools could teach Irish more effectively, we would somehow become a bilingual society. Those of us who work in the immersion sector realise that language planning is much more complicated than that. Success in converting minority language competence acquired in an education context to societal use has been very limited, particularly in the absence of a critical mass of speakers.

The personal experiences and professional challenges outlined here, prompted me to explore these questions and to undertake the studies reported in this volume. I hope that this body of research will prompt debate and discourse, and inform the future direction of immersion education in Ireland and internationally.

As the studies in this volume were conducted over a number of years, I owe a debt of gratitude to many people. It would not have been possible to conduct the research without the cooperation and participation of pupils, teachers and parents in many Irish-medium schools throughout Ireland who gave generously of their time. I am deeply grateful to them for all I learned from them. John Harris, TCD, was my doctoral supervisor and I benefited enormously from his expert knowledge, research experience and ongoing guidance and encouragement in carrying out much of the research presented here. Much of the early research presented in this volume was inspired by the work of Merrill Swain, Sharon Lapkin and Jim Cummins of the Ontario Institute for Studies in Education. I greatly appreciate the advice and support that I received from Merrill, Sharon, Jim, the Toronto District School Board and the Ottawa Carleton District School Board in conducting interviews with teachers in Toronto and Ottawa. I would also like to thank the teachers for giving so generously of their time and insights. The time spent in Ontario would not have been possible without the accommodation provided by John O'Dwyer.

The financial support and encouragement of *An Chomhairle um Oideachas Gaeltachta agus Gaelscolaíochta* and Muireann Ní Mhóráin is greatly appreciated. The governing body and research committee of St Patrick's College, DCU, also provided financial support which was instrumental in enabling me to complete many of the studies. I am grateful to Anne Looney, Daire Keogh, Fionnuala Waldron, James Kelly, Mary Shine Thompson and Pauric Travers in their various senior management roles in St Patrick's College and DCU for their support and encouragement. A research grant from the Standing Conference on Teacher Education, North and South, enabled me to extend the original corpus study to Northern Ireland with the collaboration of Jill Garland. I also drew on funding from *Gaelscoileanna* and *An Coiste Seasta Thuaidh Theas ar Ghaeloideachas*.

My colleagues in *Teagasc na Gaeilge* (Teaching of Irish), DCU, Lorraine Ní Gháirbhith, Máire Ní Bhaoill and Nóirín Ní Nuadháin, provided invaluable support, advice and motivation to continue with my research and to free me from teaching at critical times. I draw on data from various studies in this volume, some that I conducted myself and other in collaboration with co-researchers. I greatly value the contributions of Aisling Ní Dhiorbháin, Gabrielle NigUidhir, Laoise Ní Thuairisg, Jude Cosgrove and Seán Ó Cathalláin to those studies. I would like to thank Matthew Stout for drawing the map of Ireland and Deirdre Ní Chaomhánaigh and Lisa Chamard for assistance with transcription and data entry. Laoise Ní Thuairisg read early drafts of the manuscript and her insightful feedback was instrumental in bringing sharper focus and coherence to the manuscript.

Finally, my wife Pauline, has been unconditionally supportive over many years. Without her patience and tolerance over a long number of years, I would not have been able to bring much of this research to publication. Her proof reading and insightful comments as a critical friend were immensely helpful. I hope to be able to return her love and dedication in years to come. *Míle buíochas a ghrá*. My children Tríona, Caoimhe and Conall for their understanding when I was not available. May they continue to have opportunities to speak Irish to a new generation. *Gura fada buan sibh!*

1 Introduction

Setting the Context

The education system was given a central role in the Irish language revitalisation policy of the Irish Free State when it was founded in 1922. One of the key policy initiatives at that time was to introduce Irish-medium education wherever there were teachers qualified and competent to teach through the medium of Irish. The objective of this policy was to educate a bilingual generation of children who would go on to speak Irish and over time revitalise the Irish language. This early policy initiative has resulted in a long tradition of Irish-medium education in Ireland. There have been periods of growth and decline in the number of schools teaching through the medium of Irish during the intervening years. The last 40 years have seen a period of sustained growth in the number of all-Irish[1] schools, driven in the main this time by parental demand rather than by state initiative. Currently, there are 43,130 (7.97%) primary pupils (aged 4–12 years) receiving their education through Irish in the Republic of Ireland (RoI) with a further 5,854 (3.41%) in Northern Ireland, giving an overall figure of 48,984 (6.87%) for the island of Ireland (www.gaelscoileanna.ie). The remainder of pupils attend mainstream English-medium schools and learn Irish as a core subject. This all-Irish school movement is viewed by many as one of the most positive enterprises in language promotion in the history of the state (Council of Europe, 2008). Despite this growth in interest and popularity, objective evidence about the proficiency in Irish of the pupils who participate in these programmes is sparse and the contribution of this movement in enhancing the number of people using Irish on a daily basis outside of the school environment has not been adequately explored.

Research findings from a number of studies by Harris (1984) and Harris *et al*. (2006) that focused on all-Irish primary school pupils demonstrated the very positive impact of Irish language immersion. These studies indicate that all-Irish pupils significantly outperform their peers in English-medium schools in terms of their ability in Irish. This is not surprising given that pupils in all-Irish schools are exposed to approximately 6000 hours' instruction through the medium of Irish in primary school compared to just under 900 hours of Irish instruction in English-medium schools. Systematic investigation of immersion pupils' Irish and the extent to which it approaches native speaker norms has been limited. Concern has been expressed from time to time about the non-target-like nature of pupils' spoken Irish (Mac Corraidh, 2013; National Council for Curriculum and Assessment, 2006). It has been suggested that pupils speak a school dialect which is closer to English than Irish in syntactic terms (Nic Pháidín, 2003). The evidence, however, is largely anecdotal and it is not known to what extent the features of the pupils' Irish are linked to immersion specifically or to the nature of the larger sociolinguistic context within which schools operate. Notwithstanding the non-target-like nature of the pupils' Irish, there is evidence that immersion pupils achieve high levels of competence in Irish, at least compared to English-medium schools, by the end of their post-primary education (Murtagh, 2006) having participated in up to 14 years of an immersion programme. These outcomes mirror experiences in other immersion contexts, including dual-language contexts, throughout the world.

While one kind of Irish-medium school has been implicitly referred to, in reality it is necessary to distinguish between two types of Irish-medium school. The first type are Gaeltacht schools which exist solely in geographic bilingual areas where Irish is the community language for an ever-decreasing proportion of the population. These areas are mainly located along the western and south-western seaboard. The second type is all-Irish immersion schools outside the Gaeltacht where the vast majority of pupils have English as their home language. All-Irish schools are located outside the Gaeltacht areas and the vast majority of pupils are monolingual English speakers when they start school. The programme provided in all-Irish schools can be described as early immersion, where the pupils are immersed in Irish, their second language (L2), from their first day in school. It is the language acquisition of the pupils in this latter type of Irish-medium school outside the Gaeltacht that is the principal focus of this volume. English dominates the lives of these pupils and their contact with Irish is largely confined to the school. Their sociolinguistic background is similar in many respects to that of French immersion pupils in Canada or to Gaelic immersion pupils in Scotland.

A number of comprehensive studies of the Gaeltacht in Ireland have shown that these areas are becoming increasingly bilingual and that the number of native Irish-speaking children in Gaeltacht schools has declined (Mac Donnacha et al., 2005). There are also fewer families in Gaeltacht areas transmitting the language to the next generation (Ó Giollagáin et al., 2007; Ó hIfearnáin, 2007; Péterváry et al., 2014). Ó hÉallaithe (2010) estimated that 2326 (30%) such families were transmitting Irish to their children and Ó Broin (2014) suggested that there might be up to 600 families outside the Gaeltacht raising their children through Irish. The potential language revitalisation role played by all-Irish schools is all the more critical in light of this lack of transmission. This is not to suggest that former pupils of all-Irish schools are the only source of competent bilinguals. Other schools, comprising over 90% of all schools, have a critical role to play also. As Ó Riagáin (1997) argued, the education system in general in Ireland and the immersion schools in particular need to produce substantial numbers of competent bilinguals to compensate for the insufficient rate of intergenerational transmission. However, producing competent bilinguals does not necessarily guarantee language revitalisation (Baker, 2006) as linguistic competence may not transfer beyond the classroom. Experience over the last 90 years in Ireland bears this out where Irish, learned in a classroom, is not used widely in everyday life nor is there evidence of an increase in intergenerational transmission.

The government's 20-Year Strategy for Irish (Government of Ireland, 2010) recognises the roles of capacity, opportunity and desire (Grin, 2003) to speak Irish in its revitalisation efforts. These three interacting factors underpin the studies reported in this volume. Education contexts tend to address language capacity or competency, but have limited influence on opportunity and desire. In investigating all-Irish pupil competence, I am very aware that opportunities for pupils to use Irish outside the school context impact, not only on their future use of Irish, but also on their desire to learn and use Irish in the present. There is some evidence that all-Irish schools are successful 'in introducing students to Irish language-speaking networks that facilitate maintenance and use of Irish after they leave school' (Murtagh, 2007: 450). The fact that all-Irish schools are producing increasing numbers of competent bilinguals gives them a potentially critical role in the revitalisation of Irish (Harris, 2007).

An important issue arising from this level of success in producing competent bilinguals is the extent to which the Irish language skills acquired by these pupils prepare them for participation in the Irish language speech community (Ó Laoire, 2000). The greater the level of competence that pupils have in speaking Irish, the greater the likelihood that they will participate in Irish-speaking networks in the future (Ó Riagáin et al., 2007). This was borne out in the latest survey of attitudes towards the Irish language where those with higher proficiency levels in Irish were more likely to speak Irish (Darmody & Daly, 2015). For those who go on to participate in Irish-speaking networks and to set up Irish-speaking families, a high standard of Irish is critical in my view because these speakers have the potential to influence the evolving character of the language. If one subscribes to the view that new speakers of Irish and native speakers need to be mutually intelligible, then opportunities for new speakers to acquire a more native-like form are diminishing due to the decline in the number of native speakers.

An alternative view is that the Irish language may evolve to a post-traditional form, a pidgin or simplified variety may emerge. Research in other jurisdictions has compared immersion pupils' language with that of native speakers, for example, Basque (Cenoz & Gorter, 2017), French (Lyster, 2007), Swedish (Buss, 2002) and Welsh (Thomas & Gathercole, 2007). The evidence suggests that immersion schools tend to produce speakers who speak a 'school code' that deviates from native speaker norms. If this is the case in Ireland, it is likely that the variety of Irish spoken by these new speakers will be different from traditional speakers of the language and the authenticity of this variety will be contested unless it replaces the traditional variety in the future (Romaine, 2006). Indeed, evidence is emerging of new speakers of Irish who hold negative views of their fluency and this inhibits their use of Irish especially with more proficient speakers or native speakers (Walsh & O'Rourke, 2015).

Aims of this Volume

The principal aim of this volume is to synthesise a number of studies that I undertook alone or with colleagues which examine the proficiency in Irish of pupils in all-Irish schools and the attitudes of pupils, their parents and their teachers to proficiency and language use inside and outside the classroom. The studies were carried out over an eight-year period from 2007 to 2014 and are described in detail in Chapter 4. Briefly, the first two studies were corpus-based studies of all-Irish primary school pupil speech. The first study I undertook was in the RoI and the second extended this research with the assistance of a colleague, Jill Garland, to Northern Ireland. In these studies, I recorded immersion pupils spoken language, surveyed their attitudes to learning and using Irish and interviewed their teachers to ascertain their attitudes to the pupils' linguistic proficiency. Anecdotal evidence indicated that the Irish spoken by all-Irish pupils contains many non-target-like features. A comprehensive analysis of the pupils' Irish would help to establish if this is the case and to inform teachers of precisely which features are not being mastered after almost eight years of immersion. There are many factors that potentially contribute to a lack of grammatical accuracy in pupils' speech, including the nature of the immediate immersion context, the pupils' attitude and motivation to learn Irish, their lack of exposure to Irish outside the school and the pedagogical approach adopted in schools. In order to gain insights into these issues, the first two studies reported in this volume set out to compile a corpus of all-Irish pupils' speech and to analyse it.

In the third study, I investigated the attitudes of French immersion teachers towards the proficiency in French of their students in Grades 6–8 in Toronto and Ottawa and compared these to the views of Irish immersion primary schoolteachers. In the fourth study, I examined, with colleagues Gabrielle NigUidhir, Seán Ó Cathalláin and Laoise Ní Thuairisg, the attitudes and motivation of primary and post-primary all-Irish students to Irish and their use of Irish outside the classroom. I also sought to establish the degree to which their parents used Irish with the pupils. In synthesising these studies and drawing on other sources in the research literature, this volume offers the reader an in-depth description of the current state of Irish language proficiency in immersion education in Ireland and places the findings in the context of other one-way immersion programmes internationally with a particular focus on minority language settings. Such a description does not currently exist, so this volume will help to inform future teacher education strategies and provide a valuable resource to immersion teachers, teacher education students, graduate students and second language acquisition (SLA) researchers both nationally and internationally.

The creation of a corpus of Irish immersion pupil language and its subsequent analysis identifies for teachers the aspects of Irish that will not be acquired implicitly by pupils without explicit attention to form. Immersion programmes are often promoted to parents as delivering 'two for one'. The implied message being that an L2 is acquired as content is taught through the L2 and at no cost to first language (L1) attainment. While there is some truth in this statement, nothing comes free as Lyster (2011) reminds us. A large degree of attention needs to be placed on form in the L2 if a degree of grammatical accuracy is to be acquired. The language mix in Irish immersion schools differs from other immersion contexts in so far as all subjects, except English language arts, are taught through the medium of Irish. After an initial total immersion phase, this model continues throughout all-Irish schooling to the final grades of post-primary education, representing approximately 85% of instructional time. This contrasts with the majority of one-way immersion programmes which gradually increase instruction through the L1 moving to a 50:50 model in senior grades of primary school. The vast majority of all-Irish schools are immersion centres as opposed to immersion tracks, streams or units. This enables all-Irish schools to operate entirely through the medium of Irish with pupils expected to speak Irish at all times including break-time in the playground. This environment provides additional opportunities for output in the target language which might aid acquisition. The fact that the vast majority of all-Irish schools are stand-alone immersion centres enables the pupils to have communicative opportunities outside of the classroom but within the school. It is interesting to explore the extent to which these opportunities are availed of by the pupils. As all subjects, other than English language arts, are taught through the medium of Irish, the pupils require a good command of Irish in order to access all curriculum subjects. Leaving aside the desire to increase the use of Irish in society, I believe that this factor of pupils accessing the curriculum requires that we enable them to attain a high level of proficiency in Irish. This proficiency encompasses oral and written production that approximates target-like norms in terms of morphology and syntax. Much of the focus in the examination of immersion pupils' Irish in this volume is on morphology and syntax. In the corpus analysis, I investigate the linguistic errors made by the pupils and refer to their linguistic accuracy. In doing so, it is not my intention to reduce the issue to one of merely identifying the deficits in pupils' language. My concern is that their language proficiency may possibly be inadequate for the ultimate purposes of the endeavour which I believe are twofold:

(i) to experience a high-quality education in its broadest sense and (ii) to have sufficient competency in Irish and a desire to speak it when opportunities arise outside of the school context.

This leads me to the secondary aim of this volume which is to examine the potential for all-Irish school pupils to become active users of Irish outside the school environment and to increase the use of Irish in society. Ireland has a long history of immersion education. The initial immersion model used a top-down approach and was driven by the state. It enjoyed some success initially, but later lost the confidence of teachers, parents and the general public. With the more recent parent-led immersion model, one might expect parents to exercise a good deal of agency in relation to their own and their children's use of Irish in the home in particular. However, we do not know to what extent parents use the Irish that they themselves learned in school with their children.

Structure of this Volume

The studies in this volume adopt a broad-based approach and examine the variety of Irish spoken by the pupils, the extent to which the Irish spoken deviates from native speaker norms, the degree to which pupils are aware of and attempt to acquire a native-like variety and the extent to which issues of identity and motivation are involved.

The volume is set out in nine chapters. This introductory chapter gives a brief overview of the current state of the Irish language in order to place the studies in context and set out their aims. Further information on the geographical and political context of the place of Irish in the education system is presented in Chapter 2. The role of the Irish language in education since the foundation of the Irish Free State in 1922 is described and contrasted with the position of Irish in the education system in Northern Ireland. The fortunes of Irish as a vernacular from the end of the 18th century are then briefly traced before giving an account of early state polices in relation to the language. The outcome of these policies is then critiqued. This is followed by a description of a new grass-root's movement during the 1970s that saw a growing interest in all-Irish schools that has continued unabated to this day.

The field of SLA research is wide-ranging and diverse. It covers areas such as language learning in both naturalistic and instructional contexts. It is beyond the scope of this volume to review all of this literature. Instead, a number of theoretical perspectives on L2 learning with particular relevance for language learning in immersion programmes, and the unique situation in Ireland, are presented in Chapter 3. The theories that underlie SLA research are influenced by a variety of perspectives and approaches. Among these are universal grammar, sociocultural, sociolinguistic, cognitive and interactionist approaches to L2 learning. Immersion education is placed within the larger field of L2 learning and sociocultural learning. I discuss the role of interlanguage corpora in informing pedagogy in instructional settings and explore research and pedagogy in immersion education.

Chapter 4 gives an account of the research methodology I used to create a corpus of pupil speech. This corpus was analysed to provide a comprehensive description of the features of the primary pupils' spoken Irish. Speech samples recorded during a collaborative task in 13 all-Irish schools make up this first corpus of its type for Irish in the primary school. These all-Irish schools were located across the island of Ireland in the RoI and NI. As there is no standard oral corpus of Irish available for adults or for children, I deemed it necessary to compile a second corpus of 'native speaker' (Gaeltacht) pupils for comparative purposes and so three Gaeltacht schools were visited to record samples of the pupils' speech. It might be more accurate to describe these pupils as bilingual rather than native speakers. Ó Curnáin (2007) documented the decline in traditional forms of Irish and argued that a pure form of Irish no longer exists even in the strongest heartland areas. The speech of native speakers is characterised by code-mixing and there is evidence of the influence of English syntax. Nonetheless, this group was chosen for comparative purposes as all-Irish pupils are expected to reach a level of proficiency in Irish as close as possible to their bilingual counterparts in the Gaeltacht (National Council for Curriculum and Assessment, 2015). Bilingual Gaeltacht pupils have greater exposure to Irish both as a community and as a home language and are considered the closest native speaker comparison available. Pupils' speech in both school types was recorded while they were engaged in a collaborative task. In total, speech samples were gathered from 112 pupils, 89 in all-Irish schools and 23 in Gaeltacht schools.

In Chapter 5, I describe and analyse the corpus of pupils' language. The analysis focuses on the syntactic and lexical features of the pupils' Irish. Issues such as the pupils' use of the copula and the substantive verb in Irish are examined in detail, together with the morphology of verbs most commonly used. The use of prepositional pronouns, interrogative pronouns and numbers are examined and the mapping of English syntax onto Irish is considered. The most common words used by pupils in each school type are identified and the corpus is also analysed for the presence of grammatical errors. An account of the pupils' code-mixing and code-switching behaviour is also presented.

Following transcription and analysis of samples of the pupils' speech, I returned to each all-Irish school to ascertain the views of the pupils in relation to their own speech samples. I conducted a stimulated recall activity with pupils in order to gain a greater understanding of the features of their language, their opinions and insights in relation to learning Irish and their proficiency in Irish. I describe the findings of this activity in Chapter 6. The 89 all-Irish pupils who participated were shown selected excerpts from a video-recording of their interaction while they were engaged in the collaborative task. The excerpts selected contained non-target features of

Irish. Each group viewed the excerpts a number of times and were given an opportunity to assess their own proficiency in Irish, to identify what expressions and forms they saw as 'mistakes' and to establish to what extent they were capable, on reflection, of self-correction. The features that the pupils corrected and those that went unnoticed give insights into their underlying competence in Irish. Errors that could be corrected with prompting and pupils' views on code-mixing are also described in this chapter. The insights gained through this activity help to inform effective instructional strategies that seek to enable all-Irish school pupils to emulate native speaker competence.

Chapter 7 reports on a study I conducted with colleagues to examine the attitudes and motivation of all-Irish primary and post-primary pupils to learning Irish and to using Irish in the home and in the school outside the classroom. Data were gathered through questionnaires to pupils and to a matched sample of their parents. If the growth of all-Irish schools is one of the most positive developments in Irish language education according to the Council of Europe as cited above, then we might expect these immersion pupils to make a contribution to an increase in Irish language use and to become 'new speakers' of Irish. Pupil responses to the questionnaires gave insights into their attitudes and motivation to learning Irish and to their use of Irish in the home and in the school outside the classroom. The data gathered and analysed in this study provided important information about the potential of all-Irish pupils to become active speakers of Irish in the future.

I give an account in Chapter 8 of the analysis of interviews conducted with 32 immersion teachers in Ireland and Canada. I interviewed 18 teachers and principals in all-Irish schools in relation to their pupils' speech and compared their views with similar interviews I held with 14 French immersion teachers in Toronto and Ottawa. I report on the teacher satisfaction with the pupils' proficiency in Irish and French and how they respond to the pupils' grammatical errors is explored. The teachers also provide insights in relation to the pupils' willingness to speak the immersion language and the steps the teachers take to try to improve pupils oral production.

The volume concludes in Chapter 9 with a discussion of the implications of the findings of these studies for pedagogy in immersion education in Ireland, in other minority language contexts and in immersion contexts internationally.

Note

(1) The term 'all-Irish school' is favoured throughout this book over 'Irish immersion school' or 'Irish-medium school' as this is the term in common use since the 1970s to denote *scoil lán-Ghaeilge*. These all-Irish schools are similar to immersion centres as opposed to dual-track schools elsewhere. All subjects apart from English are taught through the medium of Irish, hence the term 'all-Irish school'. The term *Gaelscoil*, meaning 'Irish school', has latterly become popular also.

2 Immersion Education in Ireland: Origins and Current Context

Introduction

This chapter provides the historical context that led to the growth of a parent-led movement to establish Irish immersion schools in the 1970s. I briefly trace the development of the Irish language in education from the establishment of the national school system under British rule in 1831, when there was no place for the teaching of Irish, through the various Irish language campaigns leading up to the establishment of the Irish Free State in 1922. The newly formed Free State government set out to revive the Irish language, with significant efforts to achieve this goal through the teaching and promotion of Irish in the school system. This chapter outlines the successes and failures of these policies and the manner in which government policies helped or hindered language revival efforts.

Geographical and Political Context

It is beyond the scope of this book to provide a comprehensive account of the geographical and political context on the island of Ireland. Nonetheless, in order to understand the different Irish language education policies in Ireland, some background information is required. The island of Ireland is divided into 32 counties. Twenty-six of these counties form the Republic of Ireland (RoI) and the remaining six counties form Northern Ireland (NI) which is part of the United Kingdom. Prior to 1922, all of Ireland had been under British rule for approximately 700 years. The partition of Ireland into Northern and Southern Ireland took place in 1921 under the Government of Ireland Act 1920. After the War of Independence and the Anglo-Irish Treaty, Southern Ireland became the independent Irish Free State. Under the Irish constitution of 1937, the Irish Free State became the Republic of Ireland, commonly known as Ireland.

The division of Ireland in this way led to two different education systems on the island of Ireland. In the RoI, the Irish language is a compulsory subject on the school curriculum throughout a child's education from entry, typically at age 4 or 5, to exit at age 17 or 18. Irish is taught as a subject for an average of 30–40 minutes per day depending on age and level. In NI, Irish is an optional subject on the school curriculum and is offered mainly in schools under Catholic patronage. Irish-medium or immersion education is available in both jurisdictions. The schools in Gaeltacht areas are also officially Irish-medium schools. The level of Irish-medium provision in these schools has, however, often depended on the linguistic proficiency of teachers and on the general linguistic composition of the community (Ní Thuairisg, 2014).

Figure 2.1 shows Ireland divided into its two jurisdictions: the RoI and NI. The shaded areas, principally in the west, are officially designated Gaeltacht or Irish-speaking areas where Irish is a community language.

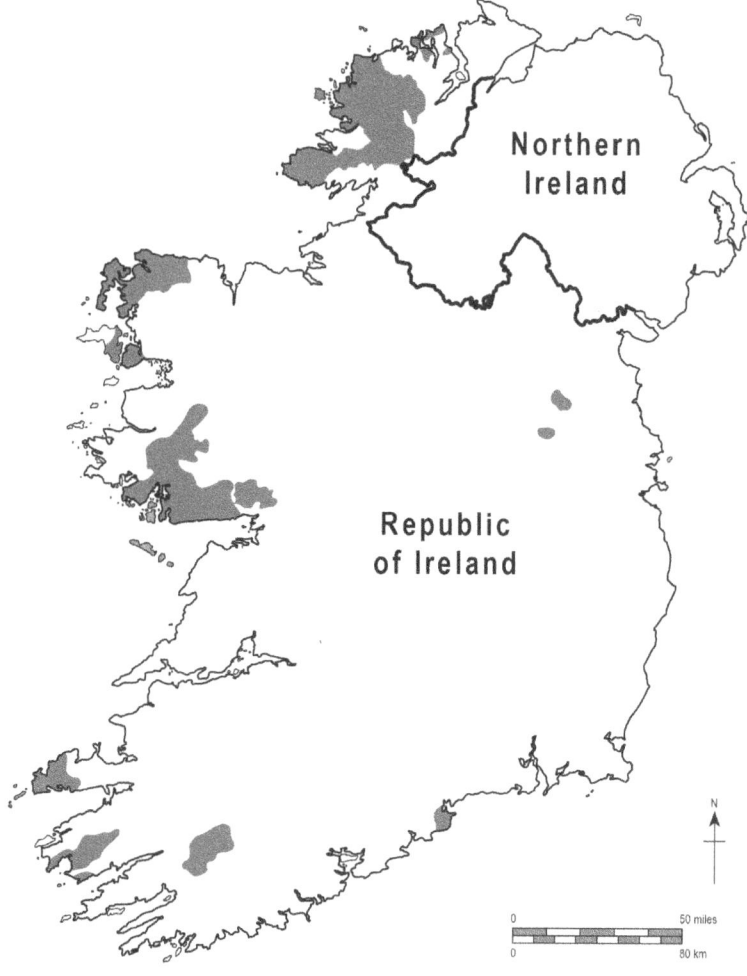

Figure 2.1 Map of Ireland. Shaded areas represent Gaeltacht communities with Northern Ireland in the north-east

The vitality of the language in these areas varies greatly and they can at best be described as bilingual communities. In a recent analysis of census data for the 155 electoral areas located within the Gaeltacht, Ó Giollagáin and Charlton (2015) could only identify 21 areas where Irish was spoken on a daily basis by 67% or more of the population in these communities. A usage rate of 67% or more is considered to be essential for the sustainability of a minority language (Ó Giollagáin *et al.*, 2007). There are no Gaeltacht areas in Northern Ireland.

The Irish Language in Education

The education system in the RoI played a significant role in language revitalisation efforts from the foundation of the Free State in 1922. During the 1960s, the states commitment to Irish-medium education waned. Less curriculum time was devoted to teaching Irish and teaching through the medium of Irish. Some parents became frustrated with the standard of Irish achieved by pupils. This prompted some to instigate a grass-roots movement to establish Irish-medium schools where a greater connection would be made between the acquisition and function of the immersion language. This new generation of schools formed the basis for Irish-medium schools as they have developed to this day. In this chapter, I will outline the growth of immersion education in Ireland and the historical context in which it developed, and I will examine how these developments have impacted immersion practices in Irish language schools today.

The Irish language is said to have been in decline in Ireland since the early 17th century. The language revivalists of the late 19th century tended to oversimplify the causes of this decline and accorded blame for the decreasing number of Irish speakers on various figures and establishments such as members of the Catholic clergy and the national school system. There are differing opinions as to the population of Irish speakers in the early 19th century. According to Wolf (2014) there were 3–4 million Irish speakers in Ireland in the 1830s out of a population of almost 8 million. He ascribes this large number to the increase in the population at that time. If this estimate is correct, this would be the greatest number of Irish speakers in the history of the language. Doyle (2015), on the other hand, suggests that the figure is likely to have been somewhat over 2 million Irish speakers. These speakers, who represented between a quarter and half the population, were widely dispersed and while they could be found in all social classes, the status of Irish was diminishing. Despite the sizable number of Irish speakers, the role of the Irish language in political, judicial and civil service business was in decline by 1800. The ravages of famine (1845–1849) and subsequent emigration resulted in the overall population of Ireland falling to approximately 6 million. Undoubtedly, this reduced the number of Irish speakers significantly.

By 1851, only 29.1% of the population spoke Irish (Central Statistics Office, 1932) and only about one third (10%) of these were monoglot speakers of Irish (Doyle, 2015). Wolf (2014) suggests that the language shift in Ireland happened later than is commonly believed and at a greater rate of decline. Doyle (2015) maintains that the decline happened more gradually over a hundred-year period from 1750 to 1850 in particular.

As no Irish was taught in the national school system established in Ireland in 1831, this probably contributed to a further decline in the use of Irish. Even in areas of the country where there were monoglot Irish speakers, only English was spoken at school. It could be argued, however, that the decline was well under way before the establishment of national schools (Doyle, 2015). The education policy relating to Irish in this era was consistent with the more fundamental British policy: to spread the use of the English language by prohibiting the use of the vernacular language in schools.

An Irish language revival movement in the final quarter of the 19th century attempted to stem the tide of decline (Ó Tuathaigh, 2008). The Society for the Preservation of the Irish Language, founded in 1876, led a campaign to introduce the teaching of Irish in national schools. As a result of this campaign, the teaching of Irish as an additional subject after school to fifth and sixth classes was permitted in 1878 (Ó Buachalla, 1984). Unfortunately, little or no effort was made at this time to train teachers to teach Irish. This had implications later when policies to extend the teaching of Irish were made without sufficient numbers of teachers competent to teach the language. The founding of *Conradh na Gaeilge* (The Gaelic League) in 1893 saw renewed efforts for further progress in teaching Irish in schools and the campaign achieved some success in 1904 when the Commissioners for National Education were persuaded to allow the introduction of a bilingual programme in areas where Irish was spoken.

When the Irish Free State gained independence from Great Britain in 1922, the Irish language was considered critically important to the new state's identity. In building a new nation, the language of the coloniser, English, was to be replaced with the local vernacular, Irish. A minimum standard of Irish was a compulsory requirement for matriculation (entry to university) and for many jobs in the public sector. National schools were identified by the newly independent Irish government as central to its policy to reverse the language shift from English back to Irish. Early in 1922, arising from the first National Programme Conference (1922), the Irish Free State government announced that Irish would be taught and used as the medium of instruction for at least one hour per day where there were teachers with sufficient Irish to implement this policy. The government also decided that Irish should be the sole medium of instruction in infant classes.

Only infant classes were initially targeted due to insufficient native speaker or near-native speaker teachers. The result of this was that the infant programme was to be taught entirely through Irish, and Irish was to gradually replace English in more senior classes over time as more teachers became fluent in Irish. While not a participant at the National Programme Conference, the Reverend Timothy Corcoran, Professor of Education at University College, Dublin, influenced the outcomes of the conference (O'Connor, 2010). Corcoran believed that the language shift of the 17th and 18th centuries from Irish to English was brought about mainly through the school system. He maintained that total immersion in Irish from an early age would reverse this language shift and achieve native speaker competence thus restoring the native language (Corcoran, 1925). Some of Corcoran's ideas were based on his observations of emigrant children from Eastern Europe in the United States who were immersed in English in school and appeared to acquire English without difficulty (O'Connor, 2010). The context of a lesser-used language such as Irish in Ireland, where there was no communicative need to be able to speak the language, was obviously very different to that of New York where there would have been parental support and constant exposure to English in the environment.

The extra burden that the programme placed on teachers appears to have been too heavy for some to bear and it was decided at the second National Programme Conference convened in 1925 that English would be used as a medium of instruction prior to 10:30 (Coolahan, 1973). Despite the easing of the requirements, the programme was overly ambitious as many teachers did not in fact have sufficient competency to teach Irish as a subject or to teach other subjects through the medium of Irish. At the time of the report of the second National Programme Conference in 1926 there were 13,000 national schoolteachers in total. Of these, 3414 (26%) held ordinary certificates in Irish, 2197 (17%) held bilingual certificates and 589 (4.5%) had an ardteastas (higher) certificate. The remaining 7390 (56.5%) teachers had no qualification in Irish (Coolahan, 1973). By 1935, only 20% of teachers had no qualification in Irish (Coolahan, 1973). One can imagine the challenges for schools in implementing the programme when so many teachers lacked basic competency in the language. Even where teachers possessed an ordinary or bilingual certificate, this did not guarantee sufficient competency. O'Connell (1968) believed that much damage was done to the progress of Irish in schools during this time because the authorities deemed that a bilingual certificate was sufficient to teach through the medium of Irish. One of the steps taken to improve teachers' competency in Irish was to establish seven Irish-speaking residential preparatory colleges, the first four of which opened in 1927 (Jones, 2006). These preparatory colleges catered for post-primary pupils who scored highly in oral Irish tests or were native speakers of Irish. The aim was to prepare them to go on to teacher training colleges and to become primary schoolteachers. The relative success of Irish language education policies in the following three decades was greatly influenced by graduates of these preparatory colleges who went on to become schoolteachers.

Despite the unease of teachers, parents and some TDs (*Teachta Dála*/ parliamentary deputy) during the early years of the Free State, the Minister for Education, Tomás Ó Deirg, took the position that schools should bear the major responsibility for the revival of the Irish language and reiterated the state's policy in relation to Irish through the Revised Programme of Primary Instruction 1934 (Coolahan, 1981). The government did not, however, succeed in replacing English instruction with Irish in the more senior classes in all schools. In 1930, Irish was the medium of instruction in 4% of national schools and by 1940 this figure had increased to 12%, but fell back somewhat to 11% in 1950 (Ó Buachalla, 1984). The 1940s were the high point for Irish language education policies with a steady decline from the 1950s onwards.

Throughout this period, there was continual criticism of the state's policy in relation to teaching through Irish, particularly from the Irish National Teachers Organisation (INTO). The teachers were particularly opposed to Irish being the sole language of instruction in infant classes. A motion was passed at the INTO Congress of 1936 to establish a committee of enquiry into the use of Irish as a teaching medium to children whose home language was English (Irish National Teachers' Organisation, 1941). One of the findings of that committee, which reported in 1941, was that 39.5% of teachers surveyed were in favour of the 'all-Irish' policy in infant classes for the sake of the revival of Irish, whereas 60.5% were in favour of the use of both English and Irish in infant classes. The committee recommended that both English and Irish be used in infant classes but this recommendation was ignored (Coolahan, 1981). There was criticism from parents also who were 'wont to say, however groundless the charge, that nothing except Irish was being taught in the schools' (O'Connell, 1968: 365). It was also believed that the pupils did not like Irish. Teachers' lack of ability and training to teach through the medium of Irish may well have been a contributing factor. These criticisms fed into the growing public protest against what became known as 'compulsory Irish' and the policy of teaching all infant classes through Irish was revisited in 1960 with the issuing of Circular 11/60 which stated that schools were no longer required to teach all subjects through Irish. There was a dramatic decline in the number of schools teaching through Irish from the high point in the 1940s to the 1970s such that by 1972 there were only 10 all-Irish primary schools outside the Gaeltacht. The 1960s marked the end of official state policy of the revival of the Irish language with the state now moving towards a position of bilingualism in the 1970s.

Although the Irish language policy in schools had on the surface been successful from 1922 to the 1950s, the revitalisation policy was not pursued with the same vigour in other domains. While schools are important for language maintenance, they cannot revive a language without support in other domains (Spolsky, 2012). In many instances, they can be overburdened with implementing state language policy, and this appears to have been the case in Ireland. When the schools did produce Irish speakers, opportunities to use the language outside the domain of the school were limited. Enabling children to acquire competence in a language, particularly a minority language, does not guarantee that they will have opportunities or choose to speak it in adult life (Ó Riagáin et al., 2007). Without links to a native speaker community and without the home functioning as a site of language reproduction, schools may not be able to revive a language that is in decline (May, 2001). Fishman (2013) cautions that an overdependence on schools as vehicles for language revitalisation rather than intergenerational transmission is unlikely to be successful. Fishman (2013: 487) cites Ireland as a prime example of this with the 'institutionalization of Irish as an occasional, formal second language among the school-focused middle classes ... rather than as a mother tongue and informal medium among members of Irish society more generally'.

The architects of the state's Irish language policy in 1922 would surely have been very disappointed with the results achieved 50 years later in 1972. It appears to have taken the state that length of time to realise the folly of over-reliance on the schools as the main agents of revival (Edwards, 2017). While they acted most vigorously in the domain in which they had the greatest capacity to influence, the policy might have been more successful if it had been supported by systematic research (Ó Buachalla, 1984) and adequate training of teachers. There is a school of thought that suggests that some of those who came to power in the Free State following the struggle for independence wished to maintain the social and educational status quo with the same class structures but to rebrand it under a new national leadership (Ó Giollagáin, 2014; Ó Giollagáin & Péterváry, 2016). The vision for the revival of Irish was compartmentalised to the education system alone. The relative neglect of native speakers of Irish in Gaeltacht areas was a feature of this mindset.

Irish-Medium Schools Since the 1970s

During the 1960s and 1970s, the belief grew among the majority of the population that educating pupils through Irish was detrimental to their English language skills. These views were influenced by the Macnamara (1966) research study of 1000 primary pupils at the time. It was claimed that competence in Irish gained by pupils taught through the medium of Irish was achieved at a cost to their English language skills. Despite this, not all parents were averse to Irish-medium schools. Cummins' (1977) critique of Macnamara's findings helped to assuage many parents' fears in this regard. When he re-examined Macnamara's data, he found that the all-Irish pupils had the same level of attainment in English as the English-medium pupils. Some parents were unhappy with the standard of Irish in English-medium schools and the change in state policy towards the Irish language in the education system. They wanted to ensure that their children would achieve a reasonable competence in Irish, and this led to the establishment of parent-led naíonraí (Irish-medium pre-schools) and gaelscoileanna (all-Irish schools). In many cases, it was the success of the naíonra in a community that led to parental demand for the establishment of an all-Irish primary school. Of course, this has also been the case in other minority language communities internationally where successful immersion education efforts at pre-school level led to the establishment of immersion primary and post-primary schools.

This new generation of all-Irish schools represented a change in direction in Irish language education. New schools emerged as a direct result of the wishes and desires of parents rather than from state policies (McAdory & Janmaat, 2015). This parent-led campaign heralded the beginning of a bottom-up movement which contrasted with the top-down approach that had existed in Ireland for the previous 50 years. The type of bilingual education offered in these schools is described in the research as immersion education.

The number of all-Irish primary schools in Ireland has grown significantly since the grass-roots movement at the beginning of the 1970s, as can be seen in Figure 2.2. There are now 232 Irish-medium schools in Ireland, 184 primary and 48 post-primary (source: www.gaelscoileanna.ie).

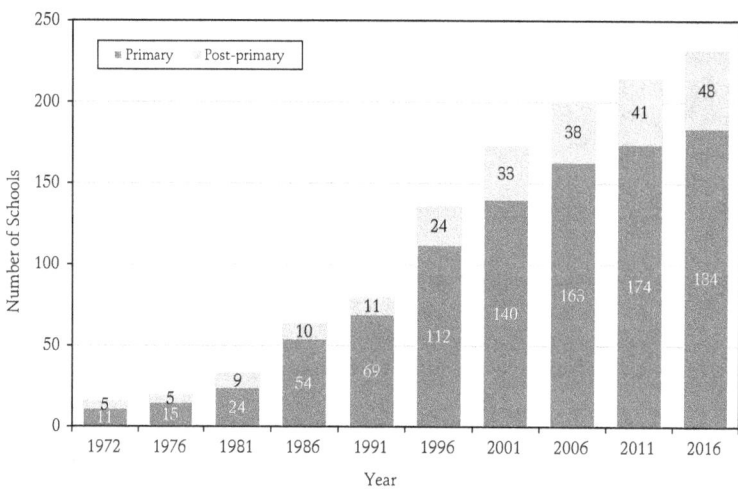

Figure 2.2 Growth in Irish-medium schools in Ireland 1972–2016

While the majority of all-Irish schools are stand-alone schools or immersion centres, a small number are Irish-medium units or streams. Pupils in an Irish-medium language unit are immersed in the Irish language for the duration of the school day. The unit is like a school within a school with a coordinating teacher and enjoys some autonomy. Irish-medium language streams, on the other hand, make limited provision for Irish-medium education within an all-English-medium school. These streams are similar to the immersion tracks found in schools in North America. There are 7 primary all-Irish units in Ireland and 14 post-primary units. It is important to note, in relation to the research presented in this book, that the studies pertain primarily to stand-alone Irish-medium schools only. For further research relating to Irish-medium streams and units at primary and post-primary levels, the reader is referred to Ó Duibhir *et al.* (2015c). Some results from this study are presented in Chapter 7.

In the 2015–2016 school year, 48,984 (6.87%) pupils attended all-Irish primary schools on the island of Ireland, as can be seen in Table 2.1. Of these, 35,613 attended Irish immersion schools in the RoI, 5,854 in NI (2016–2017) and a further 7,517 pupils attended Gaeltacht schools in Irish-speaking communities. This means that approximately 7.97% of pupils in the RoI (http://www.education.ie/en/Publications/Statistics/Statistical-Reports/Annual-Statistical-Reports.html) and 3.41% of pupils in NI (https://www.education-ni.gov.uk/topics/statistics-and-research/school-enrolments) receive their primary school education through the medium of Irish.

Survey data in the RoI consistently indicate that there is scope to increase this percentage threefold. Almost one-quarter of respondents in surveys stated that they would send their children to an all-Irish primary school if one was located near their home (Darmody & Daly, 2015; Ó Riagáin, 2007).

All-Irish schools in the RoI differ from immersion schools in other jurisdictions in three key areas. First, they are whole-school immersion centres established under the rules for national schools with an independent

Table 2.1 Pupil enrolment in Irish-medium primary schools in the Republic of Ireland in the 2015–2016 school year and in Northern Ireland in 2016–2017

	Republic of Ireland			Northern Ireland	Total for island of Ireland
	Within the Gaeltacht	Outside the Gaeltacht	Total		
Number of pupils in all-Irish schools	7,517	35,613	43,130	5,113	48,984
Total number of primary pupils	540,955	540,955	540,955	171,612	712,567
Percentage	1.39	6.58	7.97	3.41	6.87

board of management. Second, Irish is the first language of the school and this is recognised in the curriculum for Irish language (National Council for Curriculum and Assessment, 2015). Third, while practice in relation to English instruction varies in infant classes, once English language instruction commences, it amounts to approximately 14% of the school day and this remains constant thereafter until the end of primary school. All other subjects (history, geography, science, mathematics, music, drama, visual arts, physical education and social, personal and health education) are taught through the medium of Irish. Instructional time through the medium of Irish does not decrease as in some early total immersion programmes where the proportion of instructional time typically decreases to 50% by Grade 6 (Genesee, 2008).

The majority of all-Irish schools employ an 'early total immersion' model where children are immersed in Irish from their first day in school in junior infants. The introduction of English as a subject is usually delayed until some point in the child's second year in school. Approximately 10% of all-Irish schools, however, teach English from the start of the child's first year in school for 30 minutes per day (Ó Duibhir et al., 2015c). Irish is also the communicative language of the school and pupils are expected to converse in Irish at all times within the school environment including the school playground at break-time. The school curriculum is the same as that for all other primary schools except for the Irish language itself and the fact that the subjects are taught through Irish. The vast majority of pupils attending all-Irish schools speak little or no Irish at home or outside the school. All teachers are bilingual and pupil exposure to Irish is effectively confined to the school environment. Their development in English language is supported by its dominant status in the community (Figure 2.3).

The immersion model employed in NI is closer to the practice found internationally where there is a longer total immersion period and exposure to English increases over time. By the end of primary school, children in all-Irish schools in both the RoI and NI will have received approximately 6000 hours of instruction through the medium of Irish.

The expectation of the primary language curriculum (National Council for Curriculum and Assessment, 2015: 6) is that immersion pupils would achieve proficiency in Irish 'at a level appropriate to their abilities'. The learning outcomes and progression continua in the primary language curriculum delineate a trajectory which aims for near-native-like ability as the pupil progresses through school. This sets a high standard for the pupil to achieve in the absence of significant out-of-school exposure to Irish. This target is in line with current state policy which saw the goal of Irish language education as one of language revitalisation and more recently as producing competent Irish speakers who could extend the use of Irish more widely in society. The NI curriculum for Irish-medium schools

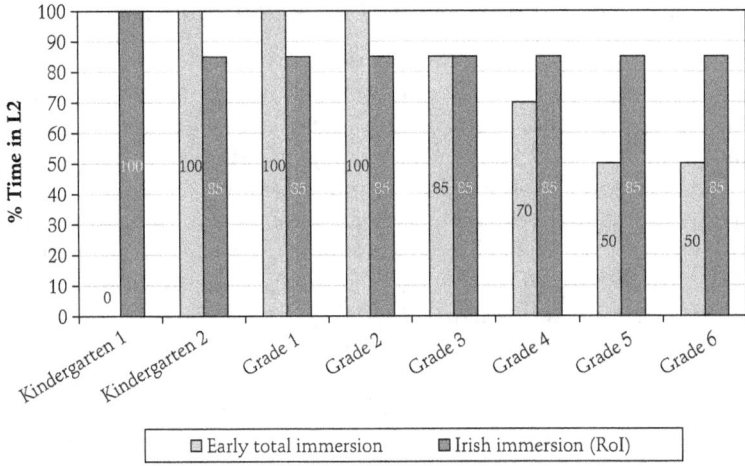

Figure 2.3 Comparison 'early total immersion' model and Irish immersion (RoI) by percentage of time spent in L2

sets similar standards (CCEA, 2009). In a review of different primary second language (L2) programmes, Genesee et al. (1989: 262) concluded that: 'If the goal is native-like second language proficiency, then serious consideration needs to be given to how to extend the language environment of programs that lack peer models'. This view supports Fishman's (2013) advice of guarding against an over-reliance on the school as the site for language revitalisation.

Given the amount and intensity of exposure to Irish that all-Irish pupils have, is it realistic to expect that they would be able to speak Irish fluently with a good degree of accuracy in their final year of primary school? The research carried out in this area to date indicates that all-Irish schools have been reasonably successful in this respect. Pupils in their final year in all-Irish primary schools, their eighth year of immersion education, appear very successful in their acquisition of basic literacy and conversational skills. It is argued that their competence at this juncture enables them to function effectively in an Irish-speaking setting and to learn through the medium of Irish (Harris et al., 2006). It is recognised, however, that they often succeed in getting their meaning across in a way that is grammatically inaccurate, using language that would not be viewed as acceptable by native speakers. Harris et al. (2006) identify specific areas of concern. Mastery of the objective of *understanding the morphology of verbs* on a listening test by pupils in Irish immersion in the RoI, for example, had decreased significantly since a previous study 20 years earlier in 1985. The mastery of *control of the morphology of verbs* on a speaking test had also decreased but not significantly. These concerns are not unique to the Irish context and have been well documented in the literature on immersion education in Canada, Wales and Northern Ireland.

The Sociolinguistic Context of Irish Immersion Education

While schools have a very important role to play in the revitalisation of Irish, they represent only one domain of children's lives. As noted by Fishman (2013), without exposure and opportunities to use the language in other domains such as family, peer group and society in general, revitalisation efforts are less likely to be successful.

The Irish language appeared doomed to extinction in the final quarter of the 19th century. The achievements since then which have ensured its survival to date have been described as miraculous by Fishman (1991). There are other outward signs of vitality in the Irish language in the wider society. Examples include the establishment of TG4, the Irish language television station, in 1996 and the popularity of its innovative programming; the growth of all-Irish schools since the 1970s; the volume of works of prose published in Irish in recent years; the enactment of the Official Language Act 2003; the appointment of An Coimisinéir Teanga (Language Commissioner) in 2004; the Irish government statement on the Irish language in 2006; the achievement of 'official working language' status for Irish in the European Community in 2007; the 20-Year Strategy for Irish in 2010; a policy for education in the Gaeltacht (Department of Education and Skills, 2016); and the demand for Irish language courses for adults and Gaeltacht courses for teenagers. These initiatives and innovations combined with new language planning approaches in the Gaeltacht indicate that there is considerable vitality in relation to the promotion of Irish.

Behind these outward signs, however, there are underlying trends that are less favourable. The political commitment to the language has declined in recent years in the face of an economic downturn (An Coimisinéir Teanga, 2013). The Irish language has been in competition with English as a community language for centuries. It is now categorised as a minority or lesser-used language and the threat from English has not diminished. The number of daily speakers of Irish is relatively small and thinly dispersed. In a recent survey, results show that while over half the population in Ireland have a positive attitude towards the language, this positivity does not translate into regular language use. Results show that even among respondents with basic and advanced fluency in the language, Irish is not frequently spoken on a 'weekly basis' or 'more often than that' (Darmody & Daly, 2015). Even in the Gaeltacht areas, Irish is perceived to be under threat (Ó Giollagáin & Charlton, 2015). The number of people speaking Irish on a daily basis in the Gaeltacht decreased by 2589 (11.2%) between 2011 and 2016 (Central Statistics Office, 2017). Some of this decline may be explained by emigration due to the impact of the downturn in the economy on employment opportunities in Gaeltacht regions.

Further examination of the figures from the 2016 Census of Population in the RoI reveals the fragility of the Irish language (Central Statistics Office, 2017). On a positive note, the number of people over the age of three with the ability to speak Irish was recorded as 1.76 million, representing 39.8% of the entire population. This figure is evidence of the success, albeit limited, of Irish language education policies. Over 1 million of this 1.76 million, however, rarely if ever speak Irish or speak it less than once per week. A large proportion of these speakers are primary and post-primary school pupils who study Irish as a subject in school and who may not necessarily speak Irish outside the school or language learning context. When one removes those who speak Irish within the education context only, there are 73,803 (1.7%) daily speakers and 111,473 (2.3%) weekly speakers of Irish. The figure for daily speakers represents a decrease of 3382 since the previous census in 2011. Of the daily speakers, 20,586 reside in the Gaeltacht and represent just 21.4% of the total Gaeltacht population. The remaining 53,217 live outside the Gaeltacht. It is clear from these figures that the proportion of daily speakers of Irish living outside the Gaeltacht (72.1%) far outweighs those living within the Gaeltacht (27.9%). As can be seen in Figure 2.4, this is not a new trend as the proportion of daily speakers outside the Gaeltacht has been rising since 2006.

The Northern Ireland Census 2011 recorded the percentage of the population aged 3 years or over with some ability in Irish as 10.65% (Northern Ireland Statistics and Research Agency, 2012). The optimistic view of the future of Irish has been that as the language declines in the Gaeltacht, the number of new speakers in urban areas will increase to take their place, in part due to the growth in Irish-medium schools. The census figures reported here confirm that native speakers in the Gaeltacht are

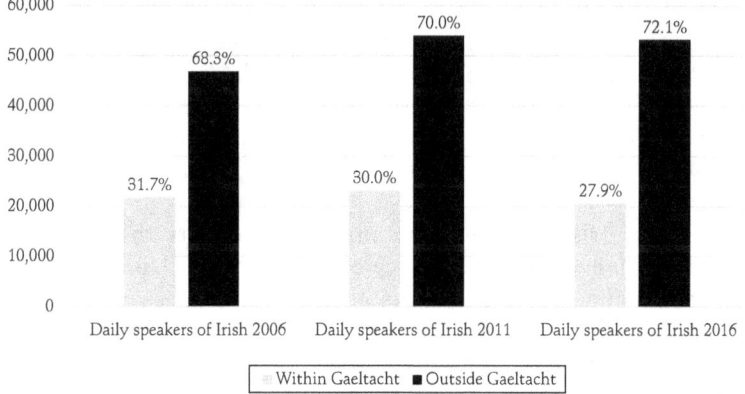

Figure 2.4 Number of daily speakers of Irish outside the education system by region – within Gaeltacht or outside of Gaeltacht[1] (Source: www.cso.ie)

declining as is the overall number of daily speakers of Irish. If the number of daily speakers of Irish continues to decline, it would not bode well for the future of the language. Questions and concerns have been raised about the variety of Irish spoken by new speakers (Ó Gairbhí, 2017). I discuss this issue further in Chapter 7.

The Irish Language Survey of 2013 sought to provide greater detail than available from the 2011 census data on the use and level of Irish competency in both jurisdictions (RoI and NI) (Darmody & Daly, 2015). There were 2255 participants over 18 years in the survey, 1045 in the RoI and 1215 in NI. The results showed that 57% of respondents in the RoI and 17% of respondents in NI reported having either basic or advanced fluency in the language. In relation to attitudes to the language, 67% of respondents in the RoI and 45% of respondents in NI reported being either strongly in favour or somewhat in favour of the language. It is interesting to note that 68% of Catholic participants in NI had favourable attitudes to Irish which is very close to the RoI figure. As the survey was confined to adults over 18 years, it is likely to have excluded the majority of those in full-time education other than those studying Irish at third level or those working in the education sector. This high level of self-assessed ability in Irish indicates that there is potential to expand existing Irish speaker networks. The '20-Year Strategy for the Irish Language 2010–2030' (Government of Ireland, 2010) seeks to tap that potential and has set an ambitious target of 250,000 daily speakers of Irish by the year 2030. However, progress in achieving this goal and indeed instigating the necessary steps towards this progress has been slow and the strategy has been criticised by many who fear that the government in the RoI lacks the will and resources to bring the strategy to fruition (Ó Cuirreáin, 2014).

Pupils in all-Irish schools, located outside the Gaeltacht, depend on dispersed networks of Irish speakers to come in contact with Irish. In circumstances where the language is not visible to pupils outside the context of the school, their motivation to learn the language may weaken as the language structures become more complex. Pupils may not sustain the effort required to acquire the more difficult structures of Irish if they do not see a practical application for their efforts in their lives outside of school.

Most active Irish speakers live in social contexts that are heavily influenced by the increasing language contact between Irish and English. The global dominance of English is also increasing the extent of code-mixing of the two languages which is a common feature of the speech of Irish speakers (Nic Eoin, 2005). O'Malley Madec (2007) noted in her research that native speakers of Irish in all age groups use a significant amount of English words and phrases in their speech. Her study of English discourse markers led her to classify them as borrowings rather than code-switches and found that the more formal an interaction was, the fewer borrowings there were. Speakers appeared to use English discourse markers to denote a speaker style. In a study of adult native speaker Gaeltacht pre-school *stiúrthóirí* (leaders), Hickey (2009) found that over three-quarters of their code-switches were made up of a small number of English discourse markers. This use of English has led writers such as Nic Pháidín (2003) to refer to the Irish spoken in the Gaeltacht areas as a creole. The language lacks the richness that it once had and is now heavily influenced by English syntax (Ó Baoill, 1981), and indeed Mac Mathúna (1997) goes so far as to state that one cannot be certain that native speakers have even a grasp of correct grammatical structures.

A comprehensive linguistic survey of young people of post-primary age in Gaeltacht areas highlighted the process of language shift and a decrease in their levels of proficiency (Ó Giollagáin *et al.*, 2007; Ó Giollagáin & Charlton, 2015). While 67% of young people in the Gaeltacht describe their level of proficiency in the Irish language as 'fluent' or 'very good', only 10% claim their proficiency in Irish is greater than in English. This contrasts with Wales where 89.4% of pupils from Welsh-speaking homes felt more comfortable speaking Welsh than English while only 5.6% of pupils from English-speaking homes and attending Welsh-medium education felt the same (Thomas & Roberts, 2011). A significant number of young people in the Gaeltacht also have difficulty with written language. Among the language areas proving most difficult were spelling, grammar and a deficient vocabulary, particularly in school-related topics (Ó Giollagáin *et al.*, 2007). Further research analysed bilingual competence and language acquisition among young children in the Gaeltacht, whose home language was Irish and who would be classed generally as native speakers (Péterváry *et al.*, 2014). This research reported that pupils exhibited a lower level of ability in Irish than in English with an average difference of 15% between their ability in English and Irish. Areas where the English language held an advantage included: vocabulary, functional code-switching, grammatical accuracy in morphology and syntax and phonetic accuracy. Concern has been expressed that the decline in the traditional variety of spoken Irish in the Gaeltacht, will give way to a variety spoken by new speakers of Irish that may gain a higher status (Nic Fhlannchadha & Hickey, 2016). Native speaker pupils in Gaeltacht schools are certainly exposed to a greater amount of Irish and enjoy acquisition opportunities not afforded to those pupils in all-Irish schools outside the Gaeltacht. It appears, however, that the level of exposure to the English language has significantly impacted their acquisition of Irish.

Although the number of all-Irish schools is increasing, the pupils in these schools have limited access and exposure to Irish outside of school-based activities apart from some exposure to TG4, the Irish language television station. Murtagh (2003, 2007) found, however, that pupils who had attended an all-Irish school were more likely to participate in Irish-speaking networks outside of school than pupils who had attended English-medium schools. Access to these networks is extremely limited, however. The variety of Irish spoken by pupils in all-Irish schools has been referred to as Géarla (mix of Gaeilge 'Irish' and Béarla 'English') (Mac Síomóin, 2014), a type of interlanguage similar to Hammerly's (1991) 'Frenglish'. This interlanguage is characterised by a high level of fluency but a lack of grammatical accuracy with many borrowings from English. Although the promotion of fluency may be a necessary first step for immersion pupils, many involved in immersion education believe it must not be at the expense of grammatical accuracy. While the lack of grammatical accuracy has led some to consider the possibility that a new creole will emerge from all-Irish primary and post-primary schools (Ó Cíobháin, 1999), others praise the creativity of the language use of these immersion pupils and the variety of Irish that they are creating through a creolisation process (McCloskey, 2001).

The issue of errors in Irish usage generally is a topic of greater concern and sensitivity than it might be in other sociolinguistic contexts due to the perceived fragile status of the language. While in other more widely used languages, caregivers are not unduly concerned about developmental errors, there is a heightened sense of alarm that young speakers of Irish may not go on to become fluent accurate speakers (Harrington, 2006). This concern applies to all-Irish school pupils in particular since all-Irish schools are the source of a greater number of competent bilinguals than the Gaeltacht schools. The evidence from Wales (Jones, 1996), Northern Ireland (Henry *et al.*, 2002), Scotland (Johnstone *et al.*, 1999) and Canada (Lyster, 1987) indicates that developmental errors are a feature of immersion programmes and that it is realistic to only expect pupils to achieve a 'high, though not native-speaker, level of proficiency...' in the target language (Swain & Johnson, 1997: 7). Pupils in all-Irish schools may in fact be performing as well as can be expected.

Notwithstanding this, it is worrying that these non-target-like features appear to be a common characteristic of the language, particularly among L2 learners. These linguistic features don't typically lead to a breakdown in communication and therefore remain an integral part of their language acquisition and use. With little opportunity for the pupils to use the language outside of the educational domain, they do not gain experience of the levels of proficiency normally associated with native speakers of a language. However, as discussed above, developmental errors are also to be heard in the speech of young native speakers of Irish with incomplete acquisition of the language.

In the next chapter, I examine the progression of immersion education and the practice of L2 learning in the classroom in both the Irish and international context. I also examine some of the most important research studies conducted in immersion education and discuss how these studies have impacted pedagogical practices in the classroom.

Note

(1) In Figure 2.4, 72.1% appears smaller than 70.0% because the total number of daily speakers of Irish declined from 2011 to 2016. It is therefore a higher proportion of a smaller number.

3 Language Learning in Immersion Education in Ireland and Internationally

In the previous chapter, I discussed immersion education in Ireland, its development as an educational approach and its popularity today among parents who wish their children to experience a bilingual educational environment. Achieving a level of second language (L2) proficiency in a sociolinguistic context where the target language, a minority language, is not broadly used or heard in everyday life, poses challenges for learners and teachers alike. In this chapter, I explore the origins and features of immersion education in Ireland and internationally, and present important research studies that have informed the development and progression of immersion and bilingual education, and pedagogical strategies that facilitate second language acquisition (SLA). I review research studies that examine the acquisition of the Irish language and those factors that can obstruct successful acquisition, particularly in the case of a minority language. Firstly though, let us look at the theoretical framework surrounding L2 learning.

Second Language Learning

Chomsky observed that children appear to acquire their first language (L1) relatively quickly and effortlessly and that they could not do so, based solely on the input that they have received, without the assistance of some innate language ability. Even if L2 learners do not achieve native-like mastery of the target language, an explanation is required as to how learners know more about the language than could be expected from the limited input that they have received. DeKeyser (2003) argues that children's access to universal grammar (UG) is outside their awareness, whereas adults use their analytical abilities to compare structures in the L2 with their L1. A study by Harley and Hart (1997) compared the French proficiency of continuing early immersion pupils with that of late immersion pupils in an eleventh-grade class. They found that L2 proficiency outcomes in early immersion tended to be more connected with memory ability whereas the late immersion pupils drew more on analytical language ability (Harley & Hart, 1997: 397). These findings may provide evidence to support DeKeyser's (2000: 518) position that between the ages of about 6 and 16 years, 'everybody loses the mental equipment for the implicit induction of the abstract patterns underlying a human language, and the critical period really deserves its name'. The notion of a critical period in L2 language learning is contested, with researchers drawing attention to the 'importance of quality and amount of input and learners' attitudes and orientations' (Muñoz & Singleton, 2011: 25). DeKeyser (2000) believes that children are better at acquiring a language implicitly, while acknowledging that they require a large amount of input to do so and that only a total early immersion programme can provide this amount of input. This view may lend support to those writers (Harley, 1993; Lyster, 2007; Stern, 1990) who cite the need for a more analytical approach to immersion pedagogy.

Effect of previously acquired languages

Although young children in an early immersion programme may be able to acquire a language implicitly, a key difference for them when compared to children acquiring their L1 is that as L2 learners they have already acquired their L1. Because they already know one language, the way in which they experience the acquisition of the L2 is different to that of native speakers (NSs) (Pinter, 2011). The immersion context puts pressure on the learner to comprehend the input being received. However, comprehension is not the same as speech and a listener may make meaning from the input through vocabulary, lexical information, extra-linguistic information or a combination of these. In speech or production, on the other hand, the speaker must utilise aspects of grammar such as concord, definite/indefinite distinctions and singular/plural in order to be easily understood. Pupils, using their L1 processing strategies, may not pay attention to all the information regarding L2 structures and forms available to them in the input, as they did when they acquired their L1 (Doughty, 2003).

It could be argued that the learner in an immersion context may be principally decoding while listening, but unless those language structures are being encoded also, the learner will not have access to them when speaking. If DeKeyser (2000) is correct, then this encoding will happen implicitly. The evidence of early immersion research, however, shows that learners develop their receptive skills to a greater degree than their productive skills (Allen et al., 1990; Lapkin & Swain, 2004). Language learning that leads learners to develop their productive skills requires them to attend to relevant language features in the input and on restructuring their knowledge. L2 learners may need to have their attention drawn explicitly to features of their L2 that are grammatically incorrect, as they may be influenced by structures from their L1. One way to achieve this is to focus learners' attention on form, which may lead them to notice a 'hole' or gap in their 'interlanguage' (Swain, 2000).

Language learning from a cognitive perspective

A cognitive approach to L2 learning views language learning as being similar to any other type of learning. The more we know about how the brain processes and learns new information, the greater our understanding will be of the processes involved in L2 learning.

VanPatten (1996) recognised the role of input in SLA and developed a model for input processing as shown in Figure 3.1.

VanPatten's studies of how learners process language have shown that learners have a tendency to process input for meaning rather than for form. This view is supported by Sharwood Smith (1993) who maintains that learner's attention will be on content words first in order to negotiate for meaning. VanPatten's (2002) model explains that if the input is processed successfully it might lead to intake. By processing, he means 'moment-by-moment operations during comprehension which can encompass everything from syntax to morphology to lexicon to interfaces' (VanPatten & Jegerski, 2010: 5). In order to hold information in the working memory, learners need to have sufficient attentional resources available from their limited attentional capacity. VanPatten (2002) was primarily interested in the first stage of the process outlined above where input may lead to intake, though he acknowledges a role for output as well. He wanted to affect the ways in which learners managed input and devised tasks by manipulating learner attention. To do this, learners received processing instruction on how to notice structural features available in the input as well as negotiating for meaning. This was done by manipulating 'learner attention during IP (input processing) and/or manipulating input data so that more and better form-meaning connections are made' (VanPatten, 1996: 763). While the results of research in this area have tended to support VanPatten's theories, it is generally accepted that if we want learners to process for form, some pedagogical intervention is necessary (Doughty, 2003). Attention to form could be taught through explicit grammar teaching and explicit error correction or indirectly through input enhancement. While VanPatten's theory is useful for the understandings that it provides in relation to incomplete input processing, it does not explain how intake may be incorporated into the developing interlanguage system. Schmidt (2001) formulated the noticing hypothesis whereby learners must pay attention to structural elements of utterances in the language input. Noticing can be influenced by instruction frequency and salience, while individual differences among learners also play a role in how input is processed. Skehan (1998) suggests that noticing must take place within short-term

input ⟶ intake ⟶ developing system ⟶ output

Figure 3.1 VanPatten's model of processing and acquisition (Adapted from VanPatten, 1996: 41)

or working memory. If the learner has sufficient attentional resources available within his/her working memory to notice form in the input, it may be incorporated and coded into long-term memory.

Learners draw on their developing language system when producing output and one of the most important ways that Native Speakers (NSS) are able to speak at normal rates in real time, according to Skehan, is by drawing on lexical modes of communication. He suggests that in order to maintain a free flow of speech when speaking, speakers do not create each utterance 'mint fresh' (Skehan, 1998: 3). NSs' speech, according to this view, is derived from a mixture of creativity and prefabricated chunks and this is also the case with young children and L2 learners. However, L2 learners will initially be more dependent on controlled processing. Lantolf and Thorne (2006: 298) maintain that declarative knowledge is converted to procedural knowledge through restructuring and fine-tuning and 'converted in production' rules. This procedural knowledge is accessed initially through controlled processing and places a heavy burden on short-term memory. With repeated practice, these rules become automatised and are stored in long-term memory. Once automatised, these forms are less susceptible to change.

Skehan (1998: 4) conceptualised a dual-coding approach to language performance and language learning incorporating the use of a rule-based and a memory-based system. The rule-based system follows the pattern of restructuring under the operation of a UG or other cognitive process where rules are developed over time as the learner's language capacity develops. The memory-based system, on the other hand, relies on the accumulation of formulaic language chunks that can be accessed from long-term memory. When coding takes place, it can lead to restructuring in the interlanguage system. The use of language chunks frees up time for planning the rest of what a speaker wishes to say, which may entail shifting to analytical mode. Exemplar-based representations can also become rule based, and unanalysed chunks that learners have memorised may be analysed at a later stage and lead to productive rules.

Skehan cautions, however, that these memorised chunks drawn from the exemplar-based system may not necessarily be coded correctly. If optimum language learning conditions prevail, more accurate forms will replace premature lexicalisations. However, if the learner finds these lexicalisations useful and communicatively effective, then '… the erroneous exemplar may survive and stabilize, and become a syntactic fossil. In this case paradoxically, the usefulness in communication of a premature lexicalization is the source of the enduring problem' (Skehan, 1998: 61).

If the language chunks that learners draw upon are inaccurate forms of the target language, there is a danger that habitual practice of these will lead them to become rule based prematurely. Evidence of this outcome is examined when student speech is analysed in Chapter 5. This can lead to a degree of permanence or stabilisation that is difficult to modify even if there is ample contrary evidence in the input. Learners may continue to produce these inaccurate forms particularly if they do not cause a communicative difficulty.

Many researchers have studied the fluency of immersion pupils and commended the creative way in which they use the target language (Harley *et al.*, 1990; Nadasdi *et al.*, 2005). One aspect of this creativity is the manner in which young L2 learners will draw on features of their L1 to produce structures that are too complex for their level of L2 proficiency. An example of this is the way that children may carry L1 word order into their L2. This is a trait common also among L2 learners of Irish, where L1 English language word order is impressed upon their L2, examples of which we examine in Chapter 5. If these structures become embedded in the memory-based system, it may appear at a later stage that learners are translating from their L1 although this may not be the case.

Others have been more critical of the language use of immersion pupils, suggesting that it would be more desirable if pupils were encouraged to think before speaking so that their utterances might be more accurate (Hammerly, 1989). The communicative demands of the immersion classroom put pressure on pupils to express ideas and concepts that are sometimes ahead of their L2 ability. In such situations, their limited processing capacity may be directed more towards communicating their intended meaning than towards its form. Learners in these situations are more likely to access their exemplar-based system, while interlanguage change, on the other hand, is more likely to occur when accessed through the rule-based system. L2 use or output then cannot be guaranteed to lead to greater linguistic accuracy.

In terms of production practice, a dual-coding system calls for two types of practice: communicative practice and controlled practice (Skehan, 1998). Communicative practice can promote fluency and confidence but tends not to engage the learner's language awareness, reducing the likelihood of changes to the interlanguage system. Controlled practice, on the other hand, can engage learners' language awareness and rule-based system, so that over-reliance on communicative strategies is reduced and change in interlanguage is affected (Rannta & Lyster, 2007). Controlled practice tends to take place in context-reduced situations and can provide opportunities for learners to practice new knowledge available in declarative form, leading to automaticity and its conversion to procedural knowledge. The evidence from classrooms and from processing theories suggests that learners need to have their attention drawn to form at certain times, to direct their limited attentional resources to form rather than meaning. We will now review some interactionist approaches to L2 learning.

Interactionist approaches

Interactionist approaches to L2 learning are interested in L2 input, L2 output and the interaction between learners and others. Krashen (1985) developed the 'input hypothesis' and argued that if language learners receive sufficient comprehensible input in the target language, then they should be able to acquire that language. This was conditional to some extent on the affective filter hypothesis where some negative emotions such as anxiety and boredom inhibit efficient language processing. Work by Swain (1993) found that the speaking and writing skills of French immersion students were different from their francophone peers and this caused her and others to question Krashen's input hypothesis. Swain (1993) developed the 'output hypothesis', which will be discussed below. Before that, however, we will examine the 'interaction hypothesis' which Long (1996) put forward as a development of Krashen's input hypothesis. He examined the interaction between NS, non-native speaker (NNS) and NS–NS dyads and found that not only did conversation provide an opportunity for learners to practice specific language features, but it was also a means through which learning takes place. Negotiation for meaning in particular provides the best opportunities for learning.

Links can be made between this formulation of the interaction hypothesis and the contribution of the cognitive approach discussed earlier in relation to the learners 'selective attention' and 'processing capacity'. In studying the interaction hypothesis, it is difficult to determine if learning has actually taken place as a result of the interaction. One study that claimed to demonstrate that learning had taken place as a result of interaction was a study by Swain and Lapkin (1998) with Grade 8 French immersion students. The analysis of the collaborative dialogue of one pair of pupils demonstrated that their interaction had mediated learning.

Producing language or output has a role in developing fluency and, as noted previously in the discussion of the cognitive approach, controlled processing of different structures can lead to automatisation that in turn can aid fluency. Producing language alone, however, will be insufficient in developing accuracy.

The type of output that Swain (2005) advocates is a 'pushed' output where pupils are required to reflect on their language use and to produce the target language accurately. This output is not just the product of language learning but is in fact part of the learning process. Swain describes three functions of output to illustrate this:

(1) the noticing or triggering function causes a learner to notice gaps in his/her linguistic knowledge when he/she attempts to convey something precisely in the target language;
(2) the hypothesis-testing function allows the learner to experiment with ways of expression to test if they work;

(3) the metalinguistic (reflective) function describes the use of language to reflect on the language produced by self or others and Swain claims that the process of doing this mediates L2 learning.

Swain's claim is based on studies that utilised collaborative tasks designed to encourage pupils to engage in dialogue where they were involved in problem solving and knowledge building. This type of output arises from communicative tasks rather than from grammar exercises (Ellis & Shintani, 2014). Student output was recorded in these studies. Swain analysed the recordings and traced the language used by pupils at a later stage, back to dialogues that occurred when these pupils were engaged collaboratively on a task. The dialogues involved pupils talking about their own language output recorded during the task and represents L2 learning in progress. The pupils were 'pushed toward the delivery of a message that is not only conveyed, but that is conveyed precisely, coherently, and appropriately' (Swain, 2005: 473). It has been disputed, however, whether these processes have any long- or short-term impact on interlanguage development and L2 internalisation (Shehadeh, 2002: 612).

Another role of output is to provide an opportunity for pupils to produce language that may contain errors. The errors are welcomed and recognised as part of the learning process as they give an indication of the current state of learners' interlanguages and their understanding of the rules of the target language. By monitoring pupils' output in this way, teachers can design and adapt their programmes to address pupils' needs and provide corrective feedback. This could be considered a proactive approach to developing pupils' interlanguages (Lyster & Mori, 2008). The question remains, however: How can a teacher manage this feedback effectively to facilitate SLA while at the same time maintaining learners' confidence and enabling them to attain curriculum content objectives?

Interface hypothesis

The theories discussed thus far involve different understandings on the acquisition and function of implicit and explicit knowledge. Krashen (1985) believed that implicit knowledge could be acquired through input and that explicit knowledge could never be converted into implicit knowledge. This has been described as the 'non-interface position' (Ellis, 2005). Others such as DeKeyser (2000) favoured a 'strong interface position' which posits that explicit knowledge in adults can be transformed into implicit knowledge. A third position is that of a 'weak interface position' favoured by writers such as Ellis (2005). This position subscribes to the possibility of explicit knowledge being transformed into implicit knowledge under certain conditions. Knowledge of explicit rules can assist the learner in noticing the gap (Schmidt, 2001) and may cause him/her to pay greater attention to a structure in the input and compare it to his/her own output.

The weight given to each of the above three positions has implications for how we approach instruction in an immersion setting. The non-interface position suggests that there should be no explicit teaching of grammar. The strong interface position supports the teaching of explicit grammatical structures. DeKeyser's (2000) position in relation to this derived from comparisons of adult and child learners and his investigations into the critical period hypothesis. Explicit teaching of grammar draws on learners' analytical verbal skills which may not have developed in young immersion learners who still have access to implicit learning mechanisms. The weak interface position appears to be more applicable to immersion education where the emphasis is on the development of implicit knowledge but where explicit instruction is supported when leaners are developmentally ready to acquire grammatical rules. This position also supports raising learners' awareness of linguistic problems (Ellis & Shintani, 2014) which can be facilitated by corrective feedback.

Sociocultural Theory and Second Language Learning

The language learning theories outlined above were based primarily on a cognitive, psycholinguistic view of SLA. Some L2 theorists believe that interaction and the social context in which it takes place has a more important role than merely providing input for processing. For social constructivists, interaction and living together in a society are the basis for all mental and personal development. To view acquisition from the perspective of input and output alone would be too simplistic (Tarone & Swain, 1995). Firth and Wagner (1997) criticised the conceptualisation of SLA, up to that point, as being overly individualistic and mechanistic, with insufficient attention given to language use by L2 speakers. They also criticised the manner in which L2 speakers were viewed as deficient communicators and place 'native' speakers in an idealised position. Some of this criticism resulted from an overemphasis in their view of language learning in formal learning contexts such as classrooms. This ignored language use in society outside the classroom. It will be noted in the context of the studies reported in this volume that the focus is on young immersion learners who, by and large, have little or no contact with Irish outside of the school setting. In that context, a focus on formal language learning and use in the classroom is the primary site of acquisition for these learners. Nonetheless, we cannot fully separate what happens in the classroom with the knowledge, skills, attitudes and experiences that pupils bring with them from their life outside of school. The psycholinguistic theories examined above can help to explain SLA from a cognitive perspective. I acknowledge the critical role of the social context of the classroom and the learners' contribution to this.

Vygotsky (1978) maintained that both language and learning were socially derived and his concept of the zone of proximal development (ZPD) was of particular relevance to this viewpoint. The ZPD has been defined as 'the distance between the actual development level as determined by independent problem solving and the level of potential development as determined through problem solving under adult guidance or in collaboration with more capable peers' (Vygotsky, 1978: 86). Of note here is the distinction between what has already been completed and possibilities for future development. The social nature of the process is also evident from the interaction with others. Teachers can make use of the ZPD as a conceptual tool to identify pupils' emerging capacities and to create the learning conditions conducive to the acquisition of new knowledge. Vygotsky saw development as following learning but only if the learning is internalised. Within the ZPD, the child can carry out tasks and activities under the guidance of others through a process of 'other regulation' and the adult can assist the process through scaffolding. Scaffolding is used to describe the support that the adult or teacher initially offers and gradually removes as the learner gains greater mastery of the task. Further support is offered as necessary. If these processes are internalised, the child may progress to self-regulation. When applied to L2 learning, it suggests that development can be enabled during teacher–pupil interaction. Studies such as Spielman-Davidson (2000) and those examined by Mitchell *et al.* (2013) claim to show that effective scaffolding and feedback appropriate to the learner's ZPD is more effective than randomly selected feedback. As with other L2 research, however, not all are in agreement with the causal explanations provided for these research outcomes.

Languaging

Earlier in this chapter, we discussed the role of output in the context of interaction approaches to L2 learning. Swain locates her output hypothesis within a sociocultural framework, arguing that the productive skills of speaking and writing are cognitive tools that we use to mediate learning (Swain *et al.*, 2011). Regardless of whether the first, second or third language is used, we use these tools to learn about all areas of the curriculum be it mathematics, science or language. Examples of such tools are memory, strategies, self-regulation, language itself and cooperative learning. Swain and colleagues examined L2 learners engaged in dialogue on collaborative tasks and claim that this dialogue on linguistic data can become part of their own mental activity and mediate learning (Tocalli-Beller & Swain, 2005). They elaborate further that by verbalising thought in speech and/or writing, ideas can be crystallised and sharpened and inconsistencies become more obvious. This type of activity has been termed 'languaging', 'a vehicle through which thinking is articulated and transformed into artifactual form' (Swain, 2006: 97). The implication of this for L2 learning is that conditions should be created where learners are enabled to externalise their thinking about language-related issues. These externalised thoughts can become objects upon which to reflect and mediate internalisation creating new knowledge. These studies support a view that ZPDs are not exclusively developed by expert adults but that learners in collaborative dialogue can construct ZPDs leading to learning. This type of development is facilitated through learner autonomy and agency.

Learner autonomy

Learner reflection also plays a key role in learner autonomy. The application of sociocultural theory led Little (2007: 23) to suggest that three interacting principles govern success in L2 teaching: 'learner involvement, learner reflection and target language use'. These principles can only be applied if facilitated by teachers who must enable learners to become autonomous and gradually take ownership of their own learning. This may appear daunting for a five-year-old pupil in an immersion class, but the promotion of language learning means granting freedom to learners which they gain by taking control of their own learning. While this is a challenging proposition, it is one that may have to be realised if immersion is to be more successful particularly in a context where learners may perceive the target language speech community as being quite remote. This is highlighted in the Irish language context, where geographical areas in which the Irish language speech communities are based are often remote and isolated. This is complicated further by the fact that the majority of NSs of Irish also have native-like proficiency in the English language, suggesting that English could be the lingua franca in conversations between learners and NSs of Irish. This is particularly the case when the learner's level of proficiency is lower than that of the NS (Ó Duibhir et al., 2015a). Learners of Irish must therefore rely on other tools of autonomous learning in their SLA efforts.

The early years in immersion schools promote acquisition and fluency in a naturalistic way, sometimes referred to as meaning-focused instruction (Ellis & Shintani, 2014). While this may be appropriate initially, as pupils acquire literacy skills they must be enabled to assess and critically reflect on their language learning. It is also important to ensure that the content is targeted towards the communicative needs of the children. Little (1991) maintains that the target language is often seen as the content of L2 classes but not the medium. It could be argued, however, that the target language is often the medium of the immersion class but not the content. A greater emphasis may need to be placed at appropriate times on the target language forming an equally important part of lessons in immersion schools as the subject content in order to facilitate syntactic processing. The role of enhanced input, focus on form and negative feedback (Lyster, 2011) to help pupils acquire the structures which cause them difficulty may be warranted and merit further investigation. A more fundamental requirement, however, for these strategies to be effective may be to encourage learners to be more autonomous. Immersion programmes facilitate implicit language learning through language use in communicative contexts, but there may be a need to supplement this with reflection.

Returning to Little's (2007) three interacting principles of learner reflection, learner involvement and appropriate target language use, immersion pedagogy involves the learner in his/her learning and this is done entirely through the target language. The weaknesses in immersion pupils' grammatical accuracy appear to indicate that there may not be sufficient opportunities for learner reflection in current immersion pedagogy. We will take a closer look at this when the corpus of pupil speech is presented in Chapter 5.

Sociolinguistic perspectives on second language learning

Sociolinguistic perspectives involve the study of language in use and the context in which L2 learners learn the target language. The two areas examined in this section include the acquisition of an L2 in a school setting, and the effect of immersing pupils with others who have similarly faulty interlanguages on outcomes.

Acquisition in a school setting

The school setting is limited in that it does not provide the wide range of language functions in the target language that a child encounters when acquiring his/her L1 in his/her speech community. Where exposure to the L2 is confined mainly to the school and the classroom, one cannot expect that there will be the same opportunities for output or for the diversity of input required. It has been found in relation to input that teachers, including immersion class teachers, mainly use the present tense and imperative verb forms in linguistically unplanned talk, which provides little exposure to other tenses (Harley, 1993). In such situations of limited and restricted target language exposure, it is highly unlikely that pupils will achieve native-like competence. Even some of the target language features which may be relatively common in teacher talk may not be perceptually salient to pupils. In these situations, the pupils may be learning the content but failing to learn the linguistic features of the L2.

In relation to output, it has been observed that the teacher does most of the talking in content-orientated classes with pupils having little opportunity for sustained production (Harley, 1993). Pupils' production results almost exclusively from teachers' questions and tends to be from one or two words in length to a single clause (Allen *et al.*, 1990). When the L2 is acquired solely within the confines of the school system, it is unlikely that pupils will gain complete competency in grammatical features of the language and will fail to acquire language styles useful in informal situations (Myers-Scotton, 2006).

Baker (2003) notes in this context that the vernacular of the street is different to the language of the curriculum and that in bilingual education in a minority language there is a danger that the language will never extend beyond school use into the realms of play and peer culture. Preadolescents and adolescents mark their identity with one another in different ways, through fashion, dress and music, and by using a vernacular language style (Tarone & Swain, 1995). This style can include verbal competition, argument and insult. These language functions may not be available to them in the target language. Thus, while immersion schools in a minority language context can play an important role in language revival and maintenance, they cannot be solely responsible for pupils' mastery of Irish. The success of immersion education is limited to some extent by the opportunities for language use in wider society. Another limitation in the school setting for acquiring an L2 and particularly a lesser-used language is that the integrative social motivation is absent as there is little or no exposure to the language outside of school. This is certainly the case regarding Irish language acquisition where pupils of all-Irish schools outside Gaeltacht areas have limited opportunities to use or to experience the language in any social environment unrelated to education. If the language is to live outside the school context then it is vital that plans are put in place to extend its use in the community (Ó Duibhir *et al.*, 2015b). The availability of a critical mass of peers possessing good minority language competence with whom to interact and converse is critical (Thomas & Roberts, 2011).

Pupils immersed with other learners with similarly faulty interlanguages
Weaknesses in the immersion school context for language acquisition are further compounded because the pupils in an immersion class are interacting with other pupils with similarly faulty interlanguages which only compound the difficulties of achieving greater accuracy. Such a situation exists in relation to learners of Irish where the learners' peers have the greatest influence on acquisition, particularly given the absence of social experiences of the language within the community. In a situation where pupils are influenced by their peer group, these social factors can affect the learner's choice of 'reference group' upon which to model his/her target language variety (Ellis, 2008). Although the teacher may wish to enable pupils to integrate with the Irish speech community, that community is diminishing and is remote from the majority of all-Irish primary school pupils. The speech community of the classroom is considerably more immediate and influential and it appears that as long as pupils can communicate with one another in the target language, grammatical errors do not concern them (Mac Corraidh, 2008; Maguire, 1991).

In the case where an incorrect form is used by the learner, and this form does not cause a breakdown in communication, the learner is unlikely to notice this error (Long & Robinson, 1998). Thus, after three to four years in the programme, when pupils have reached the point where they can make themselves understood by teachers and peers, these inaccuracies are a feature of their speech. There is little impetus for them to be more accurate in their language use. There may also be a lack of sociopsychological motivation within the immersion setting for the pupils to change and adjust their grammar (Day & Shapson, 1987). This outcome is entirely understandable when one draws on social as well as cognitive perspectives of SLA (Firth & Wagner, 2007). The pupils are not to be criticised for adopting such a stance which is likely to be at a subconscious level. From the perspective of language use, the pupils have gained sufficient competence through a meaning-focused approach to be mutually understood in the speech community in which they interact. In this way, they mimic, to some extent, untutored learners and their speech has characteristics of pidgin (Ellis & Shintani, 2014).

A comparative study by Baetens Beardsmore and Swain (1985) demonstrated the limitations of acquiring an L2 exclusively at school compared to a situation where there is also some exposure to the target language outside of school. This study compared pupils in French L2-medium programmes in Brussels with those in Canada. The pupils in the Brussels' school were exposed to French outside the classroom and school whereas the pupils in Canada were not. The study revealed that the pupils in Brussels achieved comparable proficiency in French in half the time it took the pupils in Canada to achieve the same level (Baetens Beardsmore & Swain, 1985).

It appears then that pupils in immersion education are very successful in achieving high levels of proficiency in the L2 particularly in their receptive skills of listening and reading. They are unlikely, however, to achieve native-like proficiency in their productive skills of speaking and listening if their only exposure to the L2 is confined to the school setting. This is a key concern in the Irish language context and, as we will see in Chapter 6, one which has a significant impact not only on their continuing proficiency but also on their attitude towards the language.

The role of attitudes, motivation and identity in second language learning

It was suggested above that pupils may lack the motivation to continue to modify their interlanguages and to speak with accuracy given the situated nature of language learning and use in an immersion setting. Motivation has been shown to be one of the key variables in individual differences that significantly affect success in L2 learning (Dörnyei &

Ushioda, 2009). Much of the original research work on motivation in SLA was first carried out by Robert Gardner and colleagues in Canada. A key element of Gardner's (1985) social-psychological model was, understandably, pupil attitude towards the L2 community, as few learners will master the language of a community with low status (Dörnyei & Skehan, 2003). Gardner (1985) divided language learner goals into two broad categories: integrative orientation and instrumental orientation. Integrative orientation concerned a positive interpersonal disposition towards the target language group and a desire to interact and even become similar to respected members of that group. Gardner suggested that language learning was different to that of science or mathematics because of this identification with other speakers and their culture. Instrumental orientation was associated with personal gains that might accrue to an individual such as a better job or higher salary. It was suggested that these categories determine an individual's motivation to learn an L2 and it is the former area of integrative motivation that has seen the greatest level of research and is, according to Dörnyei and Skehan (2003), made up of three major components:

(i) *integrativeness*, subsuming integrative orientation, interest in foreign languages, and attitudes toward the L2 community;
(ii) *attitudes towards the learning situation*, encompassing attitudes toward the teacher and the course;
(iii) *motivation*, which according to Gardner is made up of motivational intensity, desire to learn the language, and attitudes towards learning the language. (Dörnyei & Skehan, 2003: 613)

It was these components and their constituent parts that informed the development of Gardner's Attitude/Motivation Test Battery (AMTB). As research on learner motivation continued to develop through the 1980s and 1990s, a reciprocal causation between motivation and achievement was demonstrated (Gardner & MacIntyre, 1992, 1993). Prior to that point, motivation had been conceptualised as a cause or a product of success in L2 learning.

Theoretical perspectives on motivation are currently changing and there is a move away from the individual cognitive perspective to a more dynamic one where motivation emerges through internal, social and contextual processes. Dörnyei and Skehan (2003) proposed a process model of learning motivation comprising three stages: pre-actional, actional and post-actional. They did not reject Gardner's concept of integrativeness, but maintained that his approach was of most relevance to the pre-actional stage and less useful for predicting actual L2 behaviours in the classroom which tend to be rooted in the situation-specific characteristics of the learning context. The special status given to the target language in an immersion context, for example, might lead to the creation of a new L2 identity which may, in turn, positively influence the language learning process.

Dörnyei (2005) conceived a new approach to L2 motivation which he termed the 'L2 motivational self system'. Within this system, he equates integrativeness and integrative motivation with an 'ideal L2 self'. L2 motivation, according to this model, is seen as the desire on the part of the learner to bridge the gap between the actual self and his/her ideal self, the L2 user that he/she wants to become. Another facet of this model is the notion of an 'imagined community' where the idealised self can be seen as a member of an imagined community. The difficulty in minority language situations, such as Irish in Ireland, is that young learners may have no concept of an Irish-speaking community beyond the confines of the school. In such situations, Dörnyei's 'ought-to L2 self' may be more applicable. This is where the learner is motivated to meet external expectations such as examinations or to avoid negative feedback. the expectations of the L2 user's school, family and society may exert a stronger influence than an imagined language community. This notion is closer to Gardner's instrumental motivation but would appear to conflict with learner autonomy, as discussed, where the learner is encouraged to take greater control of his/her learning. Learner autonomy can be seen as 'a way of encouraging students to experience that sense of personal agency and self-determination that is vital to developing their motivation from within' (Ushioda, 2011a: 224). This, in turn, focuses on Dörnyei's situated practice in the classroom where the teacher and peers can have an impact on motivation. Motivation in this case is not just orientated towards achievement, but is value based and identity orientated (Ushioda, 2011a). There has been a move in language motivation research to link motivation with 'identity goals that are personally valued and that reflect how we relate the self to the social world' (Ushioda, 2011b: 202). While these identity goals are personally constructed, they are influenced by our interactions and by those around us in social situations. How teachers engage learners in the classroom can influence the agency they have in constructing an ideal L2 self where they may or may not view themselves as L2 users in the future.

As noted, language learning is different from other subjects as it is a means of communication and self-expression (Ushioda, 2011b). The L2 can be used to express an emerging identity. Language teaching then involves more than just developing linguistic and communication skills. This underlies the affective dimension of language learning which needs to engage the emotional as well as the cognitive. As Swain (2013) pointed out, learning can take place due to the presence of positive or negative emotions and adds that there can be both a cognitive and an emotional struggle involved. The implications for the classroom are that we need to engage the learners' identities in the learning process itself and to enable them to make connections between the learning process in the classroom and their current and future selves. Van Lier (2007: 47) suggested that 'identities are ways of relating the self to the world'. He placed agency at the centre of learning with motivation and autonomy being inextricably linked. This implies a need to encourage pupils as individuals to explore distinct attitudes, interests, motivations and identities. Norton (2013: 6) refers to this as 'investment', where the learner's commitment and desire to learn a language is linked to his/her developing identity and located within a sociological framework.

It is interesting to note in the context of the research presented in this volume that the vitality of the L2 community influences both attitudes to L2 speakers and instrumental motivation. The data from Census 2016 (CSO, 2017) reveal a fall in the number of daily speakers of Irish in Gaeltacht areas. The number of daily speakers of Irish over three years of age outside the Gaeltacht is 53,217 compared to 20,586 within the Gaeltacht. One must question in this context whether an identifiable L2 Irish-speaking community exists at all for young language learners to envisage becoming part of. This calls into question the pursuit of NS norms for immersion learners. Contrasting this, there is the situation of English as a lingua franca where it is estimated that there are more NNSs of English in the world than NSs of English (Baker & Wright, 2017). In this context, integrating into a British or American English-speaking community may not be the goal of English language learners in China for example (Wang & Jenkins, 2016). Another point of interest is the distinction that Dörnyei and Csizér (2002) make in the context of the global status of English between world language learning and non-world language learning. They consider the L2 motivational self system to apply more to the former than the latter.

Notwithstanding these developments, the AMTB is a well-developed and tested instrument that is particularly useful for survey-type approaches to examine pupil attitude and motivation The results of an AMTB survey conducted with Irish immersion pupils and presented in Chapter 6, are analysed bearing in mind the influence of identity on attitude and motivation.

Role of error correction and feedback

One aspect of interaction between teacher and L2 learners that has received a lot of attention from researchers is negotiation for meaning. Negotiation for meaning has been defined as 'the process by which two or more interlocutors identify and then attempt to resolve a communication breakdown' (Ellis, 2003: 346). Many who subscribe to an interactionist approach believe that negotiation for meaning can lead to SLA by providing learners with three essentials necessary for SLA: comprehensible input, comprehensible output and feedback (Oliver, 2002: 97). It has been argued that negative feedback available in interaction may have a role in the development of L2 skills (Gass & Mackey, 2006).

Another type of negotiation is negotiation of form. A quasi-experimental study was conducted by Van den Branden (1997) to investigate the effects of negotiation on pupils output and the extent to which they negotiate for form or meaning. The participants were forty-eight 11- to 12-year-old learners of Dutch divided into three groups of 16. Each group contained both NS and NNS pupils. They were paired into NS–NNS dyads to perform a communicative task where there was an information gap. It was found that the pupils negotiated on levels of meaning but not on form and modified their output when met with negative feedback (Van den Branden, 1997: 626). The pupils in the study sought clarification when they failed to negotiate the meaning of what their partner had said but were not concerned with ungrammatical utterances, as long they understood the meaning. Van den Branden also found that those pupils who were pushed to produce a greater quantity of output outperformed their peers when asked to participate in the same task with a new partner in a post-test. These negotiations had no effect on syntactic complexity or grammatical correctness, however. Dalton-Puffer (2007) reported similar results from a quantitative analysis of content and language integrated classes where students, according to her, either do not notice or do not care about phonological or morphosyntactic errors. She also found that many language errors went uncorrected by teachers.

Shehadeh (2002: 634) defined a hypothesis-testing episode as: 'any utterance or part of an utterance in which the learner externalizes and explicitly experiments with his or her hypotheses about the target language by (a) verbalizing these hypotheses to test which sounds better or (b) explicitly testing hypotheses against the competences of the (NS) interlocutor by means of (1) requesting confirmation or (2) appealing for help'. Shehadeh examined the hypothesis-testing role of output using a picture description task with 16 participants in eight NS–NNS dyads. The NS interlocutors only provided feedback to 13% of the learner hypothesis-testing episodes when a NNS appealed for help or sought clarification. In situations where the NNS receives no feedback, it is possible that the hypotheses tested were confirmed and led to internalisation. It can be seen then that even when L2 learners seek feedback, it may not always be forthcoming and may lead to internalisation of incorrect forms. In both Van den Branden's and Shehadeh's studies, although the L2 learners had access to NSs with whom to negotiate or to test their hypotheses, they did not always receive feedback that might alert them to non-target forms in their interlanguage.

The corrective feedback that teachers provide to learners in classroom discourse is often deemed to be reactive (Mac Ardghail, 2014) and sometimes confusing (Ó Ceallaigh, 2013). A study of immersion teachers' use of feedback found that almost half of all signs of approval happened immediately after errors (Lyster, 1998b: 70). This happens where a teacher acknowledges the content of a pupil's utterance without drawing attention to a linguistic inaccuracy. A similar pattern was noted in an observational study of nine Grade 3 and ten Grade 6 classes in French immersion schools. It was found that only 19% of grammatical errors were corrected and that the teachers' feedback lacked consistency (Harley, 1987: 12). Teachers are unable to provide feedback for every inaccurate utterance of the pupils and often show signs of approval that can be at best misleading and at worst detrimental to pupil learning.

In another French-immersion study, Lyster and Rannta (1997) investigated learner uptake in response to feedback in four Grades 4–6 immersion classes and identified six different types of feedback provided by the teachers in their study:

Explicit correction refers to the explicit correction of the correct form.

Recasts involve the teacher's reformulation of all or part of a student's utterance, minus the error.

Clarification requests indicate to students either that their utterance has been misunderstood by the teacher or that the utterance is ill-formed in some way and that a repetition or reformulation is required.

Metalinguistic feedback contains either comments, information, or questions related to the well-formedness of the student's utterance, without explicitly providing the correct form.

Elicitation refers to at least three techniques that teachers use to directly elicit the correct form from the student ... elicit completion ... elicit correct forms ... ask students to reformulate their utterance.

Repetition refers to repetition, in isolation, of the student's erroneous utterance. (Lyster & Rannta, 1997: 46–48)

Lyster and Rannta calculated an error rate of 34% in the pupils' utterances, which include unsolicited use of the L1. The predominant type of feedback provided by teachers was recasts. When teachers focused on pupil-generated repair of their utterances, they found that these recasts did not account for any repairs. In a study in a French immersion context, Lyster (2004) found that prompts were more effective than recasts. In a further study in a Japanese immersion context, Lyster and Mori (2006) found that recasts were more effective because the learners were more attuned to focus on language form. This highlights the importance of the context in which the feedback is provided.

One of the difficulties for teachers in providing corrective feedback is that although this can be implemented in a 45-minute language lesson, it may not be feasible for an immersion teacher to continually correct pupils' target language errors throughout the school day as this could disrupt the flow of a lesson and impair content learning (Ó Ceallaigh, 2013). And so, we turn to focus on form as a complementary strategy to feedback in the promotion of SLA in the immersion classroom.

Focus on form

A distinction has been made in the literature between 'focus on form' and 'focus on formS'. Long (1991) suggested that learners need to have their attention shifted occasionally from meaning to linguistic form which he referred to as focus on form. This shift in attention can occur in the context of meaningful interaction which can be more beneficial than decontextualised grammar lessons, where attention shifts from meaning to particular linguistic code features (Long & Robinson, 1998). Focus on formS, on the other hand, is understood as a more traditional focus on presenting grammatical structures to pupils in an isolated and decontextualised way (Long, 1991).

Others have supported the merits of a focus on form approach and some studies have found evidence that incidental correction carried out regularly in context was more effective than explicit form-focused instruction (Ellis *et al.*, 2006; Swain & Lapkin, 2001). However, there needs to be more than merely incidental correction, and an explanation of some selected forms is required bearing in mind the maturity of the learners and their metalinguistic ability. Many researchers have suggested that focus on form activities can help focus learners' attention on the desired features in the input (Nassaji & Fotos, 2007; Ó Duibhir *et al.*, 2016). Even within the context of a meaning-focused approach, encouraging learners to pay attention to form can influence the degree to which the input is processed and thus may lead to uptake. While it may not be possible for teachers to correct all the pupil target language errors that they hear, they must nonetheless address the learners' linguistic weaknesses in a systematic way. It could be argued that the immersion context produces a natural focus on language use and meaning, but it appears to lack a focus on form. Cummins (1999) maintains that if pupils in an immersion context are to acquire more target-like forms in the L2, then teachers must focus on language also, and within this he includes awareness of language forms. The challenge, however, is to determine the most effective way in which to focus on form. Research shows that teachers frequently do focus on form within meaning-focused contexts, and this results in pupil learning. Pupils working in small groups in the same contexts are less likely to focus on form (Ellis & Shintani, 2014).

Doughty and Williams (1998) argue that focus on form activities are useful in drawing learners' attention to grammatical errors as they occur incidentally in classroom use. They found that a combination of communicative pressure such as the need to use particular forms in reporting experiments and narrowly focused frequent recasts, were effective in drawing learners' attention to form.

While focus on formS may be as effective as focus on form in a meaningful context, it may not be as easy to implement focus on formS instruction with young children in an early immersion programme. It is interesting to note that explicit techniques have been found to be more effective than implicit ones (Norris & Ortega, 2000). If pupils receive help in focusing on the information present in the input, i.e. making the form more explicit through guided discovery, they may be enabled to process it in a different way and to acquire the target structures. This has been described as moving the learner from semantic to syntactic processing (Kowal & Swain, 1997). In order to master the L2 structures, their existing knowledge must be reorganised in order to accommodate the new knowledge and pupils will require analytical learning strategies in order to do this. Indeed, there are certain features of the target language where comprehensible input alone, which of its nature is implicit, will not suffice. These are the features of the target language which are 'semantically lightweight, and/or perpetually nonsalient, and/or cause little or no communicative distress' (Long & Robinson, 1998: 23). It appears, however, that immersion education in its current approach fosters an emphasis on semantic processing to the detriment of syntactic processing.

A critical issue for teachers in early immersion programmes is the timing of the introduction of these types of activity. It may not be appropriate to introduce these activities in the early grades as pupils may not be cognitively ready. At a later stage, when pupils have attained basic communicative competence, error correction and feedback could be used to encourage them to reflect on their language use. Harley *et al.* (1998) conducted research with Grade 2 French immersion classes in five schools, and hypothesised that if the gender of French nouns was made more salient in the input, it would lead to more effective learning of this form. Age-appropriate materials such as games, songs and the creation of personal dictionaries were designed for use in the experimental classes over a five-week period. At the end of the school year, when the results of delayed post-tests were examined, it was found that the pupils in the experimental classes were more successful in assigning the correct gender to familiar nouns indicating item learning. There was no evidence, however, that they could generalise this knowledge and apply it to new nouns unfamiliar to them. While the latter result may be disappointing, the overall outcome of the study indicates that focus on formS such as noun gender in French can be an effective learning experience for relatively young children in Grade 2.

An examination of focus on form cannot be isolated from social, cultural and sociocultural perspectives. As noted above, the pupils in an immersion context are situated in the speech community of the classroom where target-like forms may not be seen as important by the learners provided they can communicate their intended meaning. It cannot be assumed that drawing learners' attention to form will be successful unless sociocultural factors are addressed also. Facilitating learner autonomy may engender greater commitment and desire on the part of pupils to learn more target-like features of Irish if it is connected to their developing identity and located within a sociological framework.

Interlanguage corpora and second language learning

The language produced by learners provides a valuable object of study where researchers wish to explore the underlying mental representations and developmental processes that may influence L2 production. The compilation of large datasets of learner language can help to inform not only linguistic research but also the content of L2 curricula and teacher education. The availability of such a large interlanguage corpus allows more effective and efficient evaluation of curriculum proposals in the context of what we know about learner development (Rule, 2004). With the aid of computer technologies, large amounts of data can now be reduced to manageable lists and concordances which can facilitate the identification of patterns in the text (Scott & Tribble, 2006). The identification of these patterns can enable generalisations about learner development and oral data are often ranked above written data as being particularly useful in this regard.

Ellis (1994) distinguishes three types of data for SLA research: language use, metalingual judgements and self-report data. Much of the data used by researchers to date tend to favour elicited introspective and experimental data due to the difficulty associated with controlling variables affecting learner output in 'non-experimental contexts' (Granger, 2002: 6). One of the disadvantages associated with experimental data is that they tend to be based on limited numbers of subjects, as it is difficult to conduct this type of research with large numbers. This results in research findings being reported from a narrow empirical base. A beneficial aspect of compiling learner corpora is that they provide samples of learner output for analysis that can be collected in relatively natural contexts, and so redress the balance with experimental data. Another benefit of learner corpora is their utility in documenting and explaining learner development over time which can be facilitated by longitudinal oral corpora. It must be remembered, however, that the evidence from corpora on underlying L2 competence is indirect and some criticise studies that tend to be descriptive in nature where differences between learner and native language are documented but not explained (Myles, 2005). It is clear, nonetheless, that good quality oral corpora, longitudinal if possible, have a contribution to make to research in SLA.

Research and Pedagogy in Immersion Education

'Immersion education', sometimes classed as a strong form of bilingual education, is the term used to describe L2 programmes that were introduced in 1965 in Montréal, Québec, Canada. Parents of English-speaking children felt that their children were not achieving sufficient proficiency in French in mainstream schools in order to participate fully and function in a French-speaking community and to compete for jobs with their francophone peers. It could be described as a pedagogical approach that promotes L2 learning rather than a particular teaching methodology. Instead of just teaching the L2, the L2 itself becomes the medium through which all other subjects are taught.

In French early total immersion programmes in Canada, for example, pupils enter the immersion programme in senior kindergarten and no English is taught until Grades 2, 3 or 4, depending on the region, and pupils are introduced to literacy in French before English (Genesee, 1998). Immersion education was not an entirely new phenomenon, however, when introduced in Montreal in 1965 as teaching through the medium of an L2 has been part of education systems for many centuries. It has also been a feature of the Irish education system since 1922.

Immersion education has a number of defining features that distinguish it from merely teaching through the medium of an L2:

1. The L2 is the medium of instruction
2. The immersion curriculum parallels the local L1 curriculum
3. Overt support exists for the L1
4. The program aims for additive bilingualism
5. Exposure to the L2 is largely confined to the classroom
6. Students enter with similar (and limited) levels of L2 proficiency
7. The teachers are bilingual
8. The classroom culture is that of the local L1 community

(Swain & Johnson, 1997: 6–8)

These features have been subject to change in different contexts in recent times. The changes in the ethnic diversity of pupils in immersion schools in Canada in the last decade, for example, have led Swain and Lapkin (2005) to revise these core defining features somewhat. The main revisions are that as the immersion language is often the pupils' third or fourth language, Statement 1 above has been revised as 'the immersion language is the medium of instruction'. In the case of French immersion pupils who come from a non-English-speaking home, there may not be overt support for English in the home. This has implications for pedagogy and thus Statement 3 becomes 'overt support needs to be given to all home languages'. The culture of the school may no longer reflect that of the pupils from ethnically diverse backgrounds and so Statement 8 becomes 'the classroom culture needs to recognise the cultures of the multiple immigrant communities to which the students belong'.

There has been a large increase in immigration to Ireland from a wide variety of countries since the turn of the century (Central Statistics Office, 2017) and this has impacted on pedagogy and language support in schools.

There is no evidence to date, however, that a substantial number of parents from diverse ethnic backgrounds are choosing all-Irish schools for their children (Ní Thuairisg & Ó Duibhir, 2016; Ó Duibhir *et al.*, 2015c). This may change, however, in the future and so international experiences and thinking may become more significant.

Academic achievement of pupils in immersion programmes

Target language proficiency

One of the defining feature of immersion education as quoted above is that of additive bilingualism (Fortune & Tedick, 2008). This implies that by the end of the programme: 'L1 proficiency should be comparable to the proficiency of those who have studied through the L1. In addition, a high, though not native speaker, level of proficiency is achieved in the L2' (Swain & Johnson, 1997: 7). The construct of additive bilingualism has been challenged in recent years with greater globalisation and migration. Many pupils start school with knowledge of more than one language. The notion of 'adding a language' as connoted in additive bilingualism no longer suffices for the complex sociolinguistic background of learners. García (2009) introduced the construct of 'dynamic bilingualism' to take cognisance of this new context. Nonetheless, despite the greater ethnic and linguistic diversity of Irish society, this has not been reflected to any great extent to date in all-Irish schools. In a recent study involving sixth-class pupils ($n = 284$), two (0.7%) reported speaking a language other than English or Irish at home (Ní Thuairisg & Ó Duibhir, 2016). As immersion pupils in the Irish context develop their linguistic skills in Irish, they draw on their prior knowledge of English. So, while the term 'additive bilingualism' is used in this volume, it is recognised that there is a dynamic nature to this term where learners draw on their full linguistic repertoire (García & Wei, 2013), which for the vast majority of pupils will be the named languages of English and Irish.

Internationally, immersion pupils achieve high levels of fluency in the target language and their receptive skills of listening and reading are close to those of NSs. Their productive skills of speaking and writing, however, contain many non-target-like forms that appear to persist over time (Tedick & Wesely, 2015). Harley (1991) noted that the productive skills of pupils at the end of Grade 6 had not reached NS levels on grammatical and sociolinguistic measures. Lapkin *et al.* (1990) also found that second-level students were well behind their francophone peers in the acquisition of these skills. Bibeau (1984) maintained that immersion students' French contained many syntax and vocabulary errors of a serious nature which resembled an artificial language or code. This code is used for communication but it is not like a real language with social and cultural value. While recognising that immersion pupils achieve high levels of fluency and communicative competence in the target language, these writers have highlighted areas of concern that are of relevance to all immersion and bilingual education contexts, including Irish immersion.

Studies that have investigated French immersion primary pupils' L2 development have shown the following characteristics:

- they have excellent understanding of the target language in context,
- they extract unanalysed meaningful chunks from the input they receive and use them correctly in their production,
- they make use of 'high coverage' items (e.g. chooses 'things' or general verbs such as *aller* or *faire* in French) which they stretch to cover a variety of contexts,
- they are adept at using communication strategies which allow them to circumvent their lack of a word with for example mime, gesture or the substitution of an English word,
- they can produce certain forms in the target language that have been learned as formulas without necessarily understanding their functional range. In other words, they do not wait until they fully comprehend a structure before they start producing it. This indicates that comprehension and production may be developing simultaneously.
- there is mother tongue influence on French language use.

(Based on Harley, 1991: 15)

Some studies in Canada, such as Spilka (1976) and Adiv (1980), have attempted to measure the error rates of French immersion pupils over time. The findings of these studies and others appear to challenge Krashen's (1985) input hypothesis which claimed that learners would acquire the target language and its grammar if they received sufficient naturalistic input. Despite these immersion students' prolonged exposure to the target language, their output contains a high percentage of errors. It appears that early immersion programmes are successful in achieving their aim of additive bilingualism where content learned through an L2 has no adverse effect on L1 skills. They are also very successful in producing L2 speakers who are very fluent in the target language. Where they are less successful is in the area of grammatical accuracy that is non-target-like and there is some evidence that this does not develop over time. Classroom observation studies of immersion classrooms have also found that teachers tend not to put sufficient pressure on their pupils to speak with grammatical accuracy (Genesee, 1987; Swain, 1998).

If immersion pupils are not required to speak with grammatical accuracy, they may be operating from Skehan's (1994) 'least effort' principle where the learner says what is necessary to communicate but feels little pressure to adhere to NS norms and grammaticality. Their output is not of the 'pushed' variety advocated by Swain (2005). When pupils commence an early total immersion education programme, there is pressure on them to communicate meaning through the target language. Skehan (1994) argues that situations such as this can lead to fossilisation as the pressure to extract meaning and to express oneself overrides the motivation to restructure the interlanguage system. Pupils may lack opportunities for reflection partly because they may be too young to engage in such reflection and also because of pressure on the teacher to implement all aspects of the school curriculum (Mac Ardghail, 2014). The emphasis in the early years of immersion is focused on encouraging the pupils to produce language that communicates meaning. Teachers may not consider error correction and feedback, which requires learners to reflect on language structures, as appropriate or crucial at this stage.

If the pupils in an immersion programme are truly to discover what the target language norms are, they may need feedback that alerts them to forms that are incorrect or opportunities to reflect on their output. The pupils may communicate successfully with one another, but if they do not receive feedback as to whether their message has been communicated accurately and appropriately, they are likely to continue to communicate in this way and not develop their interlanguages (Swain, 2005). There is little motivation for them to stretch their use of language and they are likely to restrict themselves to syntax and lexis that they are comfortable and familiar with and thus gain little in terms of language learning (Turnbull, 2002).

Vygotsky (1978) suggested that knowledge is constructed as learners engage in social interaction and that this knowledge can be internalised at a later stage. It could be argued that in order for learners to operate in the ZPD they need to interact with other learners or a teacher with greater linguistic expertise than themselves. In a study that has relevance for all-Irish schools, Genesee et al. (1989) compared the attainments in French of English L1 pupils in francophone (all-French) schools in Quebec with those of English L1 pupils in early immersion schools. The all-French schools resemble all-Irish schools in that English language arts were not introduced until Grade 4 and only amounted to 2.5 hours per week until the end of Grade 6. All other subjects were taught through the medium of French. This contrasts with the early total immersion programme where instruction is 50% in English and 50% in French by Grade 6 (see Figure 2.3). It was found that the early immersion pupils performed as well as the pupils in the all-French school on French proficiency tests. While it might be expected that the all-French pupils would have outperformed their early immersion peers due to greater exposure to French in the school context, Genesee et al. (1989: 260) suggested that an 'upper limit may exist to the second language proficiency that can be attained in school programs that do not provide substantial opportunities for peer interaction in the second language'. In other words, the early immersion exposure may not have been sufficient to gain the maximum impact from this type of programme. The type of interaction that he envisaged was with French NS peers. There is some evidence to support the merit of this suggestion from a study conducted by Harris and Murtagh (1987). They administered tests of mastery of various objectives in spoken Irish to pupils in second (8-year-old) and sixth classes (12-year-old) in both all-Irish and Gaeltacht schools. The objectives covered the broad areas of general comprehension of speech, understanding the morphology of verbs in listening and control of the morphology of verbs in speaking. They expected that equal percentages per group would achieve mastery of these objectives in spoken Irish over time (Harris & Murtagh, 1987: 116). While this expectation was confirmed for all-Irish school pupils, the mean percentage attaining mastery in Gaeltacht schools increased significantly over time. They offer the following as the most plausible explanation for this: '... that children from English-speaking homes will be motivated to acquire native-like competence in Irish where there are substantial numbers of native Irish speakers in the class or where Irish is the dominant language in the community outside the home' (Harris & Murtagh, 1987: 119).

Due to the small number of native Irish speakers, and the distance of most all-Irish schools from Gaeltacht areas, it is difficult to imagine how interaction with NSs could be facilitated on a large scale for the majority of all-Irish school pupils. The use of electronic media and class trips to the Gaeltacht could provide some possibilities. However, as Genesee et al. (1989: 262) concluded: 'If the goal is native-like second language proficiency, then serious consideration needs to be given to how to extend the language environment of programs that lack peer models'. Consideration must also be given to the current sociolinguistic situation in Gaeltacht areas where the majority of pupils' proficiency in English is greater than that of their L1 home language, Irish (Ó Giollagáin & Charlton, 2015; Ó Giollagáin et al., 2007; Pétervári et al., 2014). This further highlights the challenges faced by immersion educators in seeking to enable pupils to achieve native-like proficiency in Irish when their counterparts in Gaeltacht schools, with the benefit of home and some community exposure to Irish, are struggling to achieve these levels. Various pedagogical studies offer other insights that deserve consideration.

First language proficiency

Many parents with children in immersion programmes are attracted by the claim of additive bilingualism (Ó Duibhir et al., 2015c). Notwithstanding this, they are often concerned initially that while their children acquire competency in the L2, their L1 skills will suffer as a result. Many studies have been conducted to investigate this area, particularly in Canada and the United States, and the results have shown consistently that not only do

L1 skills not suffer but that their L1 skills may be even better than those of their monolingual peers (Bournot-Trites & Tellowitz, 2002; Tedick & Wesely, 2015). Many international studies have examined the effect of a world language such as French or Spanish on pupils' English language skills. The situation regarding Gaelic-medium education in Scotland is closer to that which pertains to Irish in Ireland as both Irish and Scots Gaelic could be described as minority languages. A comprehensive study of the attainment of Gaelic-medium P7 pupils in Scotland concluded that:

> At the very least it may be claimed that children educated through the medium of Gaelic are not disadvantaged in comparison with their counterparts who are educated through the medium of English and that in the process they have gained the advantage of becoming bilingual and bicultural. (Johnstone et al., 1999: 67)

The researchers also stated that the Gaelic-medium pupils' attainments in English were most encouraging.

Reference was made in Chapter 2 to the Macnamara (1966) study which claimed that teaching through Irish, the weaker language, was having a detrimental effect on the pupils' achievement in English. When the data from Macnamara's study were re-examined by Cummins (1977), it was found that the immersion pupils had the same level of attainment in English as the non-immersion pupils. These results were replicated in another study of attainments in English reading of third-class pupils (91 all-Irish and 76 English-medium) (Cummins, 1982).

The Department of Education in Ireland carried out a national reading survey of the attainments of primary school pupils in English reading in 1988. A total of 476 fifth-class pupils in all-Irish schools were tested as part of this survey. When these pupils were compared to the national sample, it was found that the pupils in the all-Irish schools gained higher scores (Department of Education and Science, 1991). One must be careful, however, in interpreting these results as neither the socioeconomic status of the children nor their intelligence levels were controlled for. A more recent study of English reading and mathematics attainment (Shiel et al., 2011) showed that pupils in second and sixth classes in all-Irish schools achieved significantly higher mean scores on English reading than pupils in the national sample. In relation to mathematics, pupils in second class in all-Irish schools achieved significantly higher mean scores than pupils in the national sample whereas there was no significant difference in the performance of sixth-class pupils relative to the national sample. When school socioeconomic background factors were considered, it was concluded that the average school-level sixth-class English reading score in all-Irish schools was about what would be expected, whereas the sixth-class mathematics scores were somewhat lower than what would be expected. The authors recommend that teachers pay 'particular attention to developing and using mathematical language in Irish as pupils engage in reasoning and problem solving' (Shiel et al., 2011: 36). Another study that examined sequencing of formal reading instruction, found that the sequence, i.e. Irish first or English first, was not critical to later reading attainment in the L1 (Parsons & Lyddy, 2009). While there were initial advantages in each language when formal reading commenced in that language, these advantages declined and evened out by later grades. These findings are supported by Kennedy (2012) who also reported positive results for the executive functioning of Irish-medium pupils.

The 'interdependence' or 'common underlying proficiency' principle developed by Cummins (1981) helps to explain how pupils learning through the medium of their L2 can attain skills in their L1 equal or better than their peers who have been educated through their L1. According to the interdependence principle: 'transfer across languages of conceptual knowledge and academic skills (such as learning and reading strategies) compensates for the reduced instructional time through the majority language' (Cummins, 2000: 186). The implication of this principle is that in immersion settings such as all-Irish schools, pedagogy that develops oral and literacy skills in the L2 is not just developing L2 skills, 'it is also developing a deeper conceptual and linguistic proficiency that is strongly related to the development of literacy in the majority language' (Ó Duibhir & Cummins, 2012: 31). While the surface aspects of individual languages are quite different, underlying features at a conceptual level can be transferred across languages. These features pertain not only to literacy skills but also to learning strategies. This common underlying proficiency has been given other terms such as 'common operating system' (Baker & Wright, 2017) and 'a common underlying reservoir of literacy abilities' (Genesee et al., 2006). Regardless of the label, this principle involves both procedural and declarative knowledge.

Academic achievement in other areas of the curriculum

A number of studies have examined the overall academic achievement of immersion pupils relative to their non-immersion peers. In an early, large-scale study, the Bilingual Education Project in Toronto and Ottawa, Swain and Lapkin (1982) compared the achievement of early French immersion pupils in mathematics, science and English at primary level with English programme students in the same school or school board. The tests were administered in English. When results were controlled for IQ and socioeconomic variables, no significant differences were found between the two groups for almost all comparisons. Other studies comparing the scores of immersion pupils on mathematic tests with their peers in English-medium schools confirmed Swain and Lapkin (1982) findings. There were no significant differences in the pupils' mean scores even where the tests were administered in English although French was the medium of instruction (Bournot-Trites & Reeder, 2001; Turnbull *et al.*, 2001).

Similar findings emerged from a study in Wales that compared the achievement of Key Stage 3 (11- to 14-year-old) Welsh-medium pupils in mathematics and science with English-medium pupils. No significant differences were found between the two groups for the majority of comparisons (Bellin, 1996). In a comprehensive study of the attainment of Gaelic-medium pupils in Scotland, cited in relation to English above, the researchers examined attainment in mathematics and science. In relation to mathematics, it was found that the average attainment scores of the Gaelic-medium pupils in both P4 and P7 were significantly higher than the national average and they also performed better than the English-medium pupils in the same schools (Johnstone *et al.*, 1999). The attainments in science were less impressive from an immersion perspective. While the P4 pupils' average attainment scores matched the national average, they were significantly below the average scores for English-medium pupils in the same schools. At P7 level, the Gaelic-medium pupils were still significantly behind their English-medium counterparts in the same schools in science, although their attainments were close to the national average (Johnstone *et al.*, 1999). A possible explanation for the poorer results in science offered by the research team was that there may have been difficulties with the vocabulary for science and that the science assessments were conducted in English whereas the medium of instruction was Gaelic. This issue is similar to that reported in the Shiel *et al.* (2011) study above where the language of mathematical problem solving appeared to cause a lower score for sixth-class pupils.

Overall, the results of the studies reported here indicate that learning curriculum content in the areas of science and mathematics through the medium of an L2 does not appear to hinder pupil attainment.

Language acquisition and pedagogy in immersion education

Three of the main weaknesses of immersion programmes that may be linked to unsatisfactory pupil linguistic outcomes can be categorised as follows:

(1) an over-reliance on comprehensible input where pupils acquire the target language without reflection and analysis of target language structures;
(2) acquisition takes place in a school setting that cannot provide the range of language functions required for full mastery of the language;
(3) pupils with faulty interlanguages are immersed with other pupils with similar linguistic errors and the sociopsychological pressure to speak more accurately is not there as a result.

In order to explore the possible origins of these weaknesses, it is necessary to examine how pupils acquire the target language in an immersion setting and to consider the type of pedagogy adopted in immersion education and its impact on target language acquisition.

Experiential and analytical teaching approaches

Teachers in immersion schools act as both content teachers and language teachers and they attempt to create naturalistic conditions similar to those in which L1 learning takes place (Cammarata & Tedick, 2012; Mac Ardghail, 2014). This type of teaching has been described as an experiential teaching strategy where there is a meaning-orientated teaching focus and the L2 is used naturally for subject-matter content. The interaction between the teacher and the pupils plays a key role in their SLA. The pupils are required to interpret the meaning of the teacher's verbal utterances and the non-verbal clues of the classroom context and it is through this negotiation of meaning that they acquire the L2. It requires great skill on the part of the teacher to implement such a programme, achieved by choosing themes which are of interest to the pupils. This, in turn, exposes them to authentic language use because the content excites their interest above and beyond the language itself (Harley, 1993).

However, students' competence in the target language does not benefit from focus on meaning alone or on functional use of the language and unless increased demands are made on the learner's developing language system, continuous growth cannot be guaranteed (Genesee, 1987). In the absence of this increased demand, the type of learning in a meaning-orientated programme leads to the development of implicit knowledge, which is 'knowledge that learners are only intuitively aware of and that is easily accessible through automatic processing' (Ellis *et al.*, 2006: 340). While an experiential approach leads to the development of good fluency in the target language and near native-like ability in the receptive skills of reading and writing, it is less successful in developing grammatical accuracy (Allen *et al.*, 1990; Lyster, 2007). What appears to be lacking in immersion programmes are the analytical strategies for organising that learning in a more conscious way or more explicit learning. Arising from the Allen *et al.* (1990) study that examined the teaching strategies in both French immersion and core French classes, Stern (1990) made a tentative recommendation that more attention should be paid to analytical strategies in immersion programmes. He emphasised that both analytical and experiential strategies should be viewed as complementary and part of a continuum, while others have suggested that older learners can cope with a more analytical approach (Philp *et al.*, 2008).

Following Stern (1992), Lyster (1998a) suggested that teachers should endeavour to create contexts within the classroom that are most conducive to learning, maintaining that the integration of an experiential and analytical approach in an immersion programme would be most beneficial. He has refined this recommendation over time which has led to the counterbalance hypothesis:

> Instructional activities and interactional feedback that act as a counterbalance to the predominant communicative orientation of a given classroom setting will be more facilitative of interlanguage restructuring than instructional activities and interactional feedback that are congruent with the predominant communicative orientation. (Lyster & Mori, 2006: 294)

In an early immersion programme where the predominant focus is on meaning, an analytical approach is likely to be more successful in focusing learner's attention on form. When this hypothesis is applied to corrective feedback, explicit feedback or teacher prompts such as elicitation, metalinguistic clues, clarification requests and repetition have been shown to be more effective than recasts in French immersion settings (Lyster *et al.*, 2013). Interestingly, Lyster and Mori (2006) found that recasts were more effective in Japanese immersion contexts in the United States where learners attended more to form. These results highlight the importance of taking contextual factors into account, and research on corrective feedback in an Irish immersion context would help to illuminate the best approach. Reflection on communication can also be a critical component in focusing the learner's attention on form. The context for this reflection on communication could be a jigsaw task as in Lyster's (1998a) study, a dictogloss (Wajnryb, 1990) task as other studies such as Kowal and Swain (1997) have demonstrated, or the reflective learning journal in Ó Duibhir *et al.* (2016) and Ní Dhiorbháin and Ó Duibhir (2017). The tasks employed in these studies have been shown to be effective in engaging learners in reflection on their language use.

Research on the Acquisition of Irish as a Second Language

Many of the studies on the acquisition of Irish as an L2 to date have been small scale in nature and have tended to have a narrow focus. In this section, we will examine the different studies and their relevance to the research presented in this book. While the focus of this volume is primarily on immersion pupils' oral production, the account of the studies below which also investigated other language skills may give an indication of the typical errors that L2 learners of Irish are likely to make.

Mastery of Irish in early immersion education

In Chapter 2, I referred to the influence of naíonraí (Irish-medium preschools) in creating a demand for the new generation of all-Irish schools.

The first naíonra was opened in 1968 and by 2016 there were a total of 300 naíonraí, 67 in the Gaeltacht and 233 outside the Gaeltacht. Two notable studies on how children learn Irish in naíonraí were conducted by Hickey (1997) and Mhic Mhathúna (2008).

The Hickey (1997) study reported on data gathered as part of a comprehensive census of 190 naíonra sessions in 1993. As well as gathering information on the number of naíonraí in operation at that time and statistics regarding the children, questionnaires were administered to parents, stiúrthóirí (leaders), stiúrthóirí cúnta (assistant leaders) and comhairleoirí (advisors to the stiúrthóirí). The census was distributed to all naíonraí in the Republic of Ireland and 225 children (58 in the Gaeltacht, 167 outside the Gaeltacht) were randomly selected and tested for achievement in comprehension, production and imitation in Irish.

The children were categorised into three groups depending on their home language background: (i) Irish only, (ii) Irish and English and (iii) English only. The researchers administered a proficiency test in Irish. Almost all the children, regardless of their home language, could answer 40% of the comprehension items successfully with all the 'Irish only homes' children scoring at least 75%. Just over half (54%) of the 'Irish and English' group scored 75% or more, but just over one-third (35%) of the 'English only' group scored 75% for comprehension. There was greater variation in the production scores where just over half (53%) of the 'English only' scored 40%, but only 6% scored 75% or more. These items were obviously more demanding as only 72% of the 'Irish only' group scored 75% or more. There were higher scores in general for the imitation items compared to production but they followed the pattern that would be expected in terms of home language.

Hickey notes that these results show that the majority of the children developed basic comprehension. More than half of the children showed an advanced comprehension and a limited ability to express themselves in Irish (Hickey, 1997). The children from these naíonraí who continue Irish-medium education in an all-Irish primary school may find the transition easier because of the comprehension skills they have acquired in Irish and, in general, the ability gained in Irish can only be advantageous to them.

Mhic Mhathúna (2008) investigated the role of storytelling as a vehicle for facilitating SLA in naíonraí. She studied and recorded storytelling sessions in an in-depth study of one naíonra, over a six-month period, using a case-study approach. She transcribed 11 hours of recorded data and, based on her analysis, she found that the pre-school teachers facilitated children's participation in the sessions and that the input received led in time to the acquisition of Irish. The teachers read the same stories repeatedly and this enabled the children to acquire formulaic utterances that they were able to segment at a later stage and to use creatively. The language of each story tended to be associated with that story only by the children, and features such as prepositional phrases did not transfer from one story to another. Where the teacher used language from the stories in interactional routines, however, the children did transfer formulaic utterances in that case. It was evident from later recordings that the children had made significant progress in acquiring Irish. Children who had substantial exposure to Irish at home and experience of being read to, benefited from the language input that they received in the naíonra and made considerable progress. Although the focus was on the language acquired from storytelling sessions, Mhic Mhathúna (2008) found that children were enriched in many ways by the experience of the storytelling sessions.

Next, we take a look at pupils' mastery of the Irish language in primary school, both in English- and Irish-medium primary schools.

Mastery of Irish in primary school

English-medium schools

The most comprehensive studies in the mastery of Irish are the evaluation studies of primary school pupils in the Republic of Ireland conducted by Harris and associates over a period of 30 years dating back to the late 1970s (Harris, 1982, 1984; Harris et al., 2006; Harris & Murtagh, 1988, 1999). Harris devised criterion-referenced tests based on the curricular objectives of the *Nuachúrsaí* [new courses] programme in use in schools at that time and which continued to be used until the advent of a revised primary school curriculum (Department of Education and Science, 1999). The tests were administered to pupils in second, fourth and sixth class. The results of the first study in late 1978 revealed that, on average, about one-third of pupils in English-medium (ordinary) schools attained mastery of the Irish language curriculum objectives, another one-third on average made at least minimal progress, while the remaining one-third failed to make even minimal progress in the objectives at each grade (Harris, 1984). A subsequent study in 1985 showed modest but statistically significant gains in the mastery of the sixth-grade objectives over the intervening seven-year period (Harris & Murtagh, 1988).

A further national survey of achievement in Irish at sixth class was conducted in 200 primary schools in 2002, 17 years after the 1985 study. The later study was more comprehensive as it included a new test of reading in Irish. As with the 1985 study, it included English-medium schools, all-Irish schools and Gaeltacht schools. The results for the English-medium schools reveal that there has been a significant decline in the level of achievement since 1985 with the most significant decline in the areas of communication and fluency of oral description (Harris et al., 2006: 56).

All-Irish schools

The results of the Irish speaking test for the same curriculum objectives in all-Irish schools are presented in Table 3.1. They reveal that the all-Irish schools maintained, to a large degree, the attainment levels of 1985 with the exception of control of the morphology of verbs in speaking and control of the syntax of statements. Harris *et al.* (2006) note in the case of the former objective that a relatively small segment of the cohort switched from mastery to minimal progress between 1985 and 2002. They caution, however, that while this change is not statistically significant, it is a cause for concern. The decline in the control of syntax in statements is statistically significant, however, with a decline of 34.2% in attainment levels. Only 59.6% achieved mastery of this objective. The figure for minimal mastery is 33.1% and for failure it is 7.3%. This level of failure is certainly a cause for concern.

More generally, the performance of all-Irish schools was quite satisfactory given the increase in the percentage of this school type from 1.1% in 1985 to 5% in 2002 (Harris *et al.*, 2006). The sociolinguistic background of pupils attending all-Irish schools had very likely changed substantially since the emergence of the new generation of all-Irish schools in the mid-1970s. For example, Ó Riagáin and Ó Gliasáin (1979) found that 51% of fathers with children enrolled in all-Irish schools in Dublin used Irish in their jobs as state employees. That situation is unlikely to pertain today. In their study, Coady and Ó Laoire (2002) found that the number of pupils from homes where Irish was spoken 'often' or 'sometimes' had fallen from 24% in 1974 to 9% in 2000.

Table 3.1 Percentage of sixth-grade pupils in all-Irish schools who attain mastery on each objective on the Irish speaking test in 1985 and 2002

All-Irish schools		Attain mastery	Difference
Irish-speaking objectives	1985	2002	(2002–1985)
Communication (second-grade objective)	99.3% a *(0.67)*	94.6% *(3.59)*	–4.7%
Fluency of oral description	95.2% a *(2.21)*	87.6% *(5.0)*	–7.6%
Speaking vocabulary	72.0% b *(5.17)*	66.4% *(6.44)*	–5.6%
Control of the morphology of verbs	65.0% b *(5.73)*	50.2% *(6.32)*	–14.8%
Control of the morphology of prepositions	85.4% b *(2.81)*	78.7% *(5.48)*	–6.7%
Control of the morphology of qualifiers	68.2% b *(7.95)*	66.5% *(5.25)*	–1.7%
Control of the morphology of nouns	49.0% b *(9.87)*	50.3% *(5.48)*	+1.3%
Control of the syntax of statements	93.8% a *(2.94)*	59.6% *(4.51)*	**–34.2%**

Source: Harris *et al.* (2006: 62).
Note: Significant differences ($p < 0.05$) are printed in bold. Standard errors are printed in italics.
N 1985: a = 145, b = 156, N 2002 = 208. 'N' represents the number of pupils who were assessed in each of the Irish speaking objectives in 1985 and 2002. In 1985, there were differences in the number of pupils tested on some of the objectives.

Effect of parental social class, ability in Irish and frequency of use of Irish

A notable finding in the Harris studies is that social class, parental ability in Irish and the frequency of use of Irish at home were all significantly correlated with pupil achievement in Irish (Harris, 2002; Harris et al., 2006; Harris & Murtagh, 1988, 1999). Use of Irish at home was also found to make a significant contribution to pupils' attitude and motivation to learn Irish (Harris & Murtagh, 1999). These findings are important for the context of the present study as parents of children in all-Irish schools generally come from higher socioeconomic backgrounds as measured by the number of parents entitled to medical cards[1]. In the Harris et al. (2006) study, the respective percentages for medical card holders in both school types were 12.8% for all-Irish schools and 19.5% for English-medium schools. In the Shiel et al. (2011) study, 45% of sixth-class pupils in all-Irish schools came from high socioeconomic backgrounds compared to 30% of sixth-class pupils nationally. Similarly, parental ability in Irish was higher in all-Irish schools with, for example, 20.3% of parents understanding most conversations or having NS ability compared to 5.9% for the same categories in English-medium schools (Harris et al., 2006). In the case of use of Irish, parents of children in all-Irish schools again used the language more often with 52% using it 'sometimes', 'often' or 'always' compared to 21.9% of parents in English-medium schools (Harris et al., 2006). However, in a study of Irish language immersion education models (2015), it was found that among parents ($n = 288$) of Irish-medium pupils, only 1.5% spoke Irish or mostly Irish in the home (Ó Duibhir et al., 2015c). According to a study by Ní Thuairisg and Ó Duibhir (2016), a similar figure of 1.5% of parents ($n = 321$) speak Irish or mostly Irish. We can speculate that as the number of all-Irish schools grows, pupils are drawn from a wider pool that is more representative of the general population of parents with a greater social class and ethnic mix and less frequent use of Irish in the home as found by Coady and Ó Laoire (2002).

Pupils' attitude, motivation and identity in relation to Irish

The role of attitude, motivation and identity in L2 learning discussed earlier was also studied by Harris and Murtagh (1999) in relation to Irish. The study, known as the Twenty Classes Study, examined sixth-class pupil attitude/motivation to learn Irish in 20 English-medium schools. The instrument used was an adapted AMTB developed by Gardner (1985) for use with French L2 learners in Canada. Harris found:

> ... that pupils were reasonably well disposed towards the Irish language itself and towards the idea of integrating with the Irish-language-speaking 'group'. But motivation, or actual commitment to learning Irish, is less

positive. Pupils with better motivation and attitudes are more successful in learning Irish. (Harris, 2002: 88)

A study of pupil attitude and motivation in the context of all-Irish schools is presented in Chapter 6.

Linguistic errors in learners' written Irish

Ó Domhnalláin and Ó Baoill (1978, 1979) and Ó Baoill (1981) analysed the examination scripts of a sample of 200 pupils who sat the Leaving Certificate Irish examination in 1975. The Leaving Certificate examination is the terminal examination at the end of post-primary education in Ireland. Pupil's scripts from both all-Irish and English-medium schools were examined and errors in their Irish language essays were recorded. The sample was evenly distributed between girls and boys and higher-level and ordinary-level papers. Of particular interest are the type of errors identified and the manner in which they were categorised for analysis. The study used the following categories: verbs, nominal words, qualifying words, prepositional words, pronouns, particles, interrogative words and conjunctions, and syntax.

In relation to verbs, the most striking aspect was that the substantive verb *bíonn*, habitual present tense 'to be', was the verb used incorrectly most often. Of all the verbs used, the verb *bíonn* was used 7.4% of the time and incorrectly used 51% of the time (Ó Domhnalláin & Ó Baoill, 1978). The verb *Bí* 'to be' is obviously one that is used frequently and its incorrect use will increase proportionately the number of errors that a learner will make. The corpus of Irish language pupils' speech presented in Chapter 5 also highlights all-Irish primary pupils' difficulty with this verb.

When the syntactic errors were examined in the same study, 76% could be traced to the influence of English. This English influence was sub-categorised as follows: direct translation, words omitted, the copula *Is*, words in the wrong order, direct and indirect speech, incorrect words and a miscellaneous sub-category (Ó Baoill, 1981). Errors in the use of the copula represented 10.3% of all errors. When students used the copula in their essays, they used it correctly 76% of the time. Ó Baoill (1981) describes the copula as an inherent part of the Irish language that frightens learners and ascribes learners' lack of grasp of this feature as being the result of a lack of practice in natural speech and an overdependence on English as a criterion.

The Walsh (2007) study examined errors in written texts collected from 17- to 18-year-old sixth-year pupils in six post-primary all-Irish schools in Dublin. She sought sample essays from the most proficient five or six pupils in Irish in each school, one Irish (as a subject) essay and another essay written in Irish from a different subject area. She analysed a total of 31 of the 60 essays submitted, 16 Irish essays and 15 in other subject areas. These samples were the work of 15 different pupils and the analysis was based on 6000–9000 words of text. She found 752 errors in total, 369 in the Irish essay and 383 in the essays from a different subject area.

The top 15 errors in the Irish essays represented 89% of the error types in the essays and there were 28 types of error in total. Some of these errors, such as spelling, pertained to writing only and either may not arise or are less obvious in the analysis of spoken language. Difficulties with lenition, eclipsis and the genitive case accounted for a significant percentage of errors (38%). Regarding the genitive case and adjectives, some writers have called for a restandardisation and a simplification of the rules associated with their use and acknowledge that the genitive case and the inflection of adjectives are undergoing change in everyday use by NSs (Ó Curnáin, 2007; Péterváry et al., 2014). A revised Irish standard was published in 2012 (Rannóg an Aistriúcháin, 2012) and a further updated standard was published in 2016 (Rannóg an Aistriúchán, 2016). Other aspects that are relevant to the present study are difficulties with the use of numbers, the use of the verb in general, translation from English, inappropriate preposition usage, the verbal noun and the copula/substantive verb.

In contrast to the Ó Domhnalláin and Ó Baoill study mentioned earlier, the error rate associated with the copula and the verbal noun was considerably lower in the Walsh study. Walsh (2007) hypothesised that there would have been a greater error rate in the case of the copula. Of note, the Ó Domhnalláin and Ó Baoill scripts were Leaving Certificate examination scripts, written under pressure without time for reflection, while Walsh's were written in a more relaxed, reflective context. Also in the Walsh study, the sample essays were from the most competent pupils in Irish. As I will highlight later on in the presentation of data in Chapter 5, reflection and time to become aware of errors can improve accuracy.

Another study that examined the use of the copula in Irish was Ó Conchubhair (2003). He designed focus on formS type tasks to teach the copula to secondary school pupils in first, third and sixth year in English-medium post-primary schools. He administered pre-tests, post-tests and delayed post-tests to the pupils. The tests were written tests as he thought that these would give pupils a greater chance of success than oral tests. Following the focus on form activities, the pupils made significant gains in their mastery of the copula and these gains were in most cases maintained in the delayed post-test. The area that showed the greatest decline in the delayed post-test was the negative form of the copula. These results suggest that focus on formS activities may be beneficial in teaching this feature of Irish.

Errors in the conversational speech of all-Irish school pupils

In this section, the findings of a number of studies that examined features of the conversational speech of all-Irish school pupils in the Republic of Ireland and Northern Ireland are explored. These studies include an in-depth investigation of the features of spoken Irish in one all-Irish school in Belfast (Northern Ireland), all-Irish school pupils' acquisition of word order or syntax in Irish and the acquisition of the copula and other features of Irish by all-Irish school pupils.

Henry *et al.* (2002) documented the variety of Irish spoken by pupils in one Irish immersion school in Belfast, Northern Ireland. The aim of the study was to identify areas of difficulty, the reasons for these difficulties and also to establish how language development could be improved. Data were gathered from 21 pupils who came from English-speaking homes and were drawn from classes P3–P5 or children in the 7- to 10-year age range. They found that the pupils in the selected school became highly competent communicators, who were able to speak Irish fluently and willingly. Most of the major aspects of Irish grammar were acquired effectively through the use of Irish in the classroom, without the need for specific grammar instruction. They found little evidence of interference from English in most major grammatical structures and many of the early errors that the pupils made seemed to disappear without specific instruction. A small number of target language errors that tended to persist for a considerable period were reported. They found no evidence that these errors were the result of errors in teacher input but rather the errors arose as part of the language development process itself. The specific areas, identified as having a tendency to fossilise, were the incorrect use of the substantive verb in place of the copula, issues concerning syntax associated with the verbal noun and the incomplete mastery of pronouns and prepositions.

A number of studies have examined word order as an aspect of Irish acquisition and all have found that children acquire this feature without difficulty and there does not appear to be any interference from English, the learners' L1. Henry and Tangney (1999) examined children in Belfast acquiring Irish at an early age in Irish-medium pre-schools and primary schools. These children had no contact with NSs of Irish outside of the school setting and their input was received from highly competent but not NSs. The immersion pupils in the Henry *et al.* (2002) study had no difficulty in acquiring the verb-subject-object (VSO) order in Irish and they displayed the ability to reset parameters for word order. Henry and Tangney (1999) believe that learners will only adopt a more complex grammar where the input they receive has strong evidence to support this. It appears that immersion pupils in all-Irish schools receive strong and consistent input regarding Irish NP (noun phrase) word order and that they acquire it without difficulty. This may not be the case with other features of the language.

The acquisition of the copula in Irish does not appear to be as consistent as word order. Sentences with *Tá*, present tense of the substantive verb *Bí* 'be', follow the expected word order VSO described above. In the case of the copula, however, 'the predicate precedes the subject, which is marked with accusative case' (Henry & Tangney, 1999: 245). For example:

Sin an leabhar.
That is the book.

Learners may not be able to reset their parameters to take account of this variation particularly when one structure in their L1 (English) has two counterparts in Irish.

Maguire (1991) examined the variety of Irish acquired by children and young adults aged 8–18 in a small urban community in Belfast, Northern Ireland. The children were raised by parents and educated by teachers in an Irish-medium school who had learned Irish as an L2. The families had limited access to other Gaeltacht areas and Irish-speaking communities. Maguire notes that it is hardly surprising then that the linguistic output of these children revealed many linguistic features associated with L2 learners. One 17-year-old in the study reflected on a trip to the Gaeltacht. The participant stated that the people spoke too quickly with peculiar accents and used words that he had never heard. It appeared that the features of the Irish that he spoke with his family and friends were communicatively sufficient for their context but that when he was confronted with NSs using Irish as their daily language, his concept of his own language competence was challenged. This reflects the situation in immersion education where many of the learners do not have an opportunity to interact with NSs or near-NSs other than their teacher. Maguire (1991) observed, however, that there was a monitoring system within the group of children from Belfast and that they would not tolerate certain irregularities. If one speaker introduced an aberrant form, another member of the group would supply the accepted form in a natural inconspicuous way. This example illustrates the social nature of language acquisition and the normative effect of a speech community.

Another study that examined the proficiency of pupils in all-Irish schools was that of Ó Catháin (2001). He gathered data from six sixth-class pupils in five different all-Irish schools in the greater Dublin area. The speech samples were collected in interviews with the subjects by the researcher. Among the features that Ó Catháin (2001) observed in these learners was the inappropriate use of the substantive verb 'Tá' instead of the copula 'Is', which was also noted by Henry *et al.* (2002) above. Other features found were the use of incorrect syntax, English words directly translated into Irish without being Gaelicised and Irish idioms being replaced by English ones. He noted that these examples were not unique to the interlanguage of all-Irish school pupils but that similar examples could be found in the speech of monolingual NSs going back 150 years. While Ó Catháin acknowledges that language change is natural and that languages are constantly changing,

Ó Dónaill (2000) maintains that the case of Irish as a minority language is not the same as that of major languages. As the vibrancy of the Gaeltacht communities diminish, there is a concern that some of the changes in Irish are the result of incomplete acquisition rather than natural changes in the language (Ó Giollagáin & Mac Donnacha, 2008).

Summary

In this chapter, L2 learning theories were examined from a number of perspectives to help identify the critical elements in the SLA of pupils in an early immersion programme. The examination of UG reveals that the knowledge of previously acquired languages can influence the learning of further languages and the cognitive perspective on L2 learning offers explanations as to how L2 input is processed. The concept of limited attentional resources is central to L2 learners' ability to process input that may lead to language development. As described, L2 learners negotiate first for meaning rather than form and they may not pay attention to all the information available in the input. This can lead to the coding in long-term memory of non-target-like interlanguage forms. When pressurised to communicate, learners may draw on these automatised forms to free up attentional resources to focus on the content of their utterances. If these inaccurate forms prove useful in communication, they may stabilise with habitual practice and may not be easily susceptible to change. We will see evidence of this in Chapter 5 when we examine the corpus of pupils' speech.

In order to get learners to notice form in the input that they receive, some pedagogic intervention is required. This is particularly relevant for features that are semantically lightweight, non-salient and do not lead to a breakdown in communication. Such intervention could be error correction and feedback, or focus on form activities that draw learners' attention to particular features. A difficulty highlighted with teacher correction is that not every error is corrected, particularly in content classes, and the feedback that pupils receive can be inconsistent. Another intervention shown to be effective in experimental studies is providing opportunities for pupils to produce 'pushed output'. This type of output can help to draw learners' attention to form in their output, leading to interlanguage development. The concept has been further developed as 'languaging' within a sociocultural framework where pupils working collaboratively with others can be scaffolded and given feedback appropriate to their ZPD. The process of verbalising their thinking about their L2 can mediate learning and just as languaging requires reflection on language use, so too does learner autonomy. It has been argued that successful L2 learning depends on learner involvement, target language use and learner reflection. It is the latter element that may be missing from immersion programmes.

In the case of a minority language where there is little or no contact with the language outside of the school, acquisition of native-like ability may be too high an expectation. The speech community of the classroom exerts its own norms that may militate against acquiring target-like forms. So, as we seek to align pedagogy with how children learn, we need to do so not just from a cognitive stance but from a socially situated one as well. The experiential nature of immersion programmes has been cited as promoting negotiation for meaning rather than form and I suggest that a more analytical approach is required where pupils would have opportunities to reflect on their interlanguage hypotheses. This could be done through interactional feedback and tasks such as dictogloss, jigsaw tasks and reflective language diaries. These strategies could help to address the overemphasis on experiential approaches in immersion programmes and on analytical approaches in traditional language classes. In implementing such strategies, learner identity would also need to be engaged to promote a greater understanding and ownership of the learning process.

Research on Irish as an L2 has highlighted areas that learners find difficult to acquire and the copula and verbal noun are two areas that have been shown to be particularly problematic. In the research on immersion education in an Irish context, pupils have been shown to attain high levels of achievement relative to their peers who learn Irish as a core subject in English-medium schools. They use non-target-like forms in their interlanguage however, and these forms persist over time similar to the findings of the general body of research in immersion programmes.

No study to date in the Republic of Ireland has provided a detailed examination and description of the features of all-Irish school pupils' spoken Irish across the range of immersion schools. If the nature of the non-target-like features is to be understood, the first step is to document and analyse these features and a suitable method is to compile an oral corpus. Such a corpus, along with analysis of pupils' attitude and motivation towards the target language and their effect on attainment levels are presented in Chapters 5 through 8. These findings provide guidance for teachers in making more informed judgements in relation to their pedagogy in immersion classes. Before we examine the data, we shall take a brief look at the research methodologies employed in the studies presented in the forthcoming chapters.

Note

(1) Medical cards are awarded to people under a certain income threshold and allow them free access to general practitioner services, community health services, dental services, prescription medicine costs, hospital care and a range of other services. In general, possession of a medical card indicates low socioeconomic status.

4 Design of Studies

Introduction

The research findings reported in this volume stem from four studies carried out in the Republic of Ireland (RoI), Northern Ireland (NI) and Canada over a period of eight years. In this chapter, I set out the research design of the studies and the rationale underpinning them. The first two studies were corpus-based studies and aimed to obtain a broad picture of the linguistic features of all-Irish pupils' Irish. The third study sought to broaden the scope of the research beyond the Irish context. The attitudes of French immersion teachers in Toronto and Ottawa towards their pupils' proficiency in French were compared to those of Irish immersion teachers towards their pupils' proficiency in Irish. The fourth study investigated the attitude and motivation of all-Irish pupils to learning and using Irish. In particular, the use of Irish by the pupils outside the classroom and in the home was explored. The home language practices of parents were also examined.

Corpus-Based Studies

The purpose of the two corpus-based studies was to obtain a comprehensive picture of Irish-medium pupils' Irish language use and to examine the range and nature of the non-target-like linguistic forms encountered. A secondary aim was to investigate pupils' awareness of and attitudes to the features of their spoken Irish. The studies recruited 16 Irish-medium schools, 13 all-Irish schools and three Gaeltacht schools. The schools were located in the RoI ($n = 12$) and NI ($n = 4$). A key focus of the research was to investigate the broader communicative and sociolinguistic context within which the variety of Irish spoken by all-Irish pupils develops. The source of these non-target-like forms was also explored. Possible reasons for their occurrence include exposure to non-target-like forms used by other immersion pupils; the limited availability of good models of correct language use reflecting the situated nature of the learning environment; and the social stimulus to correct the errors that they were aware of. Ultimately, it was intended that these studies would provide the foundation for a pedagogic approach that would improve the quality of Irish immersion pupils' Irish. It was also hoped that the studies would define more clearly the type of research programme that is needed to provide a comprehensive account of the particular variety of Irish spoken by immersion pupils.

In this chapter, I give an overview of the different components of the two corpus-based studies. In order to obtain a broad picture of the pupils' linguistic features I developed a collaborative task to administer in all-Irish schools during which typical peer-to-peer interaction occurred. Speech samples from pupils in a range of all-Irish schools were recorded and transcribed in order to describe the features of their spoken Irish. Arising from this activity, I compiled a corpus of the pupils' speech and performed a lexical and syntactic analysis on this corpus. The most common linguistic errors made by them are documented in Chapter 5. I also developed a stimulated recall activity to determine their capacity to recognise their errors and to distinguish between those errors that pupils were capable of correcting when given an opportunity to reflect on them and those that were more fundamental in character. I describe the outcomes of this activity in Chapter 6.

Participants and setting

Eleven Irish-medium primary schools in the RoI participated in the first phase of the study. Nine of these were all-Irish schools and two were Gaeltacht schools. In the second phase of the study, I extended the original research to NI, where a further four all-Irish schools participated. At a later point, I added a third Gaeltacht school in order to increase the spread of native speakers for comparative purposes. In this way, the three main Gaeltacht regions were included: Munster, Connaught and Ulster. The schools selected in all phases represent the full range of different types of all-Irish school found on the island of Ireland and were carefully chosen against a set of criteria to represent the different educational and sociodemographic variables present in all-Irish schools. Those criteria were:

- school size;
- geographical location;
- number of years established;
- socioeconomic status (SES) of school community;
- proximity or otherwise to a Gaeltacht heartland area;
- access or not to a post-primary all-Irish school.

These variables capture the range of educational and sociolinguistic circumstances that might influence pupils' proficiency in Irish. A random sample of schools would not have ensured such a broad representation.

Table 4.1 presents background information on the schools in the study. The all-Irish schools were all located in cities and small towns. This is where the vast majority of all-Irish schools are situated, as it requires a critical mass of parents to create the demand for an all-Irish school. It is not feasible to list the geographical regions in which the schools were located, as this might reveal the identity of the schools. It can be stated, however,

Table 4.1 Background information on participating schools

School ID	Access to second-level all-Irish school	Location: urban/rural	No. of years established	No. of pupils in school	Proximity to a Gaeltacht heartland (km)	Disadvantaged status
All-Irish schools – RoI						
School 1	X	Town	<20	200–300	–	–
School 2	✓	City	<20	200–300	0–15	–
School 3	✓	City	>30	>300	–	–
School 4	✓	City	>30	200–300	–	DEIS Urban 2
School 5	✓	Town	20–30	>300	30–45	–
School 6	X	Town	<20	<200	–	DEIS Urban 2
School 7	✓	Town	20–30	>300	–	–
School 8	✓	City	20–30	200–300	–	DEIS Urban 1
School 9	X	Town	20–30	200–300	–	–
All-Irish schools – NI						
School 13	✓	City	>30	>200	–	Low SES
School 14	X	City	<20	<200	–	Low SES
School 15	X	Town	<20	<200	–	Low SES
School 16	X	Town	<20	<200	–	Low SES
Gaeltacht schools						
School 10	✓	Rural	>30	<200	Category A[a]	DEIS Rural
School 11	✓	Rural	>30	<200	Category A	DEIS Rural
School 12	✓	Rural	>30	<200	Category A	DEIS Rural

[a] A Category A Gaeltacht area is defined as one where 67% or more of the population speak Irish on a daily basis (Ó Giollagáin et al., 2007).

that of the 13 all-Irish schools, 5 are located in Ulster, 2 in Connacht, 2 in Munster, 2 in Leinster outside Dublin and 2 in Dublin.

All schools are co-educational and employ an early immersion policy. Some of the schools adopt an early total immersion policy where no English is taught to the pupils until sometime in the pupils' second, third or fourth year in school. When the teaching of English commences, it is taught for approximately 3.5 hours, or 12.5% of the school week. Other schools adopt an early partial immersion approach where English is taught for 2.5 hours per week in infant classes with all other subjects taught through the medium of Irish. Ten schools in low SES areas were included in the studies. Low SES schools in the RoI participate in a scheme titled 'Delivering Equality of Opportunity in Schools' (DEIS). There are three bands within this programme: 'Band 1' and 'Band 2' for urban schools and 'Rural' for rural schools. Band 1 is considered to have a higher degree of educational disadvantage than Band 2.

The 89 all-Irish primary school pupils outside the Gaeltacht who participated in the two corpus-based studies were drawn from sixth class in the RoI and from seventh class in NI and ranged in age from 11 to 13 years. They had been exposed to approximately 5000 hours of instruction through the medium of Irish prior to the study. The pupils featured in the transcripts had little or no contact with Irish outside of school activities and came from English-speaking homes. Pupils from homes where Irish was spoken often or very often were excluded as exposure to Irish outside the school may have impacted the features of their Irish.

The 23 Gaeltacht primary school pupils who participated followed the same curriculum and the vast majority came from Irish-speaking homes. The inclusion of three Gaeltacht schools enabled a direct comparison between the linguistic output of pupils in all-Irish schools located in English-speaking areas of Ireland, and that of native speaker pupils of the same age and stage of development living in Gaeltacht communities. Day and Shapson (1996) used a francophone comparison group in a similar fashion when assessing the oral communicative skills of French immersion pupils in the province of British Columbia, Canada. Other examples of this approach of comparing immersion learners' speech with that of native speakers are Björklund *et al.* (2014), Thomas *et al.* (2014), Thomas and Gathercole (2007), Thomas and Roberts (2011) and Thordardottir (2011). The Gaeltacht schools were chosen from areas where 67% or more of the community spoke Irish on a daily basis. Areas with this level of daily Irish usage have been identified by Ó Giollagáin *et al.* (2007) as the strongest areas in which Irish is spoken. While these areas may be the strongest Gaeltacht areas still extant, they are in fact bilingual communities where the pupils experience extensive contact with English. It is not suggested that the pupils in the three Gaeltacht schools represent a pure form of Irish. As Ó Curnáin (2007) demonstrated in great detail, the Irish spoken in the Gaeltacht has entered what might be classed a 'post-traditional' stage. Recent research supports this view indicating that native speaker acquisition of Irish may be incomplete, with Gaeltacht pupils (7- to 12-year-olds) having a greater vocabulary knowledge in English than in Irish (Péterváry *et al.*, 2014). Every effort was made to recruit participants who were the strongest available in terms of linguistic competence in Irish. In consultation with the class teachers, I specifically targeted pupils with Irish as their home language. Bearing in mind the small sample size and the context of the communicative task, it is argued here that the speech samples of these pupils are representative of the most competent Irish speakers available in this age group. Among the factors that distinguish the Gaeltacht pupils in the study from their immersion counterparts is greater exposure to Irish, access to a speech community outside the educational setting and contact with more competent adult speakers. A strong relationship has been found in studies between exposure to the target language and the acquisition of linguistic forms (Thomas *et al.*, 2014; Thordardottir, 2011).

Corpus-based study 1: Collaborative task (Chapter 5)

For the first corpus-based study, I developed a collaborative task and invited the pupils to work in groups of three. Once occupied in the task, I recorded their conversations which consisted of typical language behaviour in a reasonably naturalistic setting. The task challenged the pupils to design a playground for children in a school in Zambia. A story about a girl called Maggie attending a school in Zambia was read to the pupils. Maps and photographs supported the story. The story was chosen in order to introduce an affective dimension into the task. The girl in the story was of a similar age to the children, but her life experience had been very different to that of children in a developed country. Following the story, the pupils worked together in groups of three, to design a playground for Maggie's school with a budget of €3000/£3000. A list of equipment and prices was supplied. As they designed the playground, the pupils had to bear in mind the ages of the children, the weather in Zambia and safety issues. The context created by the task was one that was as close as possible to typical peer-to-peer interaction. By and large, the groups worked independently of me and of one another, with occasional enquiries made to other groups regarding how much money they had spent or the number of swings they had included, for example. Recording took place while the pupils created the playground design on an A3 sheet. In each class, I video-recorded three groups and audio-recorded the remainder. Only the video recordings were transcribed to create the corpus.

The task activities were conducted during regular class time and all pupils in each class participated in them. Similar tasks could be easily replicated in any classroom. The speech samples collected in the video recordings were transcribed verbatim and provide, for the first time, an extensive corpus of Irish immersion learner language. The focus of the analysis of these data was on lexical and syntactic items and the pupils' language use rather than a conversational analysis and communicative interaction-type approach. The transcribed samples of the pupils' speech gathered through the collaborative task were analysed using WordSmith tools. This enabled the most common features of the pupils' spoken Irish to be quantified, thereby providing a list of the high frequency words used by the pupils, and a comparison of the correct and non-target-like use of these words.

The collaborative task used in this study was designed to focus the pupils' attention on the assignment in hand and on communicating their thoughts rather than on the linguistic form in which they were communicating them. An initial perusal of the corpus may lead the reader to assume that the pupils only had access to a narrow range of vocabulary. However, when two or more people interact, they do not express every single aspect of their intended meaning, but rely on mutually understood features of the context and background (Seedhouse, 2004). During the collaborative task, pupils were located in the here and now and this facilitated the use of non-verbal messages, where much of the meaning between the pupils was relayed.

The task differed significantly from typical teacher–pupil dialogues that often generate an initiation-response-feedback pattern generally controlled by the teacher. The dialogues generated had a much looser structure involving unfinished utterances and switches of topic (Maybin, 2006). The recordings gave insights into the features of the pupils' Irish while engaged in communicating with one another in situations not supervised by a teacher. The task designed was in keeping with a sociocultural view of learning where '[...] learning is dependent on the socially structured exchange of information between learners in groups ...' (Olsen & Kagan, 1992: 8). It was not a 'collaborative dialogue' as defined by Swain *et al*. (2011: 41) where the 'speakers engage jointly in problem solving and knowledge building'. The emphasis here was on peer-to-peer communication where the pupils were not pushed to communicate with a high level of grammatical accuracy unless they chose to do so, as this was not the purpose of the task. The samples of learner speech provided valuable insights into the communicative performance of the pupils which informed the stimulated recall exercises with the pupils at a later stage.

Corpus-based study 2: Stimulated recall (Chapter 6)

One means of enabling pupils to reflect on their language use is to video-record their communication and to allow them to view it a short time later. The recordings can then be used to ask participants to recall and explore their perceptions of their linguistic performance while performing the task (Sato & Lyster, 2007). This type of study can be classed as a retrospective study, where the exploration takes place after data collection, referred to in this case as a stimulated recall exercise (Ellis & Barkhuizen, 2005; Gass & Mackey, 2000; Polio *et al*., 2006). Another feature of this type of exercise is that it allows pupils to have a voice in the research. As a former immersion teacher, I was very aware of the insightfulness of pupils and viewed them as co-researchers in these studies (Pinter, 2014). I also believed that any measure to address the perceived inaccuracies in pupils' immersion language would need to engage them as active agents in their own learning.

The second corpus-based study used a stimulated recall design in which the researcher prompted participants to express their thoughts about their language use during the task. While asking 11- and 12-year-old pupils to explore their states of consciousness may not be possible or reliable, the recorded extracts allowed the pupils to reflect on their performance of the task and on the language used. The stimulated recall presented the pupil with his/her own speech as an object upon which to reflect and the researcher attempted to help the learner to externalise his/her thinking and to gain insights into the current state of the learner's interlanguage. The pupils were given an opportunity to reflect on their output and to correct any errors apparent to them, thus providing evidence of their underlying linguistic competence. This yielded richer data than would have been available if one relied merely on the evidence of the linguistic performance in the initial recordings.

The interactive task designed for this study focused pupils' attention on the completion of the exercise itself rather than on the language being used. The stimulated recall process allowed the researcher to seek clarification of issues that might not otherwise be capable of interpretation. The issues that the learners noticed in a stimulated recall are important as these gave an indication of where their attention was focused during the interaction. There were three phases to the stimulated recall activity in these studies. In the first phase, the pupils viewed recorded video excerpts and gave their general thoughts on their speech in the extracts. As they cited language-related issues, the researcher directed the focus of the reflection onto these issues, easing them into the stimulated recall activity. This was achieved in a non-threatening way and involved gaining their confidence and trust. I did this by affirming how well they had been able to communicate with one another. When some of the pupils were very critical of their accuracy and code-mixing, I sought to balance that by pointing out the strengths of their Irish. In this way, they were enabled to share their observations and insights into their thought processes concerning their use of Irish with an interested enquirer. In the second phase, the pupils were given a transcript of the excerpt that they had just viewed and were shown the recording a second time. After the second viewing, they were invited to correct any mistakes that they had noted in the recording or in the transcript. The third phase focused on the mistakes that the pupils identified and corrected. The issue of why they made mistakes when they knew the correct form, at some level, was explored with them. As it transpired, the pupils engaged in the stimulated recall exercise with enthusiasm and appeared to enjoy the experience.

Other Studies

Study 3: Teachers' attitudes towards pupils' proficiency in immersion language (Chapter 7)

The collaborative design task described above enabled the recording of the unplanned oral production of selected groups of pupils engaged in a collaborative task. Immersion teachers and principals observe their pupils' progress and development in the target language over the course of a school year and throughout their time in school. They are likely then, to have valuable insights to offer into the characteristics of their pupils' second language, the grammatical errors they make and the educational, social and linguistic factors that shape its emergence. In parallel with the corpus-based study, the pupils' teachers and principals in the RoI ($n = 12$) and NI ($n = 6$) were interviewed regarding their attitudes towards the features of the all-Irish pupils' Irish.

In Chapter 3, I discussed how grammatical inaccuracies in immersion pupils' oral production are a common feature of immersion programmes internationally. On that basis, I thought that it would be worthwhile to compare the attitudes of Irish immersion teachers with those of their peers in French immersion schools in Ontario, Canada, to see what similarities and differences there might be. To that end, I interviewed French immersion teachers ($n = 14$) in Toronto and Ottawa about their attitudes towards their pupils' proficiency in French. I report the views of the Irish and French immersion teachers ($n = 32$) in Chapter 7.

Study 4a: Attitude and motivation to learning and using Irish (Chapter 8)

The all-Irish primary school pupils in the original corpus-based studies also completed an Attitude/Motivation Test Battery (AMTB) survey to explore their attitudes and motivation to learning and using Irish and the results are reported in Ó Duibhir (2010). Overall, the all pupils in the RoI and NI had very positive attitudes to learning Irish, but these positive attitudes did not extend to making the extra effort required to acquire native-like grammatical accuracy. While it might be assumed that all-Irish pupils would have a positive attitude to learning Irish, I don't think that this can be taken for granted. Interviews with teachers in Irish primary schools where English is the medium of instruction reported negative attitudes to Irish and a lack of motivation to learn Irish among pupils as they see little value in learning Irish when everyone can speak English (Hickey & Stenson, 2016). Teachers in that study also reported low levels of interest among their teacher peers in teaching Irish. Smyth and Darmody (2016) report that children attending all-Irish primary schools tend to have more positive attitudes to Irish than those in English-medium schools. They also found that while 13-year-olds at post-primary all-Irish schools 'are much less likely to find Irish not interesting but no such difference is found for reported interest in Irish' (Smyth & Darmody: 6). All-Irish pupils can use Irish as a means of communication within the school which grants the language some utility value but it may not engender interest. The all-Irish pupils live in the same communities as their English-medium school counterparts and are not immune to the sociolinguistic reality that surrounds them. Evidence of this is reported by pupils in the Ó Duibhir (2010) study who revealed that they had little exposure to Irish outside the school context.

This can lead to a situation, similar to the subject in Smith-Christmas' (2017) study, where use of Irish outside the domain of the school has not been normalised. The pupils may possess the ability to speak Irish but lack the desire to do so.

In order to study these issues, the Attitude Motivation Test Battery (AMTB) previously used by Harris and Murtagh (1999) and Ó Duibhir (2010) was administered to primary and post-primary all-Irish pupils. Harris and Murtagh's version had 77-items and Ó Duibhir previously used 57-items. In this study, the AMTB was further reduced to 37-items, as part of a wider study with colleagues (Ó Duibhir et al., 2015c) which examined models of provision for Irish-medium education in 20 stand-alone schools and units on the Island of Ireland. The 37-items, related to various aspects of pupil's attitudes and motivations in relation to learning and using Irish, were spread across these 5 scales.

(1) Desire to learn Irish (six items).
(2) Attitude to learning Irish (seven items).
(3) Parental encouragement to learn Irish (five items).
(4) Irish-ability self-concept (six items).
(5) Use of Irish (13 items).

New items related to out-of-classroom use of Irish, not previously investigated, were included in the revised AMTB. Each item was answered by pupils using a five-point Likert-type response ranging from *Easaontaím go mór* 'strongly disagree' to *Aontaím go mór* 'strongly agree'. Recruitment occurred at 20 stand-alone schools and units in the RoI and NI.

Although a causal connection cannot be demonstrated between attitudinal variables and proficiency, these attitudinal variables may help to support and maintain motivation to learn a second language over the long period required to attain mastery (Harris & Conway, 2002). The degree to which pupils in all-Irish schools were motivated to attain communicative competence in Irish and the levels of motivation to acquire grammatical accuracy was the focus of this study.

Table 4.2 Participants in AMTB

School type (jurisdiction)	No. of participants	Age of participants (years)
Fifth class primary (RoI)	128	10–11
Seventh class primary (NI)	69	10–11
Year 4 post-primary (RoI)	101	15–16
Year 12 post-primary (NI)	75	15–16
Total	373	

Study 4b: Home language practices of all-Irish school parents (Chapter 8)

As a parent-led movement, the role of parents in their children's acquisition and use of Irish merits investigation. As part of the Ó Duibhir *et al.* (2015c) and Ní Thuairisg and Ó Duibhir (2016) studies, questionnaires were also sent to pupils' parents to investigate a range of issues pertinent to parents and their children's education through Irish. For the purposes of this volume, I will confine the analysis to the language medium of parents' schooling and their home language practices. The combined data from both studies create a sample size of 670 parents.

Conclusion

The results of the studies described above (corpus based, teacher attitude, pupil/parent attitude and use of Irish) provide the content for the remaining chapters of this volume. Based on the analysis of the corpus, the syntactic and lexical features of the pupils' Irish are analysed in Chapter 5. This is followed by a description of the insights of the pupils gleaned from the stimulated recall activity in Chapter 6. In Chapter 7, I compare the attitudes of the Irish and French immersion teachers to the features of their pupils' immersion language. Chapter 8 reports on the results of the analysis of the pupils' AMTB combined with key data from a questionnaire to their parents. The implications of the research findings presented in this volume are discussed in Chapter 9.

5 An Analysis of a Corpus of the Spoken Irish of All-Irish Pupils

A primary objective of this body of work was to gather speech samples from pupils in all-Irish schools in order to study and describe the features of their spoken Irish. In this chapter, I explore the corpus of the pupils' speech based on transcribed recordings that were made during collaborative tasks conducted with 89 pupils in 13 all-Irish primary schools and 23 pupils in 3 Gaeltacht schools. A description of how the corpus was collated is contained in Chapter 4.

I will begin with a description of the corpus and present a quantitative analysis of the data. The most common words used by the Gaeltacht and all-Irish school pupils will be described to highlight similarities and differences that occur in the words in each school type. Word lists of the English words used by the pupils are examined to determine the level code-mixing or code-switching occurred. Code-mixing and code-switching will be explored relative to non-target forms. I will also report pupils' responses to their peers' code-mixing and code-switching and highlight instances where pupils self-correct, correct others or question the language use of another pupil during the task.

Corpus Analysis

Analytical systems

The combined corpus of pupils' speech in all-Irish and Gaeltacht schools in this study contains 53,763 words. I used WordSmith software to carry out a comprehensive quantitative analysis of the corpus. WordSmith has the ability to reduce large amounts of language to manageable lists and concordances that facilitate the identification of patterns in the text (Scott & Tribble, 2006). Two WordSmith tools were particularly useful in this study. The first, WordList, produced word frequency lists and allowed the range of vocabulary used by the two groups (Gaeltacht and all-Irish pupils) to be identified and compared. It also counted the number of tokens (words) and types (distinct or different words) in a selected text, calculated the percentage of each word and provided a type/token ratio. The other useful tool was Concord. This allowed the corpus to be searched

Table 5.1 School by school summary of the basic features of the corpus of all-Irish and Gaeltacht pupils' spoken Irish

School ID	No. of pupils whose speech was transcribed	No. of minutes of speech transcribed	No. of tokens (words) transcribed	No. of types (distinct) words	Standardised type/token ratio
All-Irish schools					
School 1	6	40	2,504	348	22.0
School 2	9	55	4,286	523	23.1
School 3	6	26	2,933	395	23.9
School 4	9	60	5,438	648	25.4
School 5	9	56	4,334	453	22.8
School 6	11	51	4,144	489	22.0
School 7	6	40	3,482	428	22.6
School 8	6	31	2,388	396	23.0
School 9	3	21	1,274	274	23.2
School 13	6	40	2,945	397	22.7
School 14	9	60	6,168	539	21.5
School 15	6	40	3,578	361	18.0
School 16	3	20	1,693	388	24.9
Total	89	540 (9 hours)	45,177	1,826	22.6
Gaeltacht schools					
School 10	6	17	1,451	330	29.2
School 11	9	43	3,106	408	23.4
School 12	8	40	4,029	523	23.8
Total	23	100 (1 hour 40 minutes)	8,586	831	24.3
Combined all-Irish and Gaeltacht schools					
Total	112	440 (10 hours 40 minutes)	53,763	2,061	22.8

by word or phrase. Using concordances, it was possible to examine a listing of each word or pattern of words in the corpus and the local linguistic context in which the word was used. This enabled a detailed account of the conditions under which the correct and incorrect forms were used. Table 5.1 summarises the headline statistics from these word lists. Columns 1–3 identify the school, the number of pupils whose speech was transcribed and the number of minutes of speech transcribed.

Preliminary type/token analysis

Column 4 in Table 5.1 shows the number of tokens (words) transcribed in each school. The number of types (distinct words) is shown in Column 5. As the texts were of different lengths, it was necessary to use a standardised type/token ratio (STTR) in order to compare the different texts. The tokens are the total number of words in the text and the types are the different or distinct words. WordSmith was set to compute the type/token ratio every 1000 words as it processed each text file. A running average is thus calculated, and the type/token ratio is based on consecutive 1000-word chunks of text (Scott, 2004). The median STTR for all-Irish schools was 22.8 with a range of 18 (School 15) to 25.4 (School 4). In the Gaeltacht schools, the median was 23.8 and the range was 23.4 (School 11) to 29.2 (School 10). The overall average for the two school types does not appear to differ greatly at 22.6 and 24.3 for all-Irish and Gaeltacht schools, respectively. The only STTR that stands out in Column 6 is 29.2 (School 10). This may indicate that the pupils in this school had greater lexical density than the other schools. Scott (2004) cautions, however, that the STTR value is a rather crude measurement of lexical density.

Twenty-five most common words: Variations by school type

The 25 most common words used by Gaeltacht pupils, in order of frequency, were compared with those used by all-Irish pupils and are presented in Table 5.2. The purpose of this comparison was to see if any significant variations or patterns in word usage were evident. It might be expected that native Irish-speaking pupils would use a wider range of verbs in completing the task than their peers in all-Irish schools. As noted in Chapter 3, all-Irish pupils have been found to use a number of high-coverage items and stretch these to meet their needs in a variety of contexts (Harley *et al.*, 1990). It should be borne in mind, however, in the context of this study that the two sub-corpora (Gaeltacht and all-Irish) are based on an identical task and are thus constrained by the subject matter and context of the discourse. The native speaker pupils may not have been extended in the context of the task to display the full range of their ability.

To confirm if this is the case, the most common words used in each school type were compared. The compilation of word lists sought to shed light on whether or not language use varied by school type. Column 1 in Table 5.2 sets out the 25 most common words used by Gaeltacht pupils in rank order. Column 2 provides the English translation. The word frequency order, the number of times each word is used and the percentage of the total corpus is presented in columns 3, 4 and 5 for Gaeltacht schools and columns 6, 7 and 8 for all-Irish schools. We can see in Column 5 that the 25 most common words used by the Gaeltacht pupils represent 40.6% of all the words spoken in their corpus while Column 8 reveals that the same 25 words represent 41.9% of all the words spoken by the all-Irish pupils. Only four of the top 25 words were not common to both groups. This is a significant proportion of the entire corpus when one considers that we were examining only 25 words. It appears that there is a large degree of similarity between the two school types in their frequency of usage of these common words.

Table 5.2 The 25 most common words in frequency order as used by the Gaeltacht pupils compared to the all-Irish pupils

Words	Translation	Gaeltacht schools			All-Irish schools		
		Frequency order	No. of times used	%	Frequency order	No. of times used	%
sin	that	1	501	5.70	1	2837	6.19
an	the	2	327	3.72	2	1890	4.12
tá	be (Pres. Ind. Pos.)	3	294	3.35	4	1421	3.10
é	it	4	290	3.30	3	1591	3.47
sé	six	5	196	2.23	9	684	1.49
a	a (Indef. Art.)	6	166	1.89	7	907	1.98
againn	at us (1 Plural)	7	155	1.76	29	310	0.68
agus	and	8	145	1.65	5	1196	2.61
chéad	hundred	9	128	1.46	6	1024	2.23
yeah	yeah	10	119	1.35	10	654	1.43
dhá	two	11	103	1.17	8	696	1.52
bhfuil	be (Pres. Ind.)	12	95	1.08	13	538	1.17
acu	of them	13	94	1.07	243	24	0.05
rud	thing	14	93	1.06	19	440	0.96
ag	-ing	15	90	1.02	11	621	1.35
níl	be (Pres. Ind. Neg.)	16	87	0.99	24	394	0.86
cad/céard/ cad é	what	17	87	0.99	15	488	1.06
so	so	18	82	0.93	14	534	1.16
ceann	thing	19	81	0.92	23	396	0.86
no	No	20	79	0.90	17	460	1.00
Ar	On	21	76	0.86	16	469	1.02
muid	we (First plural)	22	72	0.82	12	590	1.29
seo	this	23	72	0.82	27	319	0.70
cúig	five	24	71	0.81	28	318	0.69
go	to	25	65	0.74	22	404	0.88
		Total	3568	40.6		19,205	41.9%

When the frequency percentages in Columns 5 and 8 are compared, the most notable difference is in the use of the personal pronoun *acu* 'at/of them'. The pronoun is used over 21 times more frequently by the Gaeltacht pupils (1.07%) than the all-Irish pupils (0.05%). Apart from that example, there is a relatively high similarity between the two school types.

Analysis of Corpus for the Presence of Errors

I conducted a manual analysis for the presence of linguistic errors[1] at a lexical and syntactic level. Deviations from NS norms were marked for further investigation in both all-Irish and Gaeltacht school corpora. The purpose of the error analysis was to quantify the error rates in all-Irish and Gaeltacht schools. While there were some errors in the Gaeltacht corpus, they were few in number (see Table 5.3). The impressionistic view that the reader gets from reading through the all-Irish school corpus is that there are many deviations from native speaker norms in the pupils' speech. Excerpts of 190 utterances in length were chosen from each school. This represented 10% of the total corpus. The excerpts were sent to teachers who were native or near-native speakers. They were asked to underline an utterance that contained an error. The presence of borrowings from English in an utterance was not classed as an error.

This error analysis exercise quantified the number of deviations from native speaker norms in the all-Irish and Gaeltacht school corpus. Column 2 in Table 5.3 shows the number of utterances with errors in each of 190 utterances. Columns 3 and 4 show the percentage of incorrect and correct utterances, respectively. There was a substantial difference in the

Table 5.3 Error analysis of selected excerpts (n = 190 utterances) from the 13 all-Irish immersion schools and 3 Gaeltacht schools

School and group	No. of utterances with errors	Percentage of utterances with errors	Percentage of utterances without errors
Irish immersion schools			
School 1 Group 2	39	20.5	79.5
School 2 Group 1	46	24.2	75.8
School 3 Group 3	53	27.9	72.1
School 4 Group 1	79	41.6	58.4
School 5 Group 2	63	33.2	66.8
School 6 Group 1	45	23.7	76.3
School 7 Group 1	69	36.3	63.7
School 8 Group 1	66	34.7	65.3
School 9 Group 1	42	22.1	77.9
School 13 Group 1	52	27.4	72.6
School 14 Group 2	59	31.1	68.9
School 15 Group 1	75	39.5	60.5
School 16 Group 1	58	30.5	69.5
Total Irish immersion schools	746	30.2	69.8
Gaeltacht schools			
School 10 Group 2	0	0	100
School 11 Group 1	5	2.6	97.4
School 12 Group 2	10	5.2	94.8
Total Gaeltacht schools	15	2.6	97.4

percentage of errors across the schools. The all-Irish pupils had a mean error rate of 30.2%, which is close to 3 incorrect utterances in every 10. This error rate varied substantially from school to school; however, it is not intended to equate a lower rate of errors with a greater proficiency in Irish. School 1 Group 2, for example, had an error rate of 20.0%, whereas School 4 Group 1 had an error rate of 41.6%. This is not to imply that the quality of the pupils' Irish in School 4 is twice as poor as those of School 1. It does, however, as stated at the outset, give a measurement of the number of pupil errors and confirms the impressionistic view that there are many deviations from native speaker norms in the all-Irish school corpus.

The final three rows of Table 5.3 report the results of three Gaeltacht school groups. It can be seen that there are relatively few errors in the Gaeltacht school corpus. No errors were found in School 10 Group 2 and there were 10 errors in School 12 Group 2.

Code-Mixing and Code-Switching

An examination of the corpus reveals that pupils from both school types used English words while speaking Irish. This phenomenon is common among bilinguals (Ritchie & Bhatia, 2006). For the purposes of analysis, code-mixing was defined as 'the use of various linguistic units (words, phrases, clauses and sentences) ... within a sentence' (Ritchie & Bhatia, 2006: 337) or intrasentential use. Code-switching was understood to mean 'the use of various linguistic units (words, phrases, clauses and sentences) ... across sentence boundaries within a speech event' (Ritchie & Bhatia, 2006: 337) or intersentential use. In this next section, we will look at the prevalence of English words in the corpus, followed by an examination of code-mixing behaviour with a particular focus on the most common English words used in each school type.

Intrasentential use

A systematic examination of the all-Irish school corpus word list revealed that the seven English words most often used were, in rank order: 'just', 'like', 'no', 'okay', 'right', 'so' and 'yeah'. Two of the words, 'yeah' and 'no', are referred to as the affirmative and the negative (aff./neg.) particle, respectively. The remaining words ('just', 'like', 'okay', 'right' and 'so') are discourse or pragmatic (Andersen, 2001) markers, but the former term will be employed here. Discourse markers are common in conversational speech and are used to frame dialogue and to act as signalling statements. Alternatively, they can sit outside the clause structure and link segments of the discourse together and generally help to organise the discourse (O'Keefe et al., 2007).

The discourse markers 'just', 'like', 'right' and 'so' and the affirmative/negative particles 'yeah' and 'no', all appear in the top 50 most commonly used words of the 5 million-word CANCODE (Cambridge and Nottingham Corpus of Discourse in English) English language spoken corpus (O'Keefe et al., 2007).

It is not surprising that discourse markers were so common in the all-Irish pupils' speech. What might be deemed more surprising initially was that the discourse markers were in English rather than Irish. Evidence from Hickey (2009), however, shows that 'so', 'right', 'yeah', 'no', 'just' and 'okay' were among the discourse markers used frequently by the native Irish Gaeltacht pre-school leaders in her study. O'Malley Madec (2001) argued that 'just' had replaced the more complex periphrastic[2] equivalents in Irish. There is every possibility then that the discourse markers used by the all-Irish pupils are present in the input they receive from their teachers.

The seven words identified above represented 5.8% of the all-Irish corpus and 4.50% of the Gaeltacht corpus, as presented in Table 5.4. The difference in percentage usage is perhaps smaller than anticipated. These seven words also comprised almost two-thirds of the total number of English words in the all-Irish corpus.

One explanation for the relatively high usage of the affirmative and negative particles 'yeah' and 'no' may be the fact that no simple words exist in Irish for 'yes' and 'no'. For agreement and disagreement conversationally in Irish, it is normal to echo the positive or negative form of the verb or to use the copula (see explanation in section titled 'The Syntactic and Lexical Features of All-Irish Pupils' Irish'). This places cognitive demand on second language speakers. The practice of prefacing answers in Irish with the affirmative or negative particles 'yeah' and 'no' has also been noted in the speech of adult Gaeltacht speakers (Hickey, 2009; Ó hUiginn, 1994). The use of these particles may be for stylistic reasons or to add emphasis,

Table 5.4 The seven most common English words used by all-Irish and Gaeltacht pupils

Word	All-Irish schools			Gaeltacht schools		
	Frequency order	No. of times used	Percentage of all-Irish corpus	Frequency order	No. of times used	Percentage of Gael. corpus
Yeah	9	654	1.43	10	119	1.35
So	14	534	1.16	17	82	0.93
No	17	460	1.00	19	79	0.9
Right	32	264	0.58	57	35	0.4
Just	32	277	0.60	74	29	0.33
Okay	34	262	0.57	58	35	0.4
Like	49	212	0.46	123	17	0.19
	Total	2663	5.8		396	4.50

rather than a lack of vocabulary. Alternatively, it may be that contact with English gives speakers access to simpler one-word markers to help organise their speech.

General Use of English Words

Table 5.5 presents a summary of all the English words used in the corpus. All-Irish pupils used 549 different words in English on 4809 occasions and this represented 8.97% of their corpus. The Gaeltacht pupils used 81 different words on 556 occasions, accounting for 6.48% of their corpus.

The all-Irish school pupils used an English word for 1 in every 11 words compared to 1 in 15 words by their Gaeltacht peers. The difference is not as great as one might expect. In her corpus study of two Gaeltacht communities, O'Malley Madec (2007) found that adult speakers in the core Irish-speaking heartland community used English words 2.7% of the time. Of the English words used, 66% were discourse markers. The use of English words by pupils in three Gaeltacht schools in this study was almost two and a half times that rate. This difference may suggest evidence of the attenuation of Irish among young native speakers (Péterváry et al., 2014). It may, on the other hand, reflect the nature of the activity that elicited speech in fairly densely interactive, task-based communication. In O'Malley Madoc's corpus, the speech was drawn from informal discourse with adults. It is important nonetheless that the spoken production of all-Irish pupils is compared with their Gaeltacht peers of a similar age engaged in the same task.

Layout of Glosses

In the following sections, examples of pupils' speech are selected from the corpus to illustrate the syntactic and morphological features of the pupils' Irish. The majority of the examples are presented in three-line glosses (see example below). There are a few exceptions to this where the speech of more than one pupil is cited. Line 1 in the gloss presents the utterance. If the utterance deviates from native speaker norms it is preceded by a star '*' symbol. Line 2 provides a translation to English, and the target form is provided on Line 3. The pupils are identified by the initial letter of their first name.

Table 5.5 Gaeltacht and all-Irish school pupils' use of English words by school type

	No. of different words in English	No. of times used	Percentage of English words in corpus by school type
All-Irish schools	549	4809	8.97
Gaeltacht schools	81	556	6.48

(Example) School_Group_Line no. _Pupil initial

Line 1   *Pupil utterance as it appears in corpus.

Line 2   English translation.

Line 3   Target form if the original deviated from native-speaker norms.

Pupil–Pupil Exchanges: Language-Related Episodes

When the pupils' speech was transcribed for the corpus it was noted on some occasions when pupils code-mixed or code-switched, their peers corrected them and displayed their disapproval either verbally or with gestures. The following excerpt illustrates a typical example of this type of exchange. In this case, Pupil L used the word 'swing' instead of the Irish equivalent *luascán*, which was available on the sheet with the list of equipment.

(1) 09_01_126-129

L   *Scríobh isteach cad a bhfuil sé (sic), ó agus cuir na swings anseo. [Write in what it is, oh and put the swings here.]

   Ceart go leor.
   [All right]

C   <F points to the Irish word for swing on the sheet> Na luascáin. [The swings]

L   Na luascáin, tá brón orm. [The swings, I'm sorry.]

In Example (2), when Pupil J says 'more fun' her utterance is translated by Pupil D:

(2) 16_01_41-42

J   Agus tá sé more fun. [And it's more fun.]

D   Tá sé níos sultmhar, ní deireann tú fun. [It is more fun (using Irish equivalent), you don't say 'fun'.]

A similar instance was recorded in Gaeltacht School 10 as seen in Example (3):

(3) 10_04_35-39

P   D tá idea agam, tá idea agam. [D I have an idea, I have an idea.]

D   Smaoineamh, tá smaoineamh agat. [Idea, you have an idea.]

P   Tá smaoineamh agam. [I have an idea.]

A   *Ná abairt Béarla. [Don't speak English.]

P   Tá smaoineamh agamsa. [I have (with emphasis) an idea.]

Pupil P uses the word 'idea' and Pupil D supplies the Irish equivalent *smaoineamh*. Pupil P then rephrases in Irish to show that he has accepted the feedback. Pupil A joins in with the reprimand *Ná abairt (sic) Béarla*, and Pupil P rephrases once again.

These types of instances where learners question or correct language use have been referred to as 'language-related' episodes (Swain & Lapkin, 1998). A thorough search of the corpus revealed that there were 10 instances in total of this type of episode in the all-Irish school corpus and 1 in the Gaeltacht corpus. In all 11 cases, the pupil was corrected for using an English word or phrase. No pupil was corrected by another pupil for making an error in Irish. In one instance, however, seen in the following sample, Pupil J engaged in a hypothesis-testing episode where he checks the initial mutation of the word *picnic* by repeating *Don phicnic*. Pupil S confirmed that he was correct in the first instance.

(4) 03_03_250-252

J   ... *mar caithfidh sé bheith ar an áit don phicnic*. [...because it has to be on the place for the picnic.]

J   *Don phicnic?* [For the picnic?]

S   *Don phicnic*. [For the picnic]

The interaction in Examples (1)–(3) is typical of what occurs in negotiation of meaning-type tasks where errors may be ignored in order to create an effective social interaction. It may also be the case that because the errors in Irish did not interfere with the speakers' message and did not lead to a breakdown in communication, attention was not drawn to them. When pupils code-mix or code-switch, however, they are immediately corrected because it is against the school norms. These findings are in keeping with those of Oliver (2002) and Van den Branden (1997) who found that children did not negotiate for form in interactions with their peers.

Syntactic and Morphological Features of Irish

Thus far, we have seen similarities between the all-Irish and Gaeltacht pupils in terms of the words used in performing the task, and the manner in which code-mixing occurred. There were, however, considerable differences in the number of utterances that contained errors. Given that almost 3 in every 10 utterances of the all-Irish pupils contained errors, deeper analysis was warranted.

Before presenting that analysis, we will look at some aspects of Irish linguistics relevant to this context. This is not a comprehensive account of linguistic differences between Irish and English, but a brief account that will help the reader to appreciate some of the deviant features of the all-Irish pupils' Irish and provide a greater insight into why such deviations present in the pupils' speech.

Initial mutations in Irish

Initial consonants in Irish can undergo mutation under certain circumstances, and this is also a feature of other Celtic languages. The two mutations of interest here are lenition and eclipsis. Lenition is represented orthographically by the insertion of the letter 'h' after the initial consonant and it is said to soften the sound of the consonant. One function of lenition is to distinguish gender in Irish nouns. In the following example, the noun is feminine and feminine nouns in nominative singular are lenited after the definite article. For example, *bean* 'woman', *an bhean* 'the woman'. A masculine noun, on the other hand, is lenited in genitive singular, e.g. *bord* 'table', *barr an bhoird* 'the top of the table'. Some possessive pronouns also cause lenition, such as *peann* 'pen', *mo pheann* 'my pen'. Another instance of lenition is triggered by certain preverbal particles such as *ní* in e.g. *cuireann* 'put', *ní chuireann tú* 'you don't put'.

The effect of eclipsis is to suppress the sound of the initial consonant and replace it with a new sound. Certain words trigger an eclipsis in the subsequent word. It is represented orthographically by the insertion of the letter of the new sound in front of the initial consonant. Examples of this include where the letter 'm' is inserted before the initial consonant as in; *an bord* 'the table, *ar an mbord* 'on the table'. Certain numbers such as *seacht, ocht, naoi and deich* (7, 8, 9 and 10) and some preverbal particles such as *an* 'is' (an interrogative particle) also trigger eclipsis as seen in this example; *cuireann* 'put', *an gcuireann tú?* Do you put?

Word order principles in main clauses

Syntax plays a crucial role in the acquisition of Irish, where the typical subject, verb and object (SVO) order that applies to English and other languages differs from Irish. Basic sentences in Irish have a VSO (verb-subject-object) order where the verb comes before the subject and the verb raises out of verb phrase (VP). Other aspects of Irish that differ from English are that adjectives generally follow the noun and a high incidence of prepositional pronouns are inflected.

Word order principles in infinitival or verbal noun clauses

Another feature of Irish that differs considerably from English and other languages is the word order of infinitival or verbal noun clauses. This type of clause has been described as 'one of the most complex categories of Irish grammar' (Bloch-Trojnar, 2006). I illustrate this in Example (a) below. In English, the object comes after the verb and that order is reversed in Irish with the insertion of the preposition *a* + lenition. Thus, the syntax in Irish is: object + *a* (preposition) + verbal noun.

(a) We are going to put them beside the school.
Táimid chun iad a chur in aice na scoile.

In order to translate 'to put' into Irish in the sentence above, the verbal noun *cur* is used and preceded by the preposition *a*. This preposition causes initial mutation of the verbal noun where possible, hence *a chur*. Other phrases that are followed by the verbal noun in this way are: *Caithfidh ...* 'I have to' and *An bhfuil cead agam...?* Have I permission ...? When the substantive verb *Bí* follows *Caithfidh mé ...* or *An bhfuil cead agam...?* the following structure is used:

(b) It must be very clear in your head.
Caithfidh sé a bheith an-soiléir i do cheann.

When *caithfidh* is followed by other verbs such as *déan* 'do', *cuir* 'put', *tarraing* 'draw/pull', the object must be placed before the verbal noun with the insertion of the preposition *a* as in (a) above.

(c) We have to draw a picture.
Caithfimid pictiúr a tharraingt.

As noted by Bloch-Trojnar (2006), this configuration is also found in other modal constructions expressing ability, success or failure. Where the pupils use the following verbs, similar configurations would be expected: e.g. *Is féidir liom...* 'I can...', *Tá orm...* 'I must...', *Ba mhaith liom...* 'I would like ...' and *D'éirigh liom...* 'I succeeded...'.

Another aspect of the verbal noun that can cause difficulties is where a pronoun is the object of the verbal noun. An example of this would be when a pupil expresses 'doing it' in Irish as *ag déanamh é* instead of *á d(h)éanamh*. This construction has been found in the early speech of native first language Gaeltacht children (Harrington, 2006) and may be a developmental error rather than the influence of English.

The copula *Is* and substantive verb *Bí*

A further area of difficulty for English speakers who are L2 learners of Irish is the use of a substantive verb and a copula to express 'to be'. Irish is similar to Spanish in this respect in that there are also two verbs in Spanish to express 'to be': *ser* and *estar* (Genesee, 1998). The two lexical items in Irish to express the verb 'to be' are *Bí* and *Is*. Some writers have remarked that the use of the copula is an aspect of the language that has long been identified as difficult for learners to master (Ó Domhnalláin & Ó Baoill, 1978). Research in both all-Irish and English-medium post-primary schools revealed that many pupils had difficulty with the correct use of the copula and substantive verb (Walsh, 2007). It might be hypothesised that this aspect of Irish would emerge as a difficulty for the pupils in this study. An understanding of copular forms and the substantive verb described below is crucial for the investigation of how pupils use these forms and the analysis that follows.

The commonly held view is that the substantive verb *Bí* can generally though not exclusively be used to express 'it is ...' or 'he is ...' in cases such as the following, where temporary states are being described:

It is raining. = *Tá sé ag cur báistí*.
He is in the house. = *Tá sé sa teach*.

It cannot be used, however, where a permanent state is described such as for classificatory purposes where one wishes to describe what 'a noun or a pronoun is or is not' (Mac Congáil, 2004: 165). In such instances, the copula *Is* must be used.

He is a teacher. = *Is múinteoir é*.
It's a ball. = *Is liathróid í*.

To make matters more complicated for the learner, when the copula is used with the demonstrative pronoun *sin* 'that', the copula and the personal pronoun can be omitted. Thus, the following three sentences are all acceptable ways to express the same thing, i.e. 'That is the table'.

Sentence (a) contains the copula *Is* and the personal pronoun *é*:
(a) *Is é sin an bord*.

Sentence (b) omits the copula *Is* but contains the personal pronoun *é*:
(b) *Sin é an bord*.

Sentence (c) omits both the copula *Is* and the personal pronoun *é*:
(c) *Sin an bord*.

Irregular verbs

As well as the substantive verb *Bí* which is irregular, there are 10 other irregular verbs in Irish. The main verbs that are of interest to this study are *faigh* 'to get' and *déan* 'to do' or 'to make' as they were the most common irregular verbs used by the pupils in completing the task in the study. A verb is considered irregular if its root changes from tense to tense and in the case of *déan* the root changes in the past tense and there is both an independent (*rinne*) and a dependent form (*dearna*). *Faigh* is subject to greater change than *déan* as its root changes from *faigh* to *fuair* in the past tense and there are different dependent and independent forms in the past tense (*fuair, bhfuair*), future tense (*gheobhaidh, bhfaighidh*) and conditional mood (*gheobhadh, bhfaigheadh*). I chose the verb *faigh* for in-depth analysis below and provide a summary of the use of *déan* in a later section. The analysis of the pupils' use of *faigh* examines all forms of the verb used by them, paying particular attention to the irregular forms.

Syntactic and Lexical Features of All-Irish Pupils' Irish

Here, we will examine the features of the all-Irish pupils' Irish contained in the corpus with a focus on lexical, morphological and syntactic issues. The following categories were chosen in order to analyse the features of the pupils' Irish:

- word order;
- use of copula *Is*;
- use of substantive verb *Bí*;
- morphology of the other most common verbs in the corpus;
- prepositional pronouns;
- use of numbers;
- interrogative pronouns;
- pupils use of pronoun *é* 'it';
- mapping of English syntax onto Irish.

Word order

The evidence from the data is that the children in all-Irish schools succeed in mastering word order of Irish without difficulty, i.e. VSO. English, as their first language, does not appear to interfere with the syntax of their spoken production in Irish. This may be because this aspect of Irish is salient in the input and is acquired in the early stages of acquisition.

As mentioned previously, an aspect of Irish that differs from English is noun adjective order. There are not many examples of the use of adjectives in the transcribed data, but where there are, they are used correctly. For example, 'the red table' *an bord dearg* which translates literally as 'the table red' where the adjective follows the noun in Irish.

Use of the copula '*Is*'

A copula can be defined as a word that connects the subject and predicate. Where a noun, pronoun or adjective is the predicate, then a copula is required to connect it to the remainder of the phrase. The acquisition of the copula can prove difficult for L2 learners and the pupils in this study were no exception to this. We noted in Table 5.2 that the demonstrative pronoun *sin* 'that' is the most commonly used word in the corpus of pupils' speech for both school types (5.70% of the Gaeltacht pupils' speech and 6.19% of the all-Irish pupils' speech). Although the copula is continually referred to as *Is*, it should be noted that the word *Is* does not appear in the 50 most commonly used words. *Is* was used 38 (0.43%) times by the Gaeltacht pupils and 148 (0.32%) times by the all-Irish school pupils.[3] Due to the complexities of copula use in Irish, an examination of how pupils used the two words *Is* and *sin* is particularly important.

Another aspect of relevance in the analysis of the copula is the use of the substantive verb *Bí* 'to be'. The data reveal many examples of pupils using the substantive verb *Bí* incorrectly instead of the copula. The most common reasons for this were the use of the substantive verb to describe permanent states or inserting *Tá* 'be' where the copula '*Is*' was omitted. We will now focus on examples of these features and on the different ways in which all-Irish pupils and Gaeltacht pupils manage these aspects of the copula.

Use of copula for classificatory purposes

The examples of the pupil errors given below illustrate instances of the employment of the substantive verb *Bí* for classificatory purposes. They demonstrate three errors of this type. The first, Example (5), is the non-target-like insertion of the substantive verb *Tá* where the copula has been omitted:

(5) 08_02_83_A

**Tá sin an pháirc síos ansin.*

'That's the park down there'.

Sin an pháirc thíos ansin.

The second error, Example (6), is the use of the substantive verb *Tá* for classificatory purposes where the copula *Is* should have been used:

(6) 09_01_18_C

**Tá sé bord mór.*

'It is a big table'.

Is bord mór é.

Finally, in Example (7), the dependent form of the substantive verb *bhfuil* 'be' has been employed where the interrogative form of the copula *An* should have been used:

(7) 01_02_315_S

* *An bhfuil sin gaineamh?*

Is that sand?

An gaineamh é sin?

Use of Is: The present form of the copula

The target forms presented above represent basic forms of copula use in the present tense. The all-Irish pupils in this study used the present form of the copula *Is* in 137 utterances and the Gaeltacht pupils used it in 38 utterances. *Is féidir liom* 'I can/I am able to' was the most common form used by the all-Irish pupils (56). There is evidence from the work of Mhic Mhathúna (2008) that these structures are acquired at an early stage in an immersion context as formulas or unanalysed chunks. By sixth class, the children have learned to manipulate these structures by interchanging the noun and prepositional pronoun. It is not clear, however, that they recognise them as copular structures. Apart from this form, *is a* … 'and' in the context of counting was the next most frequent form used (50). There were no examples where the copula was used for classificatory purposes in the all-Irish corpus.

The corpus of the pupils' speech in Gaeltacht schools was examined to ascertain how native speaker pupils' use the copula *Is*. The results showed that the Gaeltacht pupils did not use the copula for classificatory purposes similar to their all-Irish counterparts. As the all-Irish school pupils experienced difficulty with this structure, it was considered useful to establish exactly how the Gaeltacht school pupils classified objects for use in their design.

Use of copula by Gaeltacht school pupils with demonstrative pronoun sin

In the Gaeltacht school corpus, pupils correctly used the demonstrative pronoun *sin* 'that' and omitted both the copula *Is* 'is' and the personal pronoun *é* 'it' in order to classify objects. Although the copula is omitted in these instances, it is implied, as highlighted in the following examples.

(8) 10_01_62_D

Sin an geata isteach chuig an scoil.

That is the gate into the school.

Pupil D could have said in Example (8) *Sin é an geata* (inserting pronoun *é*) or *Is é sin an geata* (inserting both pronoun *é* and copula *Is*). He chose to omit both; however, the meaning in each case would have been the same: 'That is the gate'.

(9) 10_04_26_A

…sin é an bealach isteach.

That is the way in.

In Example (9), Pupil A could have said … *sin an bealach isteach* (omitting the pronoun *é*) or …*Is é sin an bealach isteach* (inserting the copula *Is*). Once again, the meaning would have remained the same.

It should be noted that in no instance did a Gaeltacht school pupil use the substantive verb *Bí* incorrectly in place of the copula. The ability to use this feature correctly is one that differentiates the pupils in the two school types and is fundamental to mastery of Irish.

Inaccurate use of copula by all-Irish school pupils with demonstrative pronoun sin

Utterances (10) and (11) below show examples of the demonstrative pronoun *sin* 'that', where *sin* is followed by the definite article *an* 'the' and a noun. These were the only correct forms to be found in the all-Irish corpus using *sin*, where a noun or a pronoun followed *sin*.

(10) 05_03_197_S

...*sin an* tent...

...that's the tent...

(11) 07_01_149_D

...*sin an rud atá mar suí sá.*

...that's the thing that is like a see-saw.

Examples below highlight pupils' incorrect use of the substantive verb *Bí* 'to be' with the demonstrative pronoun *sin* 'that'.

(12) 15_02_171_D

*An bhfuil sin an sleamhnán?

Is that the slide?

An é sin an sleamhnán?

Pupil D in Example (12) used the dependent present indicative form (*bhfuil*) of the substantive verb *Bí* 'to be'. Had the personal pronoun *é* 'it' been used instead of *bhfuil* 'is', the utterance would have been correct.

(13) 08_01_141_C

*... *tá sin an slí isteach, tá sin an geata, tá sin an siúltán agus tá sin an scoil.*

... that is the way in, that is the gate, that is the corridor and that is the school.

... *sin an tslí isteach, sin an geata, sin an siúltán agus sin an scoil.*

In Example (13), Pupil C repeatedly used the present indicative *Tá* 'is' of the substantive verb *Bí* 'to be'. However, had *Tá* been omitted then the utterance would have been correct.

(14) 01_02_152_C

*Cad atá é sin, an bord picnic?

What is that, the picnic table?

Cad é sin, an bord picnice? or An bord picnice é sin?

Again in Example (14), if Pupil C had omitted the relative form of the present indicative *atá* 'is' of the substantive verb *Bí* 'to be', this aspect of the utterance would have been correct.

The excerpts above demonstrate the manner in which all-Irish pupils used the copula incorrectly. When examples of their speech are compared with the Gaeltacht school pupils, we see that there are three manifestations of this type of error:

(1) The insertion of the substantive verb *Bí* 'to be' instead of the copula *Is*.
(2) The failure to omit the copula.
(3) The failure to omit the personal pronoun *é* when appropriate.

We see the insertion of the substantive verb *Bí* 'to be' instead of the copula *Is* most clearly when we compare Example (4) with Example (9). Pupil D, a Gaeltacht school pupil, said: *Sin an geata ...* which is the correct form. Pupil C, on the other hand, an all-Irish school pupil, said: *...tá sin an geata...* inserting the present form of the substantive verb *Tá*.

Three forms of the copula are acceptable when used with the demonstrative pronoun *sin* 'that'. The form most commonly used by the Gaeltacht pupils to perform the task assigned was the form in which the copula *Is* and the personal pronoun *é* are omitted. It appears that the pupils in all-Irish schools may not be cognisant of this form or if they are, they do not think to use it. They tend to insert the substantive verb *Bí* before *sin*. In order to quantify the extent of this deviant form, the corpus was analysed for examples of pupils' use of the copula in different contexts.

The first feature examined was the pupils' use of the form of the copula where the demonstrative pronoun *sin* 'that' is followed by the definite article *an* 'the'. This is where the copula *Is* and the personal pronoun *é* are omitted. The all-Irish students used this form 91 times, using it correctly 63 (69%) times and incorrectly 28 (31%) times, as shown in the first column of Figure 5.1.

The second feature examined was the use of the demonstrative pronoun *sin* with numbers. Due to the nature of the task set for the pupils, they were required to compute the amount of money spent which required them to talk about numbers. There were 317 instances where pupils used the demonstrative pronoun *sin* followed by a number. In 245 (77%) cases, pupils used this form correctly and in 72 (23%) cases, it was used incorrectly (see Figure 5.1). In each case where it was used incorrectly, the pupils inserted some form of the substantive verb *Bí*.

The third aspect of the pupils' use of the copula investigated concerned the manner in which they used the copula with nouns for classificatory purposes. In total, the students used the copula with nouns on 66 occasions. They used it correctly 41 (62%) times and incorrectly 25 (38%) times as seen in the third column of Figure 5.1. These included several examples similar to Example (15). In these cases, if the pupils had used the demonstrative pronoun *sin* instead of *Bí*, they would have been correct.

(15) 14_03_199_A

*...*mar tá sé an dréimire rópa.*

... because it is the rope-ladder.

Mar sin an dréimire rópa. or *Mar is é sin an dréimire rópa.* or *Mar sin é an dréimire rópa.*

Once again, where the copula was incorrectly used the pupils inserted some form of the substantive verb *Bí*. The analysis of these three aspects of the copula revealed that pupils used them correctly more often than incorrectly. The total number of instances of these features was 474. The pupils used them correctly in 349 (74%) instances and incorrectly in 125 (26%).

Summary of copula use by all-Irish pupils

The all-Irish school pupils demonstrated partial mastery of the copula *Is* in Irish. Their use of this structure was similar to that of the Gaeltacht

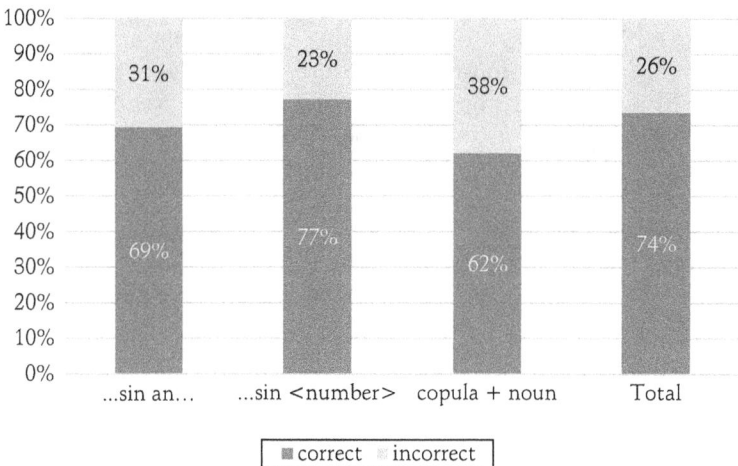

Figure 5.1 All-Irish pupils' use of aspects of the copula

school pupils and did not include use of *Is* for classificatory purposes to any great extent. Part of the difficulty for the all-Irish school pupils in attaining mastery of the copula may be that the information in the input is not salient. Although instructional grammar books such as Mac Congáil (2004) and Mac Murchaidh (2013) refer to the copula *Is*, the form of the copula *Is* was rarely used by the native speaker pupils in the unplanned oral production required for the task in the present study. For first language English-speaking all-Irish pupils, the phrase '*sin an geata*' while correct may seem incomplete as it translates literally as 'that the table'. It is as if they are not aware that the copula *Is* is implied in the phrase. The insertion of the substantive verb *Tá* may be an attempt to complete the utterance, but this results in errors such as Example (13): *Tá sin an geata* [that is the gate]. It is reasonable to conclude that the input received by the pupils may not be salient enough for them to notice this form.

The substantive verb *Bí*

There are 1388 instances of *Tá* (the present tense independent form of *Bí*) in the all-Irish school corpus. When all tenses of the substantive verb *Bí* are added together, there are 2805 instances representing 6.21% of the corpus. An analysis of the pupils' use of the substantive verb aids our understanding of this feature of their Irish. As the present form *Tá* was used most frequently by the pupils, we will analyse this form separately, followed by an analysis of *bhfuil* the present dependent form which was used 538 times.

Present tense Tá *and* Níl

There were 1760 instances of *Tá* 'Is' (1388) (present tense affirmative) and *Níl* 'Is not' (362) (present tense negative) in the corpus of all-Irish pupils' speech. *Tá* and *Níl* were used correctly with different structures on 1554 (88.2%) occasions demonstrating considerable mastery. Of the remaining 206 (11.8%) non-target-like utterances, the substantive verb was used in place of the copula in the majority of cases. Example (16) demonstrates a typical error of this type:

(16) 15_02_20_D

*... *tá sin mór ceann.*

... it is a big one.

... *sin ceann mór.*

Present tense dependent form bhfuil

The present tense dependent form of the substantive verb *Bí* is *bhfuil*. There are 481 instances of *bhfuil* in the all-Irish corpus and pupils handled most forms without difficulty. *Cá bhfuil* 'where', *go bhfuil* 'is' and *nach/*

mura bhfuil 'is not', all had very few errors, and where errors were made in the case of *an bhfuil* (the interrogative form of *bhfuil*), the pupils used the substantive verb instead of the copula as in Example (17):

(17) 09_01_123_D

*An bhfuil sin díon canvas?

Is that a canvas roof?

An díon canbháis é sin?

Another feature that caused even greater difficulty was *a bhfuil*. In this case, the most common error was the use of the dependent form of the verb *bhfuil*, instead of the independent form *Tá* as in Example (18). This incorrect form was used incorrectly 112 (81.1%) times and accounted for the majority of the errors in the use of *bhfuil*.

(18) 03_02_110_S

*Cé mhéad a bhfuil fágtha againn?

How much do we have left?

Cé mhéad atá fágtha againn?

When all examples of the use of *bhfuil* in the corpus were examined, the correct form was used in 66.3% of relevant utterances or in almost two out of every three cases. This is a higher error rate than for *Tá* as we saw above.

Past tense, future tense, conditional mood, verbal noun and present tense relative form of the substantive verb Bí

We now examine the all-Irish school pupils' use of other tenses of the substantive verb *Bí*. These include the past tense *bhí* 'was' (independent form), *raibh* 'was' (dependent form), the future tense *beidh* 'will', the conditional mood *bheadh* 'would', the verbal noun *bheith* 'being' and the present tense relative form *atá* 'are'. These forms were used correctly approximately three times out of four. The areas of greatest difficulty were the non-target-like use of the substantive verb instead of the copula as in Example (19), and the failure to use the dependent form where appropriate as in Example (20) which involves eclipsing the verb after the interrogative verb particle *an*.

(19) 06_04_35_T

*Tá é sin seacht...

That is seven...

Sin seacht...

(20) 02_01_149_Á
*An beidh spás...?
Will there be space...?
An mbeidh spás?

Pupils demonstrated reasonable mastery of the independent forms of the substantive verb *Bí* in its different tenses and forms. However, they did experience difficulty with the dependent forms. As we saw in the analysis of the copula, the substantive verb was used incorrectly on occasions where the copula should have been used. They the use of the verbal noun *bheith* was well mastered but difficulties were noted with structures where the form of the verb which follows the substantive verb was the verbal noun form. Figure 5.2 illustrates the percentage of correct and incorrect utterances involving *Bí*.

Verb morphology

Apart from the various forms of substantive verb *Bí*, we identified the most common verbs used by the pupils. The verbs *cuir* 'to put', *déan* 'to do' and *faigh* 'to get' were the three most commonly used verbs. For analytical purposes, *cuir* 'to put' was considered representative of the pupils' use of regular verbs. The pattern of use for *cuir* and *déan* were very similar and the analysis below was confined to *cuir*. Usage of *déan* is included in the summary below. The verb *faigh* 'to get' is representative of irregular verbs.

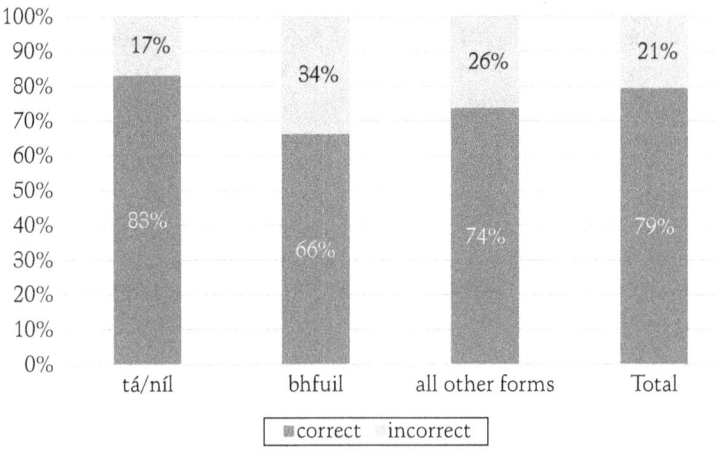

Figure 5.2 All-Irish school pupils' use of the of the substantive verb *Bí*

The regular verb cuir *'to put'*

There were 480 uses of some form of the verb *cuir* and they were used correctly 355 (74%) times by the pupils. When usage was categorised by mood (e.g. indicative, imperative, conditional) and tense, as seen in Figure 5.3, the imperative mood was used correctly by pupils 201 (92%) times out of 219 times. Incorrect use occurred where pupils pronounced it with a velarised rather than a palatalised sound as in Example (21):

(21) 04_02_193_D

*Cur é sin isteach.

Put that in

Cuir isteach é sin.

Figure 5.3 outlines the correct and incorrect utterances of the verb *cuir* in the various tenses and moods. When the past, future and present tenses were combined, the pupils used *cuir* correctly 90 (74%) times out of 121 times. The 31 occasions where they failed to use *cuir* correctly were in the interrogative form, failure to lenite the verb and failure to use the dependent form of the verb after *cén áit* 'where', as illustrated in Examples (22)–(24), respectively:

(22) 01_02_57_C

*An cuir tú isteach sleamhnán gearr?

Did you put in a short slide?

Ar chuir tú isteach sleamhnán gearr?

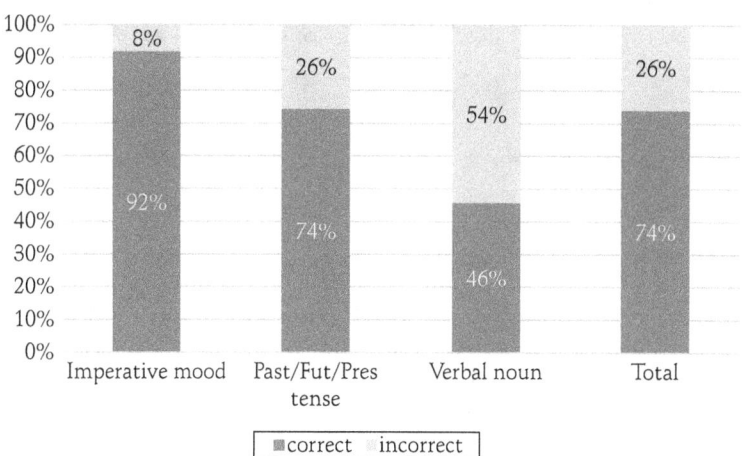

Figure 5.3 Irish immersion school pupils' use of the regular verb *cuir* 'to put'

(23) 04_02_103_D

*... cad a cuirfimid isteach?

...what will we put in?

... cad a chuirfimid isteach?

(24) 07_01_262_D

*Cén áit a chuirfimid an dréimire?

Where will we put the ladder?

Cén áit a gcuirfimid an dréimire?

As explained above, phrase structure in Irish, in cases similar to an infinitival clause in English, require a rearrangement in the word order in Irish. In these circumstances, the object is placed before the verbal noun and the preposition *a* is inserted between the object and the verbal noun *cuir*. Results show that the pupils incorrectly used the verbal noun 76 (54%) times out of 140 as shown in Example (25):

(25) 02_01_288_A

*Táimid in ann cur an díon canbháis...

We can put the canvas roof...

Táimid in ann an díon canbháis a chur...?

An examination of the Gaeltacht school corpus revealed that the verbal noun *cuir* was incorrectly used on 2 occasions out of 16 as in the following instance:

(26) 11_08_110_M

*Thig linn cur na rudaí sin...

We can put those things...

Thig linn na rudaí sin a chur...

In summary, the pupils demonstrated reasonable mastery of the morphology of the regular verb *cuir* and used it correctly almost three-quarters of the time (74%). The aspects not adequately mastered were the use of the verbal noun, the interrogative forms and the correct use of the dependent form where appropriate.

The irregular verb faigh 'to get'

The verb *faigh* is 1 of 10 irregular verbs in Irish. It is subject to substantial change between tenses. Its root changes from *faigh* to *fuair* in the past tense and there are different dependent and independent forms in the past tense, future tense and conditional mood.

There were 740 instances of various forms of *faigh* in the all-Irish school corpus. The first column in Figure 5.4 shows that the pupils used the imperative mood correctly in 99 (93.4%) out of 106 cases and appeared to have mastered this aspect of the verb. The second column shows that they used the past tense forms correctly 172 (79.6%) times out of 216. When used incorrectly, it was generally due to a failure to distinguish between the dependent and independent forms. In Example (27), for instance, the pupil failed to eclipse the verb in the interrogative form. Of note, the pupil used the correct preverbal particle *an* where *ar* would be the regular form for the past tense.

(27) 06_02_68_T

*An fuair tú ...?

Did you get...?

An bhfuair tú ...?

There were just 31 instances where the all-Irish pupils used the present tense of *faigh* and it was used correctly in just 5 (16%) utterances. The most common error was a failure to lenite the verb after the particle *a*, as can be seen in Example (28):

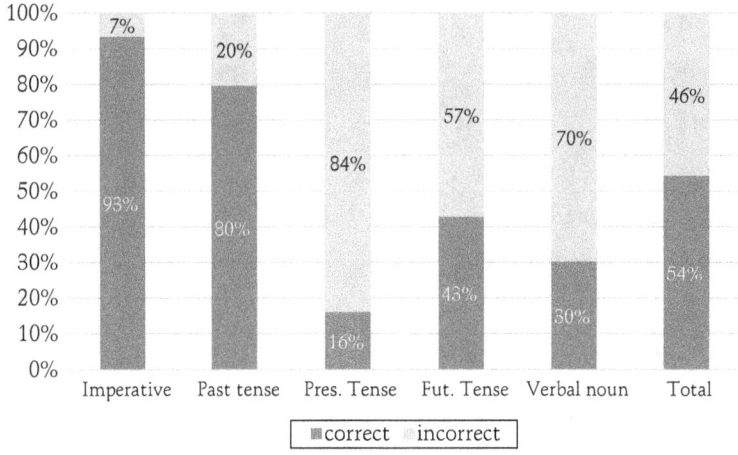

Figure 5.4 All-Irish school pupils' use of the irregular verb *faigh* 'to get'

(28) 14_03_64_N

*... *ach nuair a faigheann na páistí níos mó...*

... but when the children get bigger ...

... *ach nuair a fhaigheann na páistí níos mó...*

Pupils also had difficulties with the future tense of *faigh* and used it correctly on only 30 (43%) of 70 utterances (Figure 5.4). The inaccuracy was mainly due to a failure to distinguish between the dependent and independent forms in the future tense. In Example (29), the pupil incorrectly used the independent form where the dependent form should have been used:

(29) 03_03_123_N

**An gheobhaimid fráma dreapadóireachta eile?*

Will we get another climbing frame?

An bhfaighimid fráma dreapadóireachta eile?

The use of the verbal noun caused great difficulty for pupils resulting in a failure to use it correctly in 222 (70%) out of 317 utterances. The two most common errors with this aspect of the verb were a failure to use the correct form of the verbal noun as in Example (30) and secondly, the incorrect use of a pronoun as a direct object of the verbal noun as illustrated in Example (31):

(30) 05_03_204_S

*... *thig leo faigh isteach.*

...they can get in

... *thig leo fáil isteach.*

(31) 15_01_51_S

**An bhfuil muid ag fháil sin?*

Are we going to get that one?

An bhfuil muid chun é sin a fháil?

Summary of the morphology of the verbs cuir, déan and faigh

The three verbs most commonly used by the pupils, apart from the copula *Is* and the substantive verb *Bí*, were the verbs *cuir* 'to put', *déan* 'to do', and *faigh* 'to get'. The pupils used the correct forms of these verbs on 1198 occasions out of 1944. This represents a correct usage of 62%. The aspect of these verbs that caused the greatest difficulty was the correct use of the verbal noun. Even Gaeltacht pupils in one particular school had difficulty with this aspect. Ó Curnáin (2007) also noted this phenomenon in the speech of native speakers in the area of *Iorras Aithneach*, an Irish heartland district in Connemara, Co. Galway. Ní Dhiorbháin (2017) noted the challenge that mastery of this feature presented to initial primary teacher education students in her study also.

Use of the verbal nouns *cuir*, déan and *faigh* were incorrect on 557 (65%) occasions out of 857. If this feature could be mastered, it would greatly improve the accuracy of the pupils' Irish. Given the difficulties of other groups in mastering this feature, the pupils may require more time or some form of direct intervention before mastery can be acquired. Another area highlighted in this section was the need for improvement in the correct use of the dependent and independent forms of the three verbs examined.

Prepositional pronouns

There is a category of pronoun in Irish termed 'prepositional pronouns' where a preposition and a pronoun join together in a synthetic form. For example, a preposition such as *le* 'with' is joined to a personal pronoun *tú* 'you' and the synthetic form becomes *leat* 'with you'. This differs from English where the words remain separate. The most common prepositions used by the all-Irish school pupils in the corpus are *ag* 'at', *do* 'for', *le* 'with' and *ar* 'on'. Each preposition is inflected and can form seven prepositional pronouns: first, second and third (masculine and feminine) person singular and first, second and third person plural. The most common forms used in the corpus were the first and third person (masculine) singular and third person plural.

Henry et al. (2002) noted that pupils in Irish immersion schools sometimes failed to join the preposition and the pronoun and this was evident in this study corpus also. The most common incorrect instances were *le é/iad* 'with it/them', *faoi é* 'about it', *ar é* 'on it', *thar é* 'over it' and *de é/iad* 'of it/them'.

The first column in Figure 5.5 reflects the pupils' use of *le/leis é* and *le/leis iad*. The correct forms of these are *leis* 'with it/him' and *leo* 'with them', respectively. The main difficulty that pupils appeared to have was the insertion of the personal pronoun *é* 'it' where it is not required, as we see in Example (32). The pupils made this type of error in 17 of 25 instances.

(32) 04_02_274_D

1- *...*stop ag pleidhcíocht leis é sin*.

2- ...stop messing with that

...*stop ag pleidhcíocht leis sin*

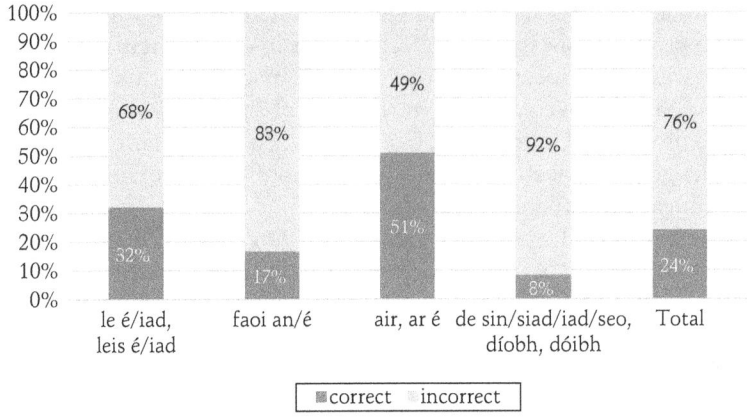

Figure 5.5 All-Irish pupils' use of the prepositions *le, faoi, air, de* and *dóibh*

The second column in Figure 5.5 reveals how the pupils handled *faoi an* 'under the' and *faoi é* 'under it'. *Faoi* and *an* are generally joined in Irish as *faoin*. The pupils did this correctly on 3 occasions in the corpus and failed to do so on 14 occasions. In the case of *faoi é* 'under it', the *é* ('it') is understood and so there is no need to insert it after *faoi*. The pupils inserted it 11 times in the corpus and omitted it correctly twice. When both types of usage of *faoi* are combined, the pupils were correct in just 5 of 30 utterances.

The third column in Figure 5.5 presents the pupils use of *ar é* 'on it' and *air* 'on it'. The latter is the correct form and *ar é* is incorrect for this purpose. The pupils used the correct form *air* on 51 occasions out of 100. We see in Example (33) an instance of incorrect use where the pupil says *ar é* instead of *air*:

(33) 07_01_155_D

3- *...cuir díon ar é.*

4- ...put a roof on it.

5- ...*cuir díon air.*

The fourth column in Figure 5.5 deals with the pupils' use of *de* 'of'. The pupils used a variety of ways to say 'of them' but 155 (92%) of 169 utterances were incorrect. The majority of errors resulted from an inability to express 'of them' accurately. The form used by Gaeltacht pupils was the prepositional pronoun *acu* 'at them'. The immersion pupils only managed to use this accurately on three occasions. An overall error rate of 76% for prepositional pronouns can be seen in Column 5.

Use of numbers

The forms of numerals in Irish differ from English. Cardinal numbers differ depending on whether the number is immediately followed by a

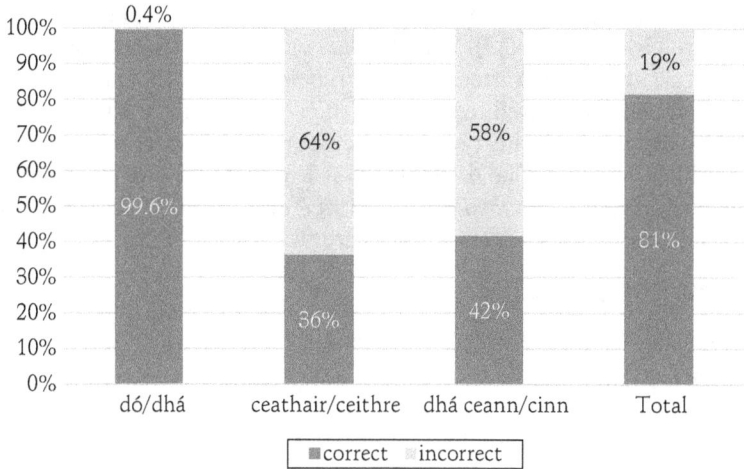

Figure 5.6 All-Irish school pupils' use of the numbers *dó/dhá*, *ceathair/ceithre* and *dhá cheann/cinn*

noun or not, and different forms for personal and ordinal numbers also exist. Due to the nature of the study task, numerals were used frequently to calculate the amount of money spent in their playground design.

Overall, mastery of the numbers in the corpus was good, but there was evidence that two exceptions in Irish had not been accurately acquired. The first issue of interest was, how the pupils handled *dhá* 'two' and *ceithre* 'four'. These numbers have other forms when not followed by a noun. The other form for *dhá* is *dó* ('two') and for *ceithre* is *ceathair* ('four'). The evidence demonstrated in the first column of Figure 5.6 is that the pupils chose the correct form of the numeral *dhá* 'two' to precede a noun in almost every situation. This contrasts with the second column where *ceathair* 'four', the incorrect form to precede a noun, was chosen 117 (64%) times out of 184.

The second area of interest was how the pupils used the word *ceann* 'thing' after *dhá* 'two'. *Dhá cheann* 'two things' is the correct form. The correct form was used in 45 (42%) cases out of 108, as shown in the third column in Figure 5.6. This form may be difficult for the pupils to master, as it is an exception to the regular form of nouns after *dhá*.

Use of Interrogative Pronouns *Cad*, *Cad é* and *Céard*

The next area to be examined is the pupils' use of the interrogative pronouns *cad*, *cad é* and *céard*. These are the three most common forms in Irish used to express 'what' in English. They each have the same meaning and are associated with the three main dialects in Irish: *cad* with Munster Irish, *céard* with Connacht Irish and *cad é* with Ulster Irish. As noted by

Mac Murchaidh (2013), *cad* may not be used as a relative particle in Irish, as illustrated in Example (34). In fact, there was no need for the pupil to use the word *cad* at all in his utterance as can be seen from the correct form in Line 3. The pupil appeared to translate the utterance from English almost word for word whereas this type of statement requires that he use the past form of the copula *ba*. The difficulty that English first language speakers experience in learning how to use *cad*, *cad é* and *ceard* is that they tend to rely on these terms exclusively to translate 'what' from English.

(34) 09_01_291_L

*Sin cad a dúirt mé.

That's what I said.

B'in a dúirt mé.

Another incorrect translation of 'what' is illustrated in Example (35). The pupil says, 'What are you like?' [meaning: What were you thinking of?] and translates it directly from English.

(35) 01_02_297_S

*Cad atá tú mar?

What are you like?

Cén sórt ceann thú féin? or *Cad atá tú ag smaoineamh air?*[4]

Column 1 in Figure 5.7 shows that errors occurred in all 21 cases where *cad/cad é/céard* was used to directly translate 'what'.

The discussion on verbs in Irish above illustrated that there is an independent and a dependent form. In the case of the substantive verb *Tá* and the irregular verbs *faigh* 'to get' and *déan* 'to do', the pupils had difficulty in choosing the correct form to use and generally used the independent form. When a verb follows *cad*, *cad é* or *céard*, it is the independent form of the verb that should be used. The second column in Figure 5.7 shows that the pupils incorrectly used the dependent form on 72 (67%) occasions out of 107. Example (36) exemplifies this error. Pupil C incorrectly uses the dependent form *bhfuil* of the substantive verb and also fails to use the correct verbal noun *rá* 'saying', and the correct syntax. There were 128 utterances containing *cad*, *cad é* or *céard* and the dependent form of the verb. Pupils failed to use them correctly on 93 (73%) occasions.

(36) 08_01_164_C

*Cad a bhfuil tú ag abairt?

What are you saying?

Cad 'tá á rá agat?

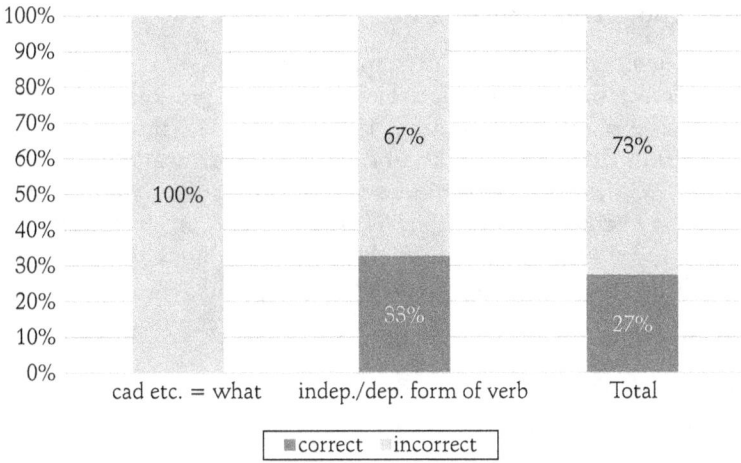

Figure 5.7 All-Irish school pupils' use of *cad, cad é* and *céard* 'what'

Pupils' Use of the Pronoun é 'it'

Another error that emerged from the examination of the corpus was the inaccurate use of the pronoun *é* 'it' or the failure to use it in certain structures. The latter was the case in Example (12) for instance, where we previously noted how Pupil D used *an bhfuil sin* instead of *an é sin*. In Example (19), Pupil T said *Tá é*, where neither word was required as the copula should have been used.

(12) 15_02_171_D

*An bhfuil sin an sleamhnán?

Is that the slide?

An é sin an sleamhnán?

(19) 06_04_35_T

*Tá é sin seacht...

That is seven...

Sin seacht...

When all 1580 instances of *é* were examined, 474 (30.0%) utterances contained the pronoun *é* 'it' incorrectly. If all-Irish pupils could master how to use this pronoun correctly, it would lead to significant improvements in their accuracy. This is not to suggest, however, that the pronoun *é* be dealt with in isolation. It would need to be addressed in the context of the other features examined earlier such as the correct use of copula, morphology of verbs and the correct syntax with the verbal noun.

Mapping English syntax onto Irish

When considering the issue of mapping English syntax onto Irish, it is worth reflecting on the influence that the English pronoun 'it' appeared to have on the pupils' Irish syntax. In Example (37), the pupil placed *é* 'it' immediately after the verb, as an English speaker would do – 'Will we leave it...?'. While this form is quite acceptable in Irish, it would normally only be used in this way to emphasise the object *é* 'it'. In Example (38), the Gaeltacht pupil placed *é* 'it' at the end of a similar utterance where emphasis is not required. This form is more target like.

(37) 09_01_1_F

An fágfaimid é mar sin...?

Will we leave it like that...?

An bhfágfaimid mar sin é...?

(38) 11_01_200_M

Fágfaimid go dtí an deireadh é.

We will leave it until the end.

As English is the first language of the vast majority of the all-Irish school pupils in the corpus, transcripts were examined for evidence of interference from English. Notwithstanding the mastery of VSO order and noun-adjective order, as discussed earlier, there was evidence that other structures in Irish present difficulties.

Some examples from the corpus suggest that the pupils may map English syntax onto Irish. This practice has also been observed in French immersion pupils in Canada (Lapkin & Swain, 2004). English influence on Irish syntax can be divided into two categories. In the first instance, English influence on Irish idiom is observed (Mac Mathúna, 2008) and a literal translation from English to Irish occurs. The second is where a sentence appears to be partially translated with the syntactic structure closer to English than Irish but with Irish words inserted.

Translation from English

The utterances highlighted in Examples (34) and (35) illustrated examples where the interrogative pronouns *cad*, *céard* and *cad é* were used to translate the English word 'what'. These represent one form of translation from English that would sound strange to a native speaker. Examples (39)–(41) show other examples of the influence of English idiom on Irish where pupils employed phrases not native to Irish to translate their utterances. Although not correct, these utterances do demonstrate the creativity of the Irish immersion speakers in complying with the school norm of speaking Irish and of communicating their message at the same time. In Example (39), Pupil D translated the slang phrase 'doing my head in' literally:

(39) 04_03_132_D

Tá mise faigh confused *le sibhse, tá an bheirt de sibh ag déanamh mo cheann isteach.*

I'm getting confused with you, the two of you are doing my head in.

Tá sibh ag cur mearbhaill orm, cuireann an bheirt agaibh soir mé. (Possible alternative)

In Example (40), Pupil S literally translated 'over' using the Irish word *thar*, but this means 'over' in an entirely different context.

(40) 03_03_9_S

*Ag déanamh troid thar an balla dreapadóireachta.

Fighting over the climbing wall.

Ag troid mar gheall ar an mballa dreapadóireachta. (Possible alternative)

In Example (41), Pupil D employed '*le* comparison', a mixture of Irish and English. There is an attempt to frame it within Irish syntax where the *le* 'with' was placed before 'comparison'. As it transpires the Irish version is *i gcomparáid le* with the '*le*' at the end of the phrase.

(41) 16_01_205_D

*Tá sí beag tiny *le* comparison *don mo cheannsa.*

It is small, tiny in comparison to my one.

Tá sí beag bídeach i gcomparáid le mo cheannsa. (Possible alternative)

Partial translation

There are numerous examples in the corpus of what appeared to be code-mixing behaviour, as discussed earlier. In many cases, however, it was not the insertion of an English borrowing into an Irish sentence, but rather the insertion of Irish words into English sentences. In Example (42), for example, Pupil A's utterance retained English syntactic structure:

(42) 05_03_228_A

No 'cos already *fuair muid sin.*

No because we already got that.

Nílimid, mar fuaireamar é sin cheana féin. (Possible alternative)

Similarly, in Example (43), although there was only one English word in her utterance, this Gaeltacht school pupil retained much of the English syntax. The exception was her partial translation of 'good idea' as idea *maith* where she employed Irish noun-adjective syntax.

(43) 11_01_80_R
Sílimse go bhfuil an túr idea *maith.*
I think that the tower is a good idea.
Sílimse gur smaoineamh maith atá sa túr. (Possible alternative)

There are many more examples of this type of error to be found in the corpus confirming the influence that English has on oral production in Irish.

A review of features such as the use of the verbal noun, the pronoun *é* 'it', indirect speech, copula, and the influence of English syntax highlight the type and frequency of inaccuracies in the corpus. If the proficiency in Irish of all-Irish pupils is to be improved, a narrow focus on particular features and structures is likely to have limited success without attention being paid to the influence of English on their lexical and syntactic choices.

Discussion

The all-Irish school corpus compiled from recordings of an activity revealed that pupils developed a high level of communicative ability after seven years in an immersion setting. The transcribed recordings gave an insight into the success of Irish-medium schools in producing pupils fluent in Irish and able to communicate with one another with ease. In most instances, the pupils demonstrated an ability to access the Irish vocabulary required to effectively carry out the task assigned to them. On average, 69.8% of their utterances were accurate from a morphosyntactic perspective, although some of these utterances were either subject to the influence of English syntax or contained English discourse markers. The areas where the pupils deviated from target-like norms will now be summarised and discussed and helpful suggestions as to how the errors might be remediated will be presented. The error rate of 30.2% for all-Irish pupils may appear high compared to 2.6% for the Gaeltacht pupils given that they had received approximately 5000 hours of instruction in Irish. However, this compares favourably with error rates in corpus studies in the French immersion context. In Chapter 3, I cited a study of Grade 12 immersion students reported to have an error rate of 54% after about 7000 hours of instruction in French (Pellerin & Hammerly, 1986). This figure resembles the 52.2% error rate found in a study of Grades 5 and 6 early French immersion pupils (Spilka, 1976). A further study in the French immersion context carried out by Lyster and Rannta (1997) reported an error rate of 34% in student to teacher interactions. This also included unsolicited uses of the first language. While it is not possible to compare these results directly due to different methodologies, they do give an indication of the extent of immersion pupils' errors in other contexts.

English words account for 8.97% of the all-Irish school corpus and 6.48% of the Gaeltacht school corpus. While the all-Irish school rate of English word usage is higher, one might have expected a greater difference. A study of native-speaking adults in the Gaeltacht only found a 2.7% rate of English word usage (O'Malley Madec, 2007), which is less than half of that found in this Gaeltacht school corpus. This reinforces the importance of comparing all-Irish pupils with native speakers of their own age rather than adult native speakers.

When code-mixing behaviour of pupils was examined, seven English words: 'yeah' and 'no' (affirmative/negative particles) and 'so', 'okay', 'just', 'like' and 'right' (discourse markers), accounted for the majority of the code-mixing and English words used by pupils in both school types. These seven words were used almost in equal measure by all-Irish pupils and Gaeltacht pupils. A factor that may influence the all-Irish pupils' code-mixing is that there is no direct translation of English 'yes' and 'no' in Irish. The case of 'yes' and 'no' could also be linked to a language contact issue where pupils use the same discourse markers in Irish as they use when speaking English, their first language. It is interesting to note that Cenoz and Gorter (2017) observed that school children who code-mixed when speaking Basque, i.e. inserting Spanish words in Basque sentences, did not usually do so when speaking Spanish, arguably the more dominant language.

Code-switching accounted for a small percentage of utterances by particular pupils rather than by all pupils. A significant finding was that there were very few examples of language-related episodes where pupils corrected one another's Irish. In all instances where correction took place, it was for code-mixing or code-switching. In no case did a pupil correct another for using an incorrect form in Irish. The school norm of speaking Irish appeared to exert a strong influence on the pupils not to speak English or use any English words. This influence does not extend to speaking Irish with accuracy. This may indicate that there is limited sociopsychological motivation to improve on this level once pupils have reached a level of communicative sufficiency in Irish (Day & Shapson, 1987).

Morphology of verbs

Incorrect use of the substantive verb *Bí* 'to be' instead of the copula *Is* 'is' manifested itself where the substantive verb *Bí* was used instead of the copula for classificatory purposes and where pupils failed to use the correct form of the copula with the demonstrative pronoun *sin*. The examination of how Gaeltacht pupils handled this feature of Irish revealed that the copula *Is* was omitted in many cases. This feature may not be salient in the input that all-Irish pupils receive and so the option to use this form goes unnoticed. There was an error rate of 26.0% by all-Irish pupils in various uses of the copula.

Cuir 'to put', *faigh* 'to get' and *déan* 'to do' were the three most common verbs used by the all-Irish school pupils apart from the copula and substantive verb. An area of particular difficulty was the correct use of the dependent and independent forms. This difficulty manifested itself with the two irregular verbs *déan* 'to do' and *faigh* 'to get' in particular. Another difficulty was the correct use of the verbal noun. Overall, across the three verbs the verbal noun was incorrectly used more than 6 times out of every 10 (62%). When all aspects of these verbs were taken together, there was an error rate of 38%.

As with the substantive verb and the copula above, improvements in these rates of error would have a significant impact on all-Irish pupils' accuracy in Irish. The challenge of this task should not be underestimated as some of the Gaeltacht pupils in School 11 were also found to have difficulty with the verbal noun. Walsh (2007) found that sixth-year (Year 14) pupils in post-primary all-Irish schools continued to have difficulties with both the copula and the verbal noun.

The pupils' use of the interrogative pronouns *cad*, *cad é* and *céard* 'what' was frequently inaccurate with the dependent and independent forms of verbs with pupils incorrectly using the dependent form instead of the independent form after these pronouns.

Prepositional pronouns

The use of prepositional pronouns presented difficulties for the all-Irish pupils. The six most common prepositional pronouns used by the all-Irish school pupils were used incorrectly 76% of the time with the pronoun *de* 'of' being most frequently incorrect. It is obvious from the corpus that the pupils have acquired the *de* form but appear to be unable to conjugate it with accuracy. Once again, it may be that the information in the input is not sufficiently salient for the pupils to notice it. The all-Irish school pupils used incorrect forms such as *de é sin*, *de iad sin*, *de sin* and *de siad* to express 'of them'. When the Gaeltacht school corpus was examined, *acu sin was* correctly used to express 'of them'. The all-Irish pupils' attention needs to be drawn to this form and other common forms of prepositional pronouns. This could be done perhaps through focus on form activities such as in the Ó Duibhir *et al.* (2016) study or in the resource designed by Ní Dhiorbháin (2014), *Bain Súp As!* (Enjoy It).

Use of numbers

In general, the all-Irish pupils achieved a good level of mastery of most of the forms of numbers examined in the corpus. Not surprisingly it was the forms that differ the most from the English number system or those with exceptions in Irish that caused the greatest difficulty. There were two main sources of error in the features examined in the all-Irish school corpus: the ability to differentiate between *ceathair* 'four' when counting and *ceithre* 'four' when followed by a noun.

The fact that the pupils learnt mathematics through the medium of Irish probably helped with their mastery of numbers in Irish. Those areas that caused difficulty could be remediated in focus on form activities as part of the mathematics class.

Influence of English

A common theme throughout the corpus was the influence of English. This manifested itself in several different ways. Code-mixing and code-switching were evident in relation to use of the interrogative pronouns *cad*, *cad é* and *céard* for 'what'. On 21 occasions in the corpus, pupils incorrectly used one of these pronouns to express 'what', which indicates that they did not fully understand the contexts in which these pronouns can and cannot be used.

Incorrect use of the pronoun *é* 'it' (30% of utterances with *'é'*) also exemplified the influence of English on the pupils' Irish. The difficulties with the pronoun *é* that this study identified intersected with areas such as incorrect copula use, incorrect syntax and the failure to use the verbal noun correctly. The three-word clusters generated using WordSmith concordance tools revealed that the English pronoun 'it' was exerting a strong influence on the use of the pronoun *é* in Irish. In many cases, pupils inserted *é* when not required either because *é* was contained as part of another word such as a prepositional pronoun in Irish or *é* was implied and so did not need to be used.

The code-mixing and code-switching behaviour of pupils caused the use of English words to interfere with Irish syntax. Although discourse markers represent 5.8% (Table 5.5) of the all-Irish school corpus, it was when the literal translation and partial translation imposed English syntax on the pupils' Irish that gave rise to the greatest cause for concern.

Analytical teaching methodology

The principal sources of the 30.2% error rate of all-Irish corpus were difficulties with the copula, the morphology of verbs, prepositional pronouns, some aspects of number use and the influence of English. These features all involve syntactic difficulties that deviate from the natural flow of the Irish language and are likely therefore to sound peculiar to native speakers. Such deviations lead to disparaging descriptions of the pupils' Irish as *Gaelscoilis or Géarla* (mix of Gaeilge 'Irish' and Béarla 'English'). Pedagogic practice needs to investigate ways to address the high incidence of errors if pupils' accuracy in Irish is to be improved. It is suggested that a dependence on a largely experiential meaning-focused approach

(Lyster, 2007) to language acquisition is likely to bring about limited improvement. Continuing to teach the copula as traditionally presented in grammar books is unlikely to help pupils acquire the correct forms. A programme in which there are 'focus on form' activities, opportunities for 'pushed' output and a more analytical approach may help to improve pupils' accuracy. Studies which examined the use of an explicit inductive approach to grammar teaching in all-Irish schools have shown promising results and merit further investigation (Ní Dhiorbháin & Ó Duibhir, 2017; Ó Duibhir *et al.*, 2016).

The non-target-like features identified in this volume need to be targeted at an earlier stage in pupils' acquisition of Irish in order to guard against their fossilisation. Sixth-year pupils in post-primary all-Irish schools still have difficulty in mastering the correct use of the copula and the verbal noun after 14 years of immersion education (Walsh, 2007). Continuing with a predominantly experiential meaning-focused approach in the hope that the non-target-like features identified in the corpus will eventually be accurately acquired over time is unlikely to be effective. Recommendations regarding pedagogy will be discussed again later in Chapter 9 in the context of the overall findings.

Notes

(1) Although a distinction has been made between mistakes and errors (Gass & Selinker, 2008), all deviations from native speaker norms are treated as errors in this stage of the analysis.
(2) A construction of two or more words would be required in Irish to replace a one-word equivalent in English.
(3) The word *is* appears more often than this in the corpus for both school types. In the other instances, however, it is used as a contraction *is=agus* 'and'.
(4) Pupil S offered this version in a stimulated recall session that followed a week later. These stimulated recall sessions are the subject of Chapter 6.

6 Pupils' Reflections on Their Communicative Performance in Irish

Introduction

From the analysis of all-Irish pupils' speech, we have established that errors occurred in 3 out of every 10 utterances among pupils during a collaborative playground design task. In choosing to study the linguistic accuracy of pupils' Irish, I felt it was important that the pupils would have a voice in the research. This was motivated by a desire to examine the issue from a sociolinguistic perspective (Tarone & Swain, 1995) and to balance the more cognitive, input interactionist-type analysis in the previous chapter. I knew from my own practice as an immersion teacher that pupils sometimes correct their grammatical mistakes when prompted by me, the teacher. In this research, I wanted to gain insights into the degree to which the pupils recognised their own errors, their ability to correct these errors and, finally, why they used inaccurate forms when they had access to more accurate language. After the corpus was gathered, transcribed and analysed, I returned to the schools to conduct stimulated recall sessions to provide the pupils with an opportunity to view a video recording of themselves engaged in the collaborative tasks and to view written excerpts of their recorded speech. This reflexive activity allowed the pupils to reflect on their use of Irish during the task and to comment on the quality of the language they used. The activity was also useful in investigating the underlying communicative competence of pupils. They were asked to identify any errors in their own speech that they recognised and to attempt to correct them. The stimulated recall sessions created opportunities for pupils' observations to act as a starting point for collaborative exploration about why their language contained certain lexical and syntactic features, such as the ones discussed in Chapter 5.

Stimulated Recall Activity

In each school, up to three groups of three pupils were video recorded as they engaged in a collaborative playground design task. The recordings of the pupils' speech during the activity were transcribed verbatim. Excerpts from the transcriptions presented in Chapter 5 highlight the most frequently occurring inaccurate features. These features (the copula, the verbal noun and code-mixing) were the focus of the stimulated recall sessions.

The stimulated recall sessions were conducted with the pupils assembled in their original groups of three in a quiet location away from the classroom. The sessions were audio-recorded and were composed of three distinct stages. In the first stage, the pupils viewed the selected extracts of the video recording of themselves engaged in the task on a laptop computer; the extracts shown contained the most commonly occurring errors in the corpus referred to above. The rationale for choosing to show the most frequent errors was that they provide the most reliable evidence of linguistic competence compared to low-frequency items (Chaudron, 2003).

Once the first viewing was complete, the pupils were asked for their initial thoughts and reactions to the video recording, followed by an invitation to comment on the quality of their Irish. In preparation for a second viewing, the pupils were given a verbatim transcript of the video excerpts they had watched. They viewed the video extracts again to check the accuracy of the transcript. They were encouraged in this activity to enter into the role of researcher assistant to ensure that their utterances had been captured correctly. This focused the pupils' attention on the language used in the playground design task. When the accuracy of the transcripts was clarified, the scene was set for the second phase of the stimulated recall exercise. The pupils were invited to identify any mistakes detected on reflection and to comment again on the quality of the Irish used now that they had access to the written transcript. I sought to be affirmative throughout the process so that pupils viewed their performance as positive. As they self-corrected mistakes, if pupils were very critical of their Irish, I mitigated this by highlighting the overall quality of their Irish even though there were some aspects that could be improved.

The final stage consisted of focused discussion on the causes of the non-target-like features that they had identified. Some groups required very little prompting to engage in this process and to reveal interesting insights, while a small number of groups, on the other hand, were more reluctant to go beyond commenting in a general way on the text of the transcript.

The non-target-like features that were self-corrected and the insights provided by the pupils highlight their underlying communicative competence and will help to inform how competence in Irish might be improved for all-Irish pupils.

Phase 1: Pupils' Perceptions of the Quality of Their Irish

The pupils responded in one of two ways when assessing the overall quality of their Irish after the first viewing of the video excerpt. The first type of response suggested general satisfaction. As Pupil A stated:

(1) 07_03

A   *Tá sé ceart go leor.*   It's all right.

Other pupils were critical of their standard of Irish. In Example (2), Pupil F appears disappointed and surprised:

(2) 09_01

F   *Cheap mise go raibh an Ghaeilge,*   I thought that the Irish, it
    ní raibh sé go maith. Ceapaim go   wasn't good. I thought that
    raibh sé níos fearr nuair atá tú ag   it was better when you are
    caint le duine.   talking to someone.

In many cases, the pupils were even more critical of the quality of their Irish when they viewed it a second time in combination with the written transcript. It appeared in some cases that until they saw their speech written down, they did not realise the level of code-mixing and the number of mistakes:

(3) 03_03

J   *Mar cheap mé go raibh Gaeilge*   I thought that we had good
    maith againn.   Irish.

N   *Yeah, nuair a féachann tú ar an*   Yeah, when you see it on
    scáileán agus atá tú in ann tú féin a the screen and when you
    chloisteáil.   can hear yourself.

S   *Agus ansin nuair a bhfuil sé scríofa* And then when it is written
    amach.   out.

Other groups made similar comments. Indeed, Pupil N was very critical:

(4) 04_03

N   *Má tháinig duine éigin isteach agus*   If someone came in and
    má chonaic sé é seo agus ní raibh a   if he saw this and didn't
    fhios aige cé raibh sé, bheadh sé ag know who it was, he would
    rá níl aon Ghaeilge ag na daoine seo say that these people have
    ... Déarfaidh siad tá siad i rang 3   no Irish ... He would say
    nó rud éigin.   they are in 3rd class or
                                            something.

When pupils made comments of this kind, they were asked to say *in what way* their Irish was not as good as they had thought it was. Pupil I in Example (5) identified the presence of English words:

(5) 05_03

R[1]	*Céard a shíl sibh faoi sin?*	What did you think of that?
A	*Coinnigh mé ag rá* 'what'.	I kept saying 'what'.
R	*An raibh fhios agat?*	Did you know? [Were you aware?]
A	*Ní raibh.*	No.
R	*Cad é a shíleann sibh anois?*	What do you think now?
A	*Tá sé níos measa ná a shíl mé.*	It is worse than I thought.
I	*Thig leis a bheith níos fearr.*	It could be better.
R	*Cén bealach, níos fearr?*	Better in what way?
I	*Gan na focla í Béarla isteach san abairt.*	Without the English words in the sentence.

The presence of English words was the source of greatest dissatisfaction among the pupils when assessing the quality of their Irish. The other general feature highlighted by the pupils was the presence of mistakes and grammatical errors.

(6) 09_01

R	*Cén bealach nach bhfuil sé chomh maith*	In what way is it not as good?
L	*Bhí cúpla mistakes ... botúin ghramadach.*	There were a couple of mistakes ... grammatical mistakes.

The pupils' comments may appear unremarkable; however, from the perspective of a former immersion teacher, I can confirm that they are indeed insightful. What they highlight is that when given the opportunity to reflect on the quality of their spoken output, many were very disappointed with it. Clearly, they had not been aware of the volume of English they were using. Awareness of the extensive use of English words and the presence of grammatical errors is the first stage in seeking to address these issues. Tapping into this sense of disappointment may be useful in motivating pupils to pay greater attention to form.

Phase 2: Correction of Mistakes Following Reflection on Output

In the second phase of the stimulated recall process, the pupils were invited to correct the mistakes that they noticed. They were asked to focus on their own utterances in particular, but the collaborative nature of the process allowed other pupils in the group to offer suggested improvements to others. This phase followed naturally from the previous one. The pupils had identified issues in their use of Irish that they were unhappy with and now they had an opportunity to address them. The transition to this phase was marked with the following question: 'Now that you have had a chance to view the DVD and your Irish written down, is there anything that you would like to change?'

In Extract (7), the text corrected by the pupils is struck out and the newly corrected text provided by the pupils is inserted and underlined. Lines 10 and 26 show the insertion of the Irish word for 'slide' and 'there', respectively. Lines 17, 18 and 27 show the correction of numbers with the word *céad* 'hundred' correctly eclipsed (*gcéad*) after *seacht* 'seven' and *naoi* 'nine'.

In Line 4, the utterance was improved by pupils but the personal pronoun *dóibh siúd* 'for them' is still not what is required in the context of the sentence. A target version *díobh sin* 'of them' was suggested to the pupils by the researcher and they were asked if they noticed a difference or if one version was more correct. They responded that they did not know.

In Line 11, Pupil J made a number of changes to the sentence that improved it. Pupil S then offered a complete restructuring which the group accepted was more accurate, which it was.

(7) 03_02

2	A	Tá … tá spás againn anseo agus…
3	J	B'fhéidir.
4	S	B'fhéidir is féidir linn ceann dóibh ~~sin ceann sin~~ siúd a cheannach.
5	A	Sea.
6	J	Sea sin díreach frámaí dreapadóireachta má chaithfimid é sin isteach níl sé ach céad eile.
7	A	Is féidir linn an sleamhnán sin a chur isteach freisin.
8	S	*No*, mar tá dréimire air sin.
9	A	Ó.
10	S	B'fhéidir is féidir linn é seo agus an ~~slide~~ sleamhnán …
11	J	~~No you see~~ má … má ~~rinn muid~~ rinneamar, má ~~fuair~~ faigh muid an túr ~~ch beidh, beidh muid~~ beimis in ann ~~ceann dóibh siúd~~ sleamhnán fada a ~~faigh~~ fháil gan dréimire agus é a cheangail don túr. S. Má fuaireamar an túr beimid in ann sleamhnán a fháil gan dréimire.
12	A	Gan dréimire, dréimire.
13	S	*No*, tagann sé le dréimire.

14	J	*No*, gan dréimire.
15	A	*No*, gan dréimire.
16	S	Ceart go leor, sin smaoineamh.
17	A	*So* seacht gcéad agus dhá chéad.
18	S	Seacht gcéad agus dhá chéad.
19	S	*Okay*, anois caithfimid na rudaí a chur isteach anois.
20	S	*So*, A an n̲déanfaidh tú é sin?
21	J	*So*.
22	A	Sleamhnán.
21	S	*Yeah*.
24	A	Agus é sin. Níl mé go maith ag tarraingt.
25	S	Sin ceart go leor, níl, níl sé ach plean.
26	A	~~*There*~~ Ceart go leor.
27	J	Tá fós naoi gcéad fágtha againn.
28	A	Dhá cinn.
29	S	Níl dhá cinn.
30	A	Ó ceart go leor.
31	S	~~Ó *wait*~~ an gceannaímid? *No*.
32	J	Tá fós naoi gcéad fágtha againn.

Correction of specific mistakes[2]

Inaccurate forms of copula

In Chapter 5, it was reported that the all-Irish school pupils used incorrect forms of the copula 26% of the time and had a 38% error rate for other verb forms depending on the form of the verb used. The stimulated recall sessions offered an opportunity to see if some of these incorrect forms were due to mistakes or if they were, in fact, evidence of underlying errors (Gass & Selinker, 2008). Many of the extracts selected for the stimulated recall sessions contained examples of the incorrect use of the copula. These generally involved the incorrect use of the substantive verb *Bí* 'to be'. In almost every stimulated recall session, pupils failed to notice these incorrect forms as mistakes; Polio *et al.* (2006) caution against drawing conclusions from what was not noticed. Consequently, the pupils' attention was specifically drawn to these errors in this phase when they did not notice them themselves. Pupil A in Example (8) was able to use the copula instead of the substantive verb when her attention was drawn to it:

(8) 02_01

R	*An bhfuil bealach eile chun, 'Tá sin an scoil', a rá?*	Is there another way to say 'That is the school' (using substantive verb)
A	*Is é seo an scoil.*	This is the school. (using copula)

In Example (9), Pupil J produced the following utterance:

J	*Agus tá sin an airgead go dtí an méid a bhí ceadaithe againn.*	And that is (substantive verb) the money to the amount that was allowed.

When he did not notice the error himself, his attention was drawn to it by way of an analogous example to establish that he had an awareness of the copula. As can be seen from the following exchange, he could use a more suitable version when he was prompted. It is also interesting to note his final comment about learning from mistakes.

(9) 07_01

R	*Má deir tú leis an múinteoir 'Tá sin an peann luaidhe' Céard a déarfadh sí?*	If you said to the teacher, 'That is the pencil'. (using substantive verb) What would she say?
J	*Is peann luaidhe é sin.*	'That is a pencil'. (using copula)
R	*An bhfuil bealach níos fearr chun 'Tá sin an airgead' a rá.*	Is there a better way to say? 'That is the money'. (using substantive verb)
J	*Sin an méid airgid a bhí ceadaithe.*	That is the amount of money that was allowed. (using copula)
J	*Caithfidh tú foghlaim ó do bhotúin.*	You have to learn from your mistakes.

Despite the fact that pupils failed in most instances to notice their incorrect use of the copula, I found that they could correct their non-target-like use of the copula in about 85% of cases but only when their attention was drawn to the error and they were prompted to do so. The prompts followed the pattern used in Example (9), where the pupils were asked what their teacher would say if they used a form such as *Tá sé ríomhaire/peann luaidhe* 'it is a computer/pencil'. When prompted in this way, they generally reformed their original utterance using the copula.

As previously reported, the Gaeltacht pupils omitted the copula *Is* and the pronoun *é* in utterances with the demonstrative pronoun *sin*. In contrast to this, when the all-Irish pupils were prompted in the stimulated recall to rephrase sentences where the substantive verb *bí* was used instead of the copula, they used *Is é* 'it is' in almost every case as in Example (8). Pupil J in Example (9) was an exception to this pattern as he said *sin an méid* 'that is the amount' when he rephrased his original utterance. It appeared that the majority of all-Irish pupils did not have access to or were unaware that this form of the copula was acceptable. The language input that all-Irish pupils receive may not be sufficiently salient for them to acquire this form of the copula where there is not a single map from English onto Irish. This finding should cause us to question if a change is needed in the way the copula is taught. Most pedagogical grammar texts will have a section on the copula *Is*. We have seen, however, that the Gaeltacht pupils rarely use that form of the copula. Instead, they omit *Is é sin* ... [that is ...], which is grammatically correct, in favour of *Sin* [that ...]. Based on the evidence of the pupils' corpus and the stimulated recall sessions, it would appear that pupils in senior classes in primary all-Irish schools have partially mastered the use of the copula with the demonstrative pronoun *sin*. In general, when prompted in a particular way, they produced the correct form but this did not appear to have been internalised as unmonitored spontaneous output.

Correction of inaccurate forms of verbal noun

The use of the verbal noun was another area of difficulty for the all-Irish school pupils and indeed on some occasions for the Gaeltacht pupils also. This issue was explored in the recall sessions in a similar way to the copula above.

In Example (10), Pupil K's attention was drawn to her utterance. She was able to correct the verbal noun error without prompting and she also replaced one instance of 'okay'.

(10) 02_02_179

K ~~Okay~~ <u>Ceart go leor</u>, *ní cheapaim*   Okay, I don't think that we are
   go bhfuil muid ~~ag faigh~~ <u>chun</u> *é sin*   going to get that, okay, wait a
   <u>a fháil</u>, *okay fan soicind*   second.

Similarly, in Example (11) Pupil I's attention was drawn to her utterance and she too was able to correct verbal noun error.

(11) 05_03_120

I *Agus thig linn* ~~fháil~~ *sin* <u>a fháil</u>   And we can get that.

Pupil A's attention was drawn to Line 147 in Example (12) and she was asked if there was a better way to express it. When she was unable to respond, I prompted her with a similar structure that was likely to be familiar to her from routine classroom conversation. She was then able to rephrase this question correctly and on hearing this, Pupil D offered the correct form for 'You can draw it'.

(12) 08_01

A 147	*Is féidir leat tarraingt é …*	You can draw it.
R	***Dá mba rud é go ndúirt tú leis an múinteoir 'An bhfuil cead agam faigh leabhar?' Céard a déarfadh sí?***	If you said to the teacher, 'Have I permission to get a book?' (said in incorrect form) What would she say?
A	*An bhfuil cead agam leabhar a fháil?*	Have I permission to get a book?
D	*Is féidir leat é a tharraingt.*	You can draw it.

Pupils were able to self-correct their incorrect use of the verbal noun approximately 50% of the time once their attention was drawn to an error. On occasions when self-correction was not possible, the researcher offered a similar phrase that used the same structure in a context with which the pupil was familiar. In many of these instances, the pupil or his/her peers realised the connection and corrected the verbal noun structure.

The exchange in Example (13) provides insight into the pupils' awareness of their mistakes. Pupil J's attention was drawn to Line 17 in the original transcript and she corrected it. I asked her why, in her spontaneous speech, she makes mistakes like that when she knows the correct form. In her response, she suggested that on occasions, mistakes were made when output was not monitored. Pupil A remarked that once their attention is drawn to a problematic feature, they know immediately that it is wrong.

(13) 07_01

J 17	*Caoga agus sin d'fhéadfadh muid ~~faigh an~~, an dréimire rópa a fháil.*	Fifty and then we could get the rope ladder.
C	*Like 'an bhfuil cead leabhar a fháil', deireann tú é sin mícheart, déarfaidh sí. 'Abair sin arís'.*	Like have I permission to get a book, you say that wrong, she (the teacher) will say. 'Say it again'.
R	*Cén fáth a ndéanann tú botún mar sin nuair atá an rud ceart ar eolas agat?*	Why do you make a mistake like that when know the correct thing?

J	*B'fhéidir tá tú ag iarraidh deir é just chun faigh é amach agus níl tú ag thabhairt a lán smaoineamh air.*	Maybe you are just trying to say it to get it out and you are not giving it a lot of thought.
R	**Nuair atá sé ráite an mbíonn a fhios agat féin go bhfuil sé mícheart?**	**And when you have said it do you know yourself that it is wrong?**
A	*Tá sé mar an gcéanna le obair scríofa, má tá rud éigin mícheart, ghlaonn an múinteoir ort agus an nóiméad a féachann tú air tá fhios agat tá sé mícheart.*	It is the same with written work, if something is wrong, the teacher calls you and the minute you look at it you know it is wrong.

This issue of pupils not monitoring their output in spontaneous production and not attending to form is a theme that arose repeatedly throughout the recall sessions. The evidence from the recall sessions was that the pupils needed to have their attention drawn to the mistake before they noticed it. Even when the error was pointed out, in many cases they were unable to correct it without significant prompting. My line of questioning of the pupils may appear somewhat intrusive when taken out of context. During the stimulated recall sessions, I framed the discussions in a way that positioned the pupils as the experts of their language use. The pupils tried to help me understand why they made certain mistakes which they themselves had highlighted and why they used a lot of English words which they themselves had also identified as problematic.

Pupils' perceptions of code-mixing

Code-mixing was common throughout the corpus and the use of English words was easily identified by the pupils. Some of the pupils' corrections are shown in Example (14). In most instances, the English word was deleted and replaced with an Irish word. The correct form for the verbal noun in Line 56 was offered.

(14) 02_02

D	~~Let's see~~ *Fan go bhfeicfimid*	Wait till we see.
B	~~O, how about like connect like cuireann tú~~ *Céard faoi má cuirfimid gach rud le chéile é seo, é seo le é seo*	How about if we put everything together this, this with this.
K	~~Yeah~~, *beidh sin* ~~class~~ *go maith/ hiontach*	That will be great.

K	*Agus ansin faigh muid* like *déanfaimid* like *rud éicint* ~~like park~~ *mar páirc do daoine beaga, páirc do daoine móra agus* ~~say~~ *deir muid...*	And then we will get like, we will do like something as a park for the small people, a park for the big people and say...
K 56	So ~~literally~~ *caithfimid* ~~fáil~~ *rud éicint* ~~atá~~ *a fháil i gcomhair gach duine agus má tá sé rud éicint mar atá* like *faigh muid rud éicint mar* like, *b'fhéidir rud mar sin* so.	So we have to get something for everyone and if it is something like, we'll get something like maybe a thing like that so.
K	~~Yeah~~, *beidh sin* ~~so class~~ *go hiontach.*	That will be great.

Pupil A commented in Example (15) that '*Tá a lán focal Béarla istigh ann*' [there are a lot of English words in it]. When questioned about this, Pupil E stated that they lacked awareness of what words they were using and that using English words was a 'habit'. It is interesting to note that the six-word sentence giving her assessment and reflection, itself contained four English words 'no', 'just', 'like' and 'habit'. This serves to highlight just how unaware the pupils were of code-mixing.

(15) 06_03

A	*Tá a lán focal Béarla istigh ann.*	There are a lot of English words in it.
C	'Like', 'oh my God', 'yeah', 'probably'.	'Like', 'oh my God', 'yeah', 'probably'.
R	*An raibh a fhios agaibh go raibh siad sin á húsáid agaibh?*	Did you know that you were using them?
E	No, *tá sé* just like habit.	No, it is just like habit.

Pupil C's response in Example (16) indicates that they (the pupils) were not aware of the volume of code-mixing that occurred and that it was a practice they were used to, confirming the notion of 'habit' expressed in Example (15).

(16) 06_04

R	*Cén fáth a bhfuil focail Bhéarla istigh ann?*	Why are there a lot of English words in it?
C	*Táimid an-*used to it.	We are very used to it.

R	*An mbíonn a fhios agaibh go bhfuil sé sin ar siúl?*	Do you know that this is happening?
E	*Ní bhíonn a fhios againn.*	No, we don't know.

The responses of the pupils above were from schools with the highest rate of code-mixing, but they were typical of the comments in all the other schools. All the pupils repeatedly stated that they were not aware that they used so many English words and it was this aspect above all others that disappointed them regarding the quality of their Irish.

Phase 3: Pupils' Insights into the Inaccurate Features of Their Irish Output

Using the reflections from Phases 1 and 2 as a starting point, the third stage of the recall sessions engaged the pupils in considering the reasons for their errors in a more general context. Questions such as why they had not spoken as accurately as they were capable and why their Irish contained so many English words were considered by the pupils. Here, we will look at the results of those discussions, beginning with monitoring of output.

Monitoring of output

When Pupil J, in the following section of Example (13), was asked why she made a mistake when she knew the correct form, her response was telling:

(13) 07_01

R	*Cén fáth a ndéanann tú botún mar sin nuair atá an rud ceart ar eolas agat.*	Why do you make a mistake like that when you know the correct thing?
J	*B'fhéidir tá tú ag iarraidh deir é just chun faigh é amach agus níl tú ag thabhairt a lán smaoineamh air.*	Maybe you are just trying to say it to get it out and you are not giving it a lot of thought.

This type of response was common in all groups and the issue of 'not thinking' as a reason for mistakes arose repeatedly during the stimulated recall sessions. The discussion between Pupils E, S and D in Example (17) also captures the notion of 'not thinking'. Pupil E was particularly critical of their Irish and had no difficulty in stating how she did not monitor her output and that she used the English version of words despite the fact that she clearly knew the words in Irish. She also observed that on occasions when writing in class, she monitors what she writes more carefully than her spoken words. Pupil S noted that she forgot about the presence of the camera, indicating implicitly that she was capable of a better 'performance' if only she had been more aware of the camera.

(17) 04_01

E	*Tá sé saghas uafásach an Ghaeilge a d'úsáid muid.*	**It was kind of awful the Irish we used.**
R	***Nach bhfuil sé chomh maith is a cheap sibh?***	**Is it not as good as you thought it was?**
S	*Níl. Tá sé go maith nuair atá tú ag scríobh é i cóipleabhar.*	**No. It is good when you are writing it in your copybook.**
E	Yeah *mar tá tú ag smaoineamh ar céard a bhfuil tú ag scríobh síos.*	**Yeah because you are thinking about what you are writing.**
D	*Ach nuair atá tú ag caint thagann sé amach.*	**But when you are talking it comes out.**
S	Like *rinne mise dearmad bhí an ceamara ansin agus …*	**Like I forgot the camera was there and …**
E	Like, *focail atá fhios agam, bhí mé ag rá iad as Béarla fiú amháin má bhí fhios agam an Ghaeilge orthu mar ní raibh mé ag smaoineamh.*	**Like, words I know, I was saying them in English, even if I knew the Irish for them because I wasn't thinking.**

In Example (18), the pupils again explained that they 'don't think' and elaborated on why that was the case. Pupil J suggested that the use of English outside of school with her friends was a strong influence. This highlights the situated nature of learning in an immersion context as discussed in Chapter 2.

(18) 07_02

R	*Cén fáth a ndeir tú an rud mícheart nuair atá an rud ceart ar eolas agat?*	**Why do you say the incorrect thing when you know the correct thing?**
J	*Mar nuair atá tú ag dul timpeall le do chairde is Béarla a bíonn á labhairt agat agus ansin nuair a thagann tú ar scoil is é Gaeilge agus caithfidh tú smaoineamh faoi.*	**Because when you are going around with your friends it is English that you speak and when you come to school it is Irish and you have to think about it.**
R	*Aon tuairim agatsa A?*	**Have you any opinion A?**

A	*Ní smaoiníonn tú.*	You don't think.
R	*An mbíonn tú ag smaoineamh níos mó nuair a bhíonn tú ag caint leis an múinteoir nó le do chairde?*	Do you think more when you are talking to the teacher or to your friends?
J	*Leis an múinteoir mar muna deir tú an rud ceart, beidh sí, déarfaidh sí tá sé mícheart.*	With the teacher because if you don't say it correctly, she will be, she will say it is incorrect.

When in conversation with the teacher, they put more effort into what they were saying. This is evident in the final comment by Pupil J. There is a subtle awareness that if you don't speak accurately, you will be corrected. Pupil D in Example (19) acknowledged that the same effort is not made when speaking with friends:

(19) 04_02

D	*Déanann muid iarracht mór sa rang leis an múinteoir ach sílim nuair atá muid lenár cairde nach ndéanaimid iarracht chomh maith.*	We make a big effort in class with the teacher but I think when we are with our friends that we don't make as big an effort.

This comment by Pupil D echoes that of a Welsh-medium pupil in Thomas et al. (2014: 353): 'when it's something I know a lot I make long sentences and try to mutate correctly with the teacher but don't really think a lot about mutation with friends'. Another pupil in the Thomas et al. (2014) study stated that they used more words in English and didn't mutate as much when they were not under pressure by the presence of the teacher. It was clear from these comments that the norm of speaking Irish as accurately as possible with the teacher was well established. It was also clear that extra effort on the part of the pupils was required to maintain this standard and that they were not inclined to make that effort when speaking with friends at school. This finding is supported by the Attitude/Motivation Test Battery (AMTB) results, where 81.7% of pupils strongly agreed that it was important for them to be able to speak Irish without mistakes when speaking with the teacher compared to 51.8% when speaking with their peers.

Correction by peers

As noted earlier, no instances of pupils correcting a peer's inaccurate use of Irish occurred during the task. Notwithstanding this, the stimulated recall groups were asked if they ever corrected each other. Pupil G in Example (20) responded:

(20) 04_02

R	*An gceartaíonn sibh a chéile riamh?*	Do you ever correct one another?
G	*Ní* it depends. *B'fhéidir* if *tá tú ag caint Béarla a lán, beidh tú ceartaithe.*	No, it depends. Maybe if you are speaking English a lot you will be corrected.

Pupil J in Example (21) responded that she would sometimes correct a peer and that she would notice a peer's inaccuracy more easily than her own.

(21) 03_03

R	*An gceartaíonn sibh a chéile riamh?*	Do you ever correct one another?
J	*Uaireanta.*	Sometimes.
J	*Cloiseann tú nuair atá daoine eile ag labhairt Gaeilge nach bhfuil cruinn. Ach ní chloiseann tú nach bhfuil tú féin ag labhairt go cruinn.*	You hear it when someone else speaks Irish that isn't accurate. But you don't hear that you are not speaking accurately yourself.
S	*Sea.*	Yes.

Pupil N in Example (22) also referred to 'not noticing' her peer's mistakes. This is interesting because earlier in the conversation, Pupil B had explained that in her view mistakes occurred *mar níl muid ag éisteacht linn féin* [because we are not listening to ourselves].

(22) 04_03

R	*Nuair a bhíonn tú ag caint le do chairde an mbeadh siad riamh dod' cheartú?*	When you are speaking to your friends would they ever correct you?
B	*Sea, uaireanta.*	Yes, sometimes.
N	*Ní thugaim faoi deara é.*	I don't notice it.
D	Only *faigheann tú an Ghaeilge maith i* like *rang 6 agus tá tú* used to *an Gaeilge eile.*	You only get good Irish in 6th class and you are used to the other Irish.
N	*Nuair a léann tú an gramadach bíonn níos mo Gaeilge maith agat.*	When you read the grammar, you have more good Irish.

R	*An gceapann sibh go bhfuil feabhas tagtha ar bhur gcuid Gaeilge.*	Do you think that your Irish has improved?
N	*Sea, feabhas mór.*	Yes, a big improvement.

This group spoke about there being two types of Irish, *Gaeilge na leanaí* 'the Irish of young children' and *Gaeilge mhaith* 'good Irish'.

The pupils were asked if they minded being corrected by their peers in class. It was clear from their responses, as in Example (23), that there were sensitivities about the manner in which corrections were carried out by a peer:

(23) 03_02

J	*Uaireanta cuireann sé isteach ort má tá duine sa rang ceapann siad go bhfuil a fhios acu gach rud ... Má cheartaíonn do chairde thú beidh siad díreach ag rá leat bí cúramach ag labhairt mar sin mar gheobhaidh tú i dtrioblóid. Mar tá do chairde ag féachaint amach duit, i mBéarla* looking out for you.	Sometimes it upsets you if there is a person in the class who thinks that they know everything ... If your friends correct you they will be just telling you to be careful speaking like that because you will be in trouble. Your friends are looking out for you, in English 'looking out for you'.
R	*Níl sé go deas a bheith ceartaithe os comhair do chairde.*	It is not nice to be corrected in front of your friends.
S	*Nó os comhair an rang.*	Or in front of the class.

These comments highlight the difficult task that immersion teachers have in striking a balance between encouraging pupils to speak the target language accurately and correcting inaccuracies, which may lead to embarrassment. Similarly, pupils' comments suggest that it is difficult for pupils to correct their peers' inaccuracies as it may appear that they are policing one another. 'Looking out' for your friends, however, legitimises drawing their attention to the use of English words. It may also be the case that the immersion variety of Irish spoken by the pupils is seen as legitimate and the accepted norm, and that pupils see no more need to correct it than they would correct a peer's English. The issue of 'getting into trouble' emerged among the pupils in the Thomas *et al.* (2014: 349) study also, with one pupil expressing the view: 'If we speak a lot in English someone will tell on us and we would be in trouble ... so no one really speaks English'. We can see in these examples the manner in which the speech community of the immersion classroom exerts a normative effect on linguistic behaviour.

Recycling of learner errors

The effect of being exposed to incorrect Irish was also commented on by Pupil K in Example (24). She explained how she 'picks up' incorrect forms from her peers and uses them herself. She goes on to explain that she would not correct her peers when they use an incorrect form because she understands what they are trying to say. The emphasis is on communicating the message.

(24) 02_01

R	*Ach uaireanta b'fhéidir go ndeir sibh an rud mícheart an ea?*	But sometimes you might say the incorrect thing, is that so?
K	*Mar cloiseann tú daoine ag rá na rudaí mícheart agus* you know just *piocann tú suas ar na rudaí sin. Agus* just *abraíonn tú iad.*	Because you hear people saying the wrong things and you just pick up on those things. And you just say them.
R	*Nuair a bhíonn tú ag caint eadraibh féin, má deir mise 'Tá sé ríomhaire' leat. Ní bheifeá do mo cheartú.*	When you are speaking among yourselves, if I say, 'It is a computer' (using substantive verb). You wouldn't correct me.
K	No. *Mar tá a fhios agam cad a bhfuil tú* like *ag iarraidh a rá, so ní dheir mé aon rud.*	No. Because I know what you are like, trying to say, so I don't say anything.

In the previous exchange, Pupil K provided an insight into one of the reasons why immersion pupils do not speak the target language accurately. Pupils immersed with other learners who also speak an interlanguage acquire one another's errors. She also explained why they do not, by and large, correct each other. The focus of their communication was on deriving meaning from the utterances of others and once this communicative need was fulfilled, accuracy was not important. It appeared that once the pupils' output conformed to the implicit norms of their variety of Irish, then a peer did not comment on it.

Translation from English

Another issue raised with pupils was translation from English. Pupil K in Example (25) responded:

(25) 02_01

| K | *Nuair a thosaigh muid ag labhairt Gaeilge* just *bhí orainn* like *smaoineamh. Céard é an focal seo? Céard é an focal sin? Ach anois tá sé* just *mar ag labhairt Béarla.* | When we started to speak Irish just, we had to like think. What is this word? What is that word? But now it's just like speaking English. |

The pupils in Example (26) recognised that they translated words from English in some contexts when the source of their conversation was in English such as a television programme in English:

(26) 04_02

R	*An mbíonn sibh ag aistriú ó Bhéarla go Gaeilge?*	Do you translate from English to Irish?
C	Say *má tá tú ag caint le do chara faoi clár teilifís agus* say *má tá an clár teilifís i Béarla. Caithfidh tú é a aistriú i do ceann roimh a deireann tú é le do chara. Ach má tá tú* just *ag caint le do cara úsáideann tú Gaeilge. Tá tú* just *ag smaoineamh ar na focail i do cheann.*	Say if you are talking to your friend about a television programme and say if the programme is in English. You have to translate it in your head before you say it to your friend. But if you are just talking to your friend you say it in Irish. You are just thinking of the words in your head.
R	*Ach an gnáthchaint sa scoil agus sa chlós tá tú ag smaoineamh…*	But the everyday language in the school and in the yard, you are thinking…
C	*Trí Ghaeilge.*	Through Irish.

This use of English is a type of 'translanguaging' where pupils hear or read something in English and reproduce it in Irish (Lewis *et al.*, 2012). Pupil C in Example (27) also reported translating from English when doing an essay in Irish:

(27) 01_02

| C | *I aiste as Gaeilge bhí mé ag smaoineamh ar rud i Béarla agus ansin aistriú mé é go Gaeilge ach ní raibh an gramadach ceart.* | I was thinking about something in English in an Irish essay and then I translated it to Irish but the grammar wasn't correct. |

Although noted previously that pupils appeared to map English syntax onto Irish, the evidence from the responses above and from other groups was that pupils did not consciously translate from English to Irish in the course of their everyday conversation. Thus, where the influence of English was detectable, it was very likely an embedded unconscious influence, not a transient effect of 'translation'. The only exception to this is where they referred to material that occurred in English. The influence of English idiom on the pupils' Irish appeared to be mostly at a subconscious level. If this is indeed the case, then pupils' attention may need to be drawn to the English influence in order to overcome it. Once again, it is suggested that an experiential approach may not be sufficient to progress pupils to speak a more native-like variety of Irish.

Focus on formS

It was observed that the pupils in some schools referred to grammar lessons more frequently than others. In the case of one particular class, their teacher engaged in 'focus on formS' lessons with a particular emphasis on the irregular verbs in Irish. The pupils were taught the conjugation patterns for regular verbs and memorised how irregular verbs differed. Pupils from these schools displayed a greater sense of awareness of the importance of grammatical accuracy than pupils from the other schools in the recall sessions.

Pupil D in Example (28) stated that:

(28) 04_03

D	Only *faigheann tú an Ghaeilge maith i* like *rang 6 agus tá tú* used to *an Gaeilge eile*.	You only get good Irish in 6th class and you are used to the other Irish.

Pupil N from the same school expressed the view that:

N	*Tá Gaeilge agus ansin tá Gaeilge níos fearr. Tá Gaeilge i gcomhair leanaí agus Gaeilge níos fearr.*	There is Irish and then there is better Irish. There is Irish for young children and better Irish.

It was evident from her other comments that she had come to this realisation through the focus on formS activities of the sixth-class teacher.

Pupil N from another school thought that despite the fact that they were learning aspects of Irish grammar, they did not always apply this learning to their speech, as she illustrated in Example (29):

(29) 03_03

N	... *nuair a bhíonn tú ag labhairt ní bhíonn tú ag iarraidh an graiméar a chur isteach, mar uaireanta bíonn tú leisciúil.*	... when you are speaking you don't want to put in the grammar, because you are lazy sometimes.
N	*Tá an iomarca rudaí sa graiméar mar an tuiseal ginideach sa chéad díochlaonadh agus an dara díochlaonadh.*	There are too many different things in the grammar like the genitive case in the first declension and second declension.

In response to Pupil N, Pupil S added in Example (30) that you forget some of the aspects of grammar when you are speaking naturally. Pupils S's second comment implied that learning grammar is like simple habit formation:

(30) 03_03

S	*Déanann tú dearmad ar cúpla de na rudaí sin nuair a bhfuil tú ag caint go nádúrtha. Caithfidh sé a bheith an-soiléir i do cheann.*	You forget some of those things when you are speaking naturally. It must be very clear in your mind.
S	*Is dóigh liom go bhfuil sé mar ag traenáil madra le an graiméar, thugann tú milseán dóibh agus ansin dhéanann siad an rud i gceart.*	I think that it is like training a dog with grammar, you give them a sweet and then they do it right.

Although the pupils in schools who had experienced grammar lessons had a heightened sense of awareness of certain features of Irish relative to their peers in the other schools, it did not appear to translate into their communicative performance. The extent to which explicit knowledge contributes to the development of implicit knowledge is contested in the literature (Ellis & Shintani, 2014; VanPatten, 2016). It may be the case, however, that this exposure to grammatical rules was an important first step in helping them to notice the gap in their accuracy (Skehan, 1998). It was noted that the pupils from one of these schools where the teacher taught focus on formS lessons, outperformed all other schools in their ability to notice mistakes in the transcripts and to correct those mistakes.

Exposure to Irish outside of school

The lack of exposure to Irish outside of school was offered as a reason for errors in pupils' Irish and for the use of English words. When asked why they thought that their Irish contained mistakes and they code-mixed, the pupils in School 06 responded as follows:

(31) 06_03

A	'Cos *táimid i gcónaí* like *ag caint Béarla agus nuair atáimid ar scoil táimid ag caint Gaeilge.*	'Cos we are always like speaking English and when we are at school we speak Irish.
C	*Níl aon Ghaeilge againn tá sé just Béarla sa bhaile.*	We have no Irish, it is just English at home.
C	*Níl aon* like *Ghaeilge in aon áit sa bhaile seo, just an Ghaeltacht* like *a bhíonn tú ag labhairt Gaeilge lasmuigh den scoil.*	There is no Irish anywhere in this town, it's just the Gaeltacht like where you speak Irish outside of school.

These views were shared by pupils in other schools who confirmed that they had no exposure to Irish outside of school and reported it as a reason why their Irish contained errors and English words. While the pupils' language behaviour in school was influenced by their home language, English, some pupils commented that sometimes they use Irish at home because of the influence of school. Pupil J in Example (32) reported that:

(32) 05_01

J	*Cúpla t-am nuair atá mé sa bhaile caintim Gaeilge mar thimpiste le mo Mham agus nil a fhios aici cad é atá mé ag rá.*	A couple of times when I am at home I speak Irish to my Mom by accident and she doesn't know what I am saying.

On the whole, the pupils experienced little exposure to Irish outside of school other than through homework. This, in their opinion, affected their ability to speak Irish accurately in school.

Discussion and Conclusions

The pupils in the stimulated recall sessions were critical of their own Irish when they were given an opportunity to view a video recording of their interaction and to see it transcribed verbatim. The aspect that they were most critical of was code-mixing. They failed to notice many grammatical errors unless their attention was drawn to them. As mentioned earlier, 8.97% of the all-Irish school corpus was accounted for by borrowings from English and English discourse markers. It appears that the pupils code-mixed considerably more than they were aware of. Indeed, they expressed surprise and disappointment at the number of English words that were present in the transcripts. When given an opportunity to correct their Irish through reflection, their most common response was to replace the English words. When questioned as to why they used so many English words, they responded that it was just a 'habit' and that they were not monitoring their output as they were focused on the task rather than form. They also cited a lack of exposure to Irish outside school as a reason for the presence of so many English words.

Apart from code-mixing, the recall sessions focused on two other features of the pupils' Irish, namely, the copula and the verbal noun. When the pupils were given an opportunity to correct mistakes in these two features in the transcripts, they rarely noticed any problem until their attention was specifically drawn to possible alternative forms. In the case of the copula, they could correct the error if prompted in a particular way using a structure similar to that in the transcript. They had more success with the verbal noun, correcting about 50% of the errors when their attention was drawn to them. The fact that the pupils were able to correct many of the mistakes that they had originally made, may indicate that they have an underlying communicative competence that is not always fully displayed in their communicative performance.

Other issues such as the morphology of verbs, prepositional pronouns, numbers and interrogative pronouns (*Cad/Céard/Cad é* 'What') incorrectly used, also arose in the stimulated recall sessions. Pupils' attention had to be specifically drawn to these issues and the pupils were unable to correct these errors until prompts were provided. When the pupils were presented with their incorrect use of the interrogative and dependent forms of verbs, they still failed to perceive them as errors and could only correct errors of this type when provided with suitable prompts.

Pupils monitored their output more carefully when they were speaking with the teacher compared to their peers. Use of Irish with the teacher, therefore, can represent 'pushed output' where the pupils are pushed to convey their intended message 'precisely, coherently, and appropriately' (Swain, 2005: 473). There was a degree of inhibition of incorrect forms by the pupils involved here which Hammerly (1989) suggests is desirable. The pupils, for their part, expressed the view that they did not like being corrected by their peers or by the teacher when it occurred in view of others, and that these encounters led to embarrassment. They rarely negotiated for form in interaction with their peers. This is in keeping with the research findings of other interaction studies with child and teenage L2 learners in English as a second language (ESL) and content and language integrated learning (CLIL) contexts (Dalton-Puffer, 2007; Oliver & Mackey, 2003). When Irish immersion pupils did negotiate for form, it was generally in instances where there was code-mixing or code-switching.

A factor that pupils believed may affect the level of errors in their output was that they acquired inaccurate forms heard frequently from their peers. As these inaccurate forms were comprehensible, they went unnoticed or were tolerated, as the emphasis was on meaning rather than on form. The role of the teacher therefore is critical in this regard in providing feedback to the pupils. Greater attention may need to be given to the potential of corrective feedback strategies in initial teacher education and professional development programmes. Due to the sociolinguistic context of Irish as a minority language, the pupils are not exposed to native speakers outside of school who might fulfil the role of maintaining the kind of implicit social pressure that promotes native speaker norms.

As outlined in Chapter 3, Skehan (1998) described rule-based and memory-based systems. According to the rule-based system, rules are developed over time as the learner's language capacity develops following the pattern of restructuring under the operation of a universal grammar or other cognitive processes. The memory-based system, on the other hand, results from the accumulation of formulaic language chunks that can be accessed from long-term memory. The unmonitored language output of the Irish immersion pupils may result from incorrect language chunks stored in their memory-based system that they retrieve automatically.

When prompted by the teacher or in anticipation of negative feedback when they make a mistake, pupils may draw on their rule-based system. It was the memory-based system, however, that appeared to be easiest for them to retrieve. This may indicate that monitoring language output required resources from working memory that reduced the attentional capacity (Skehan, 1996) at their disposal to plan for the content and form of the remainder of the utterance. If this is the case, there are implications for immersion pedagogy in raising pupils' language awareness that would lead to a restructuring of inaccurate forms in their underlying interlanguage. It would also be helpful to understand how these incorrect forms are initially miscoded, if this is indeed what is happening.

There were many examples in the transcripts where English syntax appeared to be mapped onto Irish. When the pupils were questioned about this, they stated that they did not consciously translate from English to Irish unless the source data were in English, in which case they engaged in a form of 'translanguaging' (Lewis et al., 2012). This may indicate that the inaccurate forms of the copula and verbal noun used, are forms that have stabilised in their interlanguage. If this is the case, it may be more difficult for them to notice the error and then to internalise the correct forms available to them in the input they receive from the teacher or other sources. Specific pedagogic intervention may be required. The research suggests that focus on form activities may help learners attend to form, leading to change in their underlying interlanguage (Lyster, 2007; VanPatten, 2002). Failure to address this issue may perpetuate the all-Irish pupils' propensity to habitually produce inaccurate forms. In such a scenario, errors may become embedded and lead to a degree of permanency.

Recording pupils for the purposes of the reflective activity proved very effective in drawing attention to their code-mixing behaviour. While it would not be practical for teachers to replicate this activity, they could nonetheless record their pupils engaged in regular class activities and provide opportunities to view the recordings. The pupils could transcribe short extracts of their dialogue and the teacher could provide guidance in the reformulation of this dialogue. Various research studies (Lynch, 2001; Swain & Lapkin, 2008) have shown that these strategies can lead pupils to notice gaps in their own interlanguage and has led to longer-term learning of targeted structures.

The pupils were aware of some of the linguistic errors made when given an opportunity to reflect on them. Their insights into why they don't think about form in their utterances when their attention is focused on a task can inform pedagogy. It was also evident in the pupils' comments that their exposure to Irish outside of the school context was very limited. In the examples of the stimulated recall presented in this chapter, the pupils articulated the limitations of the immersion class and school to promote accurate acquisition of Irish. I believe that this is important from a sociocultural perspective. The pupils identify with the speech community of the classroom where their output is intelligible to one another. The context outside the school clearly impacts on learning in the classroom. Regardless of the levels of target language input received by the pupils in class, without exposure to or identification with a speech community beyond the school, they are likely to lack the motivation to approximate to more target-like language norms. This factor led me to explore all-Irish pupil use of Irish outside the classroom and school and these findings are reported in the next chapter.

Notes

(1) R stands for researcher unless otherwise stated and is represented in bold type.
(2) A distinction is made between 'mistakes' and 'errors'. Learners or native speakers alike can make mistakes when speaking. These mistakes can be slips of the tongue or non-target-like forms. What distinguishes mistakes from errors is that mistakes can usually be self-corrected. The speaker usually knows the rule either at an implicit or explicit level. In the case of an error, the learner does not know the rule and cannot self-correct.

7 Use of Irish Outside the Classroom

Introduction

Many jurisdictions such as Wales, Scotland (Gaelic), the Basque Country, New Zealand (Māori) and Hawaii are trying to revive indigenous languages through the education system. In these cases, the languages are, by and large, not spoken beyond certain geographical borders. In the case of Irish, the level of intergenerational transmission is insufficient to guarantee the future survival of the language (Ó Giollagáin & Charlton, 2015). In this context, there is a significant dependence on the education system to generate new speakers of Irish (Ó Riagáin, 2008). Generating competent bilinguals is only half the battle, however. There is no guarantee that these bilinguals will become active new speakers of Irish. In order to gain a greater insight into pupils' potential use of Irish, I examined their attitudes to Irish and motivation to learn the language as part of the original corpus-based studies (Ó Duibhir, 2009). Overall, as one might expect, the all-Irish pupils ($n = 172$) in sixth-class Irish immersion had very positive attitudes and motivation to learn Irish. A full account of this element of the corpus-based study is available in Ó Duibhir (2010) and is not reported here.

In its 20-Year Strategy for the Irish Language, the government of the Republic of Ireland (RoI) affirmed the role of the education system as the primary focus for the strengthening of Irish (Government of Ireland, 2010). It acknowledged, however, '[T]he critical need to give life to the Irish language outside the classroom for the young people who study it in the formal education system' (Government of Ireland, 2010: 12). It could be argued that the state language education policy since 1922 has been relatively successful in that the numbers reporting an ability to speak Irish has increased from 18.3% in the 1926 census to 39.8% (1.76 million) in the census of 2016. However, it is the number of active speakers of a language that represent the true measure of its vitality. While there is extensive teaching and learning of Irish (Ó Laoire, 2006), and use of Irish in the domain of education should not be disregarded, I would contend that it is the use of Irish outside the classroom and school that is the ultimate objective. As noted earlier, Baker (2003) suggested that converting language learned at school to community use is very challenging. A language learned at school and not encountered outside of that domain may become associated with school only. Fishman (2013) also cautioned against an overdependence on the education system for language revitalisation and cited Ireland as a prime example of this.

The RoI government's 20-year strategy for Irish is based on the premise of three interacting factors: (i) knowledge of Irish, (ii) opportunities for the use of Irish and (iii) positive attitudes towards its use (Government of Ireland, 2010: 7). These factors have been described by Grin (2003) as capacity, opportunity and desire. The strategy seeks to improve the capacity to speak Irish principally through the education system while acknowledging that without opportunities to speak Irish and a desire or willingness to use it, improved ability may not result in increased use. Ó Laoire (2004) argued that the teaching of Irish in schools is dependent to a large extent upon its use outside the school. Grin (2003) suggested that the state, through its language policies, has a role to play in creating opportunities for language use outside the private sphere of the home. There is little evidence of this happening in Ireland. In Chapter 6, pupils highlighted the effect of the sociolinguistic environment they inhabit when they reported that they had little or no exposure to Irish outside school and that this made learning and speaking Irish more difficult as they live in a world dominated by English. Despite this, there is encouraging evidence that those who have attended all-Irish schools are more likely to participate in Irish-speaking networks as adults and to use Irish more frequently than those who attend English-medium schools (Murtagh, 2007, 2009). Ó Cathalláin (2011) found positive attitudes to speaking Irish in immersion pupils who came from homes where parents were supportive or had contact with Gaeltacht areas. Visits to the Gaeltacht provided opportunities to interact with Irish speakers and this helped to affirm the pupils' second language (L2) selves. In a recent study, Darmody and Daly (2015) reported that adult participants with a high level of ability in Irish were almost twice as likely to speak Irish 'sometimes' compared to those with basic ability. In the same study, 43% of those whose parents had a high ability in Irish, spoke Irish on a weekly or more frequent basis compared to 6% when the parents had little or no competence in Irish.

The 20-year strategy set out an ambitious target to increase the number of daily speakers of Irish from 77,185 to 250,000 by the year 2030 (Government of Ireland, 2010). That target, which I considered unrealistic from the outset (Ó Duibhir, 2012), has become even more ambitious as the number of daily speakers has declined from 77,185 in the 2011 census to 73,803 in 2016. In the remainder of this chapter, I outline a study aimed at examining what contribution Irish immersion pupils might make to achieve this target in the future. In doing so, I acknowledge that these learners are not the only source of competent bilinguals but that the studies cited above have found a strong correlation between ability in Irish, including those taught through the medium of Irish, and the use of Irish outside of the education context (Murtagh, 2007). Notwithstanding this, Ó Riagáin (2000) estimated in the 1990s that only one-quarter of those who grew up in Irish-speaking homes reproduced that subsequently in their own homes as adults. He attributed home language use at that time to three factors: (i) competent bilingual speakers generated by the school system, (ii) parents who were raised in Irish-speaking homes and (iii) others who had neither an Irish-speaking upbringing nor a strong association with Irish at school. He suggested that some of this latter group were parents who sent their children to all-Irish schools and that these schools were helping to generate some home usage of Irish. We can see then that as is the case with other minority Celtic languages, Irish is dependent on a variety of modes of transmission (Ó Murchadha & Migge, 2017).

In more recent years, active bilinguals of minority languages have been described as 'new speakers'. These are 'individuals who acquired the language outside of the home and who report that they use Irish with fluency, regularity and commitment' (O'Rourke & Walsh, 2015: 64). As noted earlier, the variety of Irish spoken by new speakers can be contested as is the case with other minority languages such as Breton (Hornsby, 2017). Some new speakers seek to approximate to native speaker norms of phonology and grammatical accuracy, whereas others consciously reject these varieties adhering to a non-traditionalist identity (O'Rourke & Walsh, 2015). Hornsby (2017) refers to this phenomenon in minority languages as a move towards post-vernacularity. He suggests that an ideology that places language users rather than the language itself at the heart of discourses is more likely to lead to positive attitudes to speaking the minority language. While some new speakers may speak a non-traditional variety of Irish, they still wish to assert their ownership of Irish and their desire to be recognised as Irish speakers (O'Rourke & Walsh, 2015). Pujolar and Gonzàlez (2013: 139) describe 'mudes' as 'specific biographical junctures where individuals enact significant changes in their linguistic repertoire'. These are transformation points that new speakers identify where they changed their language practice. Among the transformation points identified are entry to primary school, post-primary school, university and the workforce; creating a new family and becoming a parent (Pujolar & Gonzàlez, 2013: 143). These 'mudes' are not necessarily discreet points and may be interdependent. It is the school as a transformation point that is the focus of the studies reported in this volume.

The variety of Irish spoken by all-Irish primary pupils has been analysed and reported in Chapters 5 and 6. This variety was found to have morphological and syntactical features that deviated from target norms. The pupils were at the end of primary school and approximately 40% of them were likely to continue to post-primary all-Irish education (Ní Thuairisg & Ó Duibhir, 2016). Many of them will continue to develop their Irish in post-primary school and at university. From the analysis in previous chapters, we can see that the pupils demonstrated a good capacity to speak Irish, satisfying one of the three elements that Grin (2003) believes are necessary to increase minority language use. The study reported for this chapter recruited primary and post-primary all-Irish pupils and their parents. I report the pupils' desire to speak Irish and the extent to which they avail of opportunities, albeit limited, to speak Irish outside the classroom. Their parents' use of Irish is also presented.

Study Design

I conducted a large-scale study with colleagues to investigate models of Irish-medium primary and post-primary provision on the island of Ireland in 2013 and 2014. This wide-ranging study gathered the views of principals, parents and pupils in relation to Irish-medium education with a particular focus on a comparison between stand-alone schools and immersion units or streams. A full account of this study is available in Ó Duibhir *et al.* (2015c). One objective of the study was to examine the attitudes and motivation of primary and post-primary pupils to learning Irish, and to using Irish in the home and in school outside the classroom. A further objective was to investigate the home language practices of the pupils' parents. I present analysis and interpretation of these two objectives in this chapter. The findings build on my earlier work in the corpus-based studies and provide evidence of the out-of-school use of Irish by all-Irish pupils.

The pupils in the study were drawn from 20 all-Irish primary and post-primary schools across the island of Ireland. The adapted Attitude/Motivation Test Battery (AMTB) (see Appendix A) explained in Chapter 4 was administered to 373 primary pupils in fifth class (RoI) and seventh class (NI) and post-primary pupils in fourth year (RoI) and Year 12 (NI). These year groups were chosen in the two jurisdictions to match the pupils' age and stage of education. The primary pupils in the RoI and NI were age 10 or 11 years and the post-primary pupils were 15 or 16 years. The purpose of the AMTB was to quantify pupil attitude and motivation towards learning and using Irish. Motivation has been shown to be an important individual factor in L2 learning (Dörnyei, 2009). A positive attitude and motivation can help a learner sustain the effort to learn an L2 over a long period despite the challenges (Harris & Conway, 2002). There were 37 items across five scales in the adapted AMTB. The scales were: (i) desire to learn Irish; (ii) attitude to learning Irish; (iii) parental encouragement to learn Irish; (iv) Irish-ability self-concept; and (v) use of Irish. Pupils were asked to respond to each statement with Likert-type responses on a five-point scale ranging from strongly disagree to strongly agree. Each item was thus scored between 1 and 5. The range of scores for the 5-item scale was 5–25, the 6-item scale was 6–36, the 7-item scale was 7–35 and the 13-item scale was 13–65. A more comprehensive account of the test battery is available in Chapter 4 or in Ó Duibhir (2010). The number of pupil participants in each school type and the mean score for each scale are shown in Table 7.1. We tested the reliability of the scales using Cronbach's alpha and the alpha scores were very satisfactory (0.68 or greater), as reported in Table 7.1. An open-ended question at the end of the questionnaire where pupils were asked to list the factors that motivate pupils to speak Irish.

A 37-item questionnaire was also sent to each pupil's parents, but for the purposes of our discussion here we will focus on those items that relate to the linguistic background of parents, the type of school attended and their home language practices. As part of the analysis, we identified a sub-group of parents who had attended an all-Irish primary and/or post-primary school. I pay particular attention to this group in the following report.

Results

In this section, I initially report on the pupils' overall mean scores for each of the AMTB scales. Thereafter, I focus in particular on their responses to the 'use of Irish' scale and consider its relationship with 'home language use'. The degree to which pupils avail of the opportunity to speak Irish outside the classroom in the playground at school and their language practices with their parents is also explored. The linguistic background of parents and their language practice are also presented, and the pupils' language practices with their parents are explored.

A comparison of scale scores by school type and region

Table 7.1 shows the pupils' AMTB mean scores for each of the five scales by school type and jurisdiction. Score ranges varied depending on the number of items in each scale. Mean scores per scale are shown in brackets. Analysis of variance (ANOVA) tests were conducted to establish statistically significant differences in the scale scores across the different school types and jurisdictions. 'Desire to learn Irish' scores were similar regardless of school type. Primary school pupils in NI had the highest mean scores for the 'attitude to learning Irish' scale (30.28) and there was a statistically significant difference between these pupils and post-primary pupils in both the RoI and NI. The post-primary pupils in NI had the

Table 7.1 AMTB mean scores per scale by school type (average mean scores in brackets)

School type (jurisdiction)	No. of participants	Desire to learn Irish (6 items) alpha 0.75	Attitude to learning Irish (7 items) alpha 0.83	Parental encouragement to learn Irish (5 items) alpha 0.70	Irish ability self-concept (6 items) alpha 0.68	Use of Irish (13 items) alpha 0.78
Fifth-class primary (RoI); age 10–11 years	128	22.70 (3.8)	29.13 (4.2)	19.22 (3.8)	21.63 (3.6)	42.66 (3.3)
Seventh-class primary (NI); age 10–11 years	69	23.55 (3.9)	30.28 (4.3)	18.45 (3.7)	22.66 (3.8)	42.40 (3.3)
Year 4 post-primary (RoI); age 15–16 years	101	22.47 (3.7)	27.71 (4.0)	16.55 (3.3)	22.18 (3.7)	36.9 (2.8)
Year 12 post-primary (NI); age 15–16 years	75	23.23 (3.9)	27.37 (3.9)	19.97 (4.0)	21.09 (3.5)	33.07 (2.5)
Total	373	22.41 (3.7)	28.67 (4.1)	17.72 (3.5)	21.68 (3.6)	39.81 (3.1)

highest score for the 'parental encouragement to learn Irish' scale (19.97). Post-primary pupils' scores in the RoI were significantly lower than this (16.55). The scores for 'Irish ability self-concept' scale were positive overall, without significant differences between groups. Finally, in relation to the 'use of Irish', the primary pupils' scores in the RoI (42.66) and NI (42.40) were significantly higher than the post-primary pupils in both jurisdictions (RoI: 36.9 and NI: 33.07).

Pupil mean score by language spoken at home

As part of the 'language spoken at home' scale, we asked the pupils to indicate their language use at home.[1] We found that 7 (1.87%) pupils spoke Irish or mostly Irish at home. We also found that primary pupils ($n = 197$) were more likely to use some Irish at home than post-primary pupils ($n = 176$). In the parent questionnaire, we asked parents to indicate the language they spoke with their child. We conducted a regression analysis to explore student scores in relation to parent, student and school characteristics. A significant positive relationship between 'parental encouragement to learn Irish' and 'use of Irish' was apparent in the pupils' responses. However, language spoken by the parent to the child at home was no longer significantly related to the 'use of Irish scale' once the model included level of education setting, i.e. primary or post-primary. That is, it appeared that the language in which the parent communicated with the child was partly or largely mediated by whether the child was in primary or post-primary school with the greatest amount of Irish spoken with primary schoolchildren.

Use of Irish outside the classroom

The 'use of Irish' scale had two items which sought to capture pupils' language behaviour within the school but outside of class. The first item was 'To be honest, I don't make much effort to speak Irish outside of the class when I am at school'. In Figure 7.1, we can see considerable difference in the responses between primary and post-primary pupils; less than one-quarter (21.6%) of primary pupils and just under a half (49.7%) of post-primary pupils agreed or strongly agreed with this statement. This suggests that post-primary pupils make less effort to speak Irish outside of class.

The second item, on this theme was: 'I speak more English than Irish in the school playground'. While 35.5% of the primary pupils agree or strongly agree with this statement, almost double that number (70.2%) of post-primary pupils agreed or strongly agreed with the statement (Figure 7.2). These are disappointing responses when viewed from the perspective of the use of Irish outside of the classroom. The responses of the post-primary students are probably not surprising given that their Gaeltacht counterparts at a similar age were found to socialise

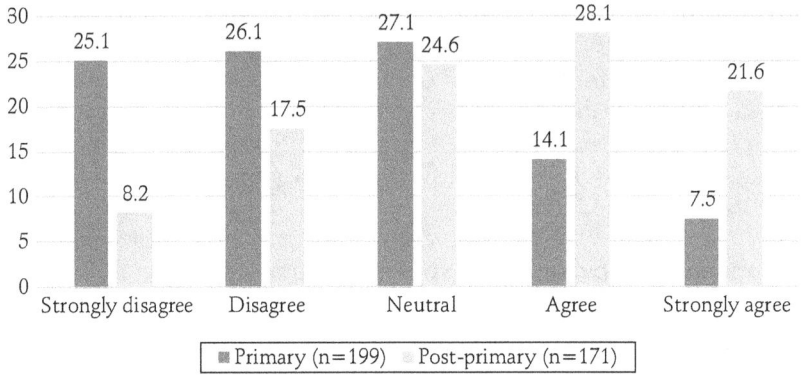

Figure 7.1 Pupils' responses in percentages to the statement 'To be honest, I don't make much effort to speak Irish outside of the class when I am at school'

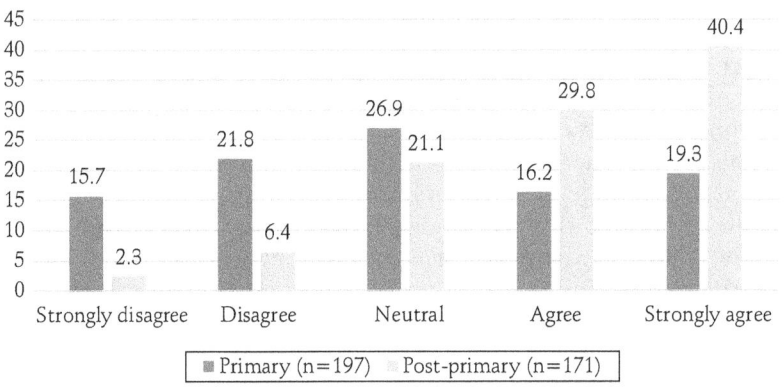

Figure 7.2 Pupils' responses in percentages to the statement 'I speak more English than Irish in the school playground'

predominantly through the medium of English, even in cases where Irish is their home language (Ó Giollagáin *et al.*, 2007). Pupils in Ó Cathalláin's (2011) study of all-Irish schools also reported resistance to the requirement to speak Irish. These findings are in keeping with evidence from Wales where pupils in Welsh-medium schools reported greater use of English when the teacher was not present (Thomas *et al.*, 2014).

These responses do not bode well as a predictor for future use of Irish when the pupils leave school. It could be argued that primary pupils take greater heed of teachers' exhortations to use Irish outside of class but that post-primary pupils are influenced more by their peer group and the norm of socialising through English. We need to be careful in our interpretation of these results as other research (Mac Gréil & Rhatigan, 2009) has shown that many adults had a more positive attitude to Irish in adulthood than they had when they were attending school. When teenagers (aged 16 years and over) in the Gaeltacht were asked in what language they would raise any future children they may have, 71% responded that they would raise them through Irish (Ó Giollagáin et al., 2007). This finding provides some hope that former all-Irish pupils may transmit Irish to the next generation despite their current disappointing use of Irish as teenagers. In order to investigate this further, we examined the school background of the pupils' parents and their use of Irish with their children. The rationale for this was to examine the impact of Irish-medium education on the previous generation to see what it might tell us about the future behaviour of the current school-going generation. In doing so, I acknowledge that language competency acquired at school is only one factor that might influence active bilingualism in adulthood.

Use of Irish by all-Irish school parents

We asked parents ($n = 288$) about language use in their home when they were growing up and about the type of school they attended. In relation to the language spoken at home, most parents came from predominantly English-speaking homes. Only 13 (3.9%) had attended all-Irish primary and post-primary school. A further 19 (5.7%) parents had attended either a primary or a post-primary all-Irish school. Overall then, 32 (9.6%) had attended an all-Irish school at primary or post-primary level or both.

The majority spoke mostly English with their children at home. Table 7.2 shows that approximately 60% of primary all-Irish parents speak 'English and Irish, but mostly English'. In the case of the post-primary parents, approximately 60.1% (RoI) and 67.0% (NI) speak 'English only'. This indicates that the amount of Irish spoken by parents with their children decreases over time and as all-Irish pupils get older, their parents speak less Irish with them.

Only 5 (1.7%) of parents reported speaking English and Irish, but mostly Irish with their children. More encouragingly, 15 (5.2%) primary RoI parents reported speaking 'English and Irish, half and half' with their children. There was a statistically significant correlation between the language the parents spoke at home growing up and the language they now speak with their children (chi-square = 173.846, df = 25, $p < 0.001$). There was no association, however, between parents' attendance at an all-Irish school and their frequency of speaking English/Irish/other language with their children (chi-square = 12.770, df = 10, $p = 0.237$). We must bear in mind that the sample size of the parents who attended an all-Irish school was small at 32 (9.6%) and the number of years in all-Irish education varied. The evidence here suggests that attending an all-Irish school did not exert a sufficiently strong influence on parents to encourage them to speak Irish at home with their children. This issue merits further examination with

Table 7.2 All-Irish parents' responses to the question: What language(s) do you speak to your child?

School type/jurisdiction (participants)	English only (%)	English and Irish, but mostly English (%)	English and Irish, half and half (%)	English and Irish, but mostly Irish (%)	Irish only (%)	Other language (%)
Primary all-Irish RoI (n = 119)	23.5	59.7	12.6	1.7	0.0	2.5
Primary all-Irish NI (n = 48)	37.5	60.4	0	2.1	0	0
Post-primary all-Irish RoI (n = 91)	67.0	33.0	0.0	0.0	0.0	0.0
Post-primary all-Irish NI (n = 30)	60.1	33.3	0.0	6.6	0.0	0.0

a larger sample of parents who attended all-Irish schools. If this pattern were to be confirmed with a larger sample, it would suggest that all-Irish pupils do not become new speakers of Irish at a rate required to increase the use of Irish in society. As noted in the literature, it is difficult to convert school use of a minority language into community use (Baker, 2003).

Language behaviour of children with their parents

A study by Kavanagh and Hickey (2012) found that children were often reluctant to speak Irish with their parents and didn't welcome parents' attempts to speak Irish with them. We wanted to investigate whether this might prevent parents speaking Irish with their children. We asked parents about their children's willingness to speak Irish with them. We can see in Figure 7.3 that parents reported that between 79.1% and 63.3% of the children, depending on school type, were very willing or willing to speak Irish with them. When we calculated the averages across school type, we found that 72.2% of pupils were very willing or willing to speak Irish with their parents, while 22.2% were unwilling or very unwilling. It is interesting to note that the level of willingness does not appear to differ greatly between primary and post-primary pupils. Overall, just under three-quarters of pupils are willing to speak Irish with their parents according to the parents.

When we analysed the responses of the pupils to the item 'I hate it when my parent speaks to me or tries to speak to me in Irish at home', 56.2% disagreed with this statement indicating that they were open to

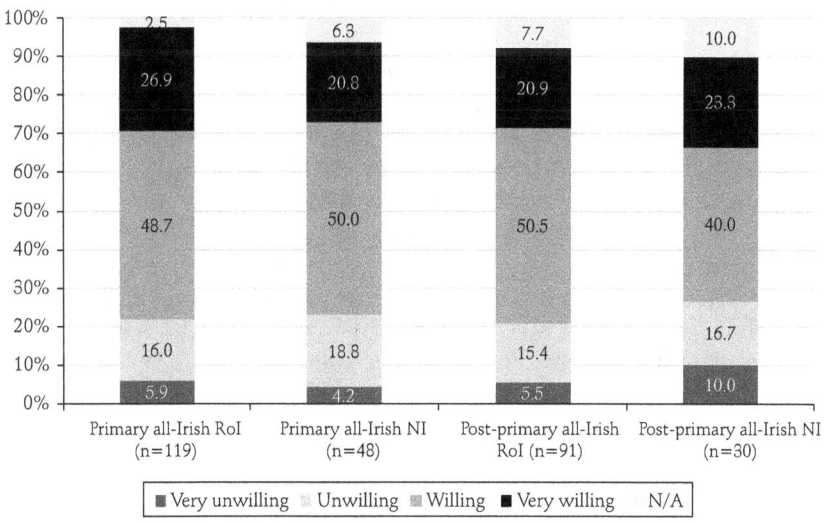

Figure 7.3 Willingness of children to speak Irish with their parents according to the parents

their parents' use of Irish. Just under one-quarter (22.1%) agreed with the statement and a further 20.7% were neutral. There is consistency across the responses of both parents and pupils to this topic. Both groups report that approximately 22% of pupils are unwilling or dislike speaking Irish with their parents. On the positive side, half to three-quarters of the pupils appear open to the use of Irish in the home. The home language practices as outlined in Table 7.2 indicate that only 20 of the 288 parents (7.9%) speak Irish half or more than half the time. There are probably many reasons why parents and pupils don't speak Irish at home. One explanation could be that Irish is normalised to some extent within the context of the all-Irish school but not outside the school or school activities. One of the aims of the 20-year strategy for Irish (Government of Ireland, 2010) is to seek to normalise the speaking of Irish in society in general. These results indicate that while some potential exists, a difficult challenge lies ahead.

Discussion

The evidence presented in this chapter is consistent with other studies which show that all-Irish pupils had a very positive attitude to Irish and to learning Irish (Harris & Murtagh, 1999; Kennedy, 2012). Their parents encouraged them to learn Irish but did not necessarily speak whatever Irish they had with their children in the home. When parents made an effort to speak Irish with their children, some children were reluctant to engage in speaking Irish and rebutted their parents' efforts. The two factors that had the greatest influence on pupils' use of Irish outside of classes and the school were (i) the amount of Irish spoken in the home and (ii) school type – primary or post-primary. Use of Irish by parents positively influenced their children's use of Irish. Those parents who had spoken Irish in their home of origin were more likely to speak Irish with their own children than parents who attended an all-Irish school. In our sample of all-Irish school parents, 9.6% had attended an all-Irish school. It would be interesting to investigate the influence of this experience on future language use among a larger sample of parents. While all-Irish pupils and some of their parents have a good command of Irish, it is still a major challenge to convert that ability to use, as attested by Darmody and Daly (2015) and Ó Duibhir *et al.* (2015c). The efforts that parents make to speak Irish with their children appear to wane as the children advance to post-primary education. A longitudinal study with a larger sample is required to verify these findings. In the meantime, we face the perennial problem of minority languages, where pupils learn the language but have little or nothing to do with it outside of the school context (Mac Aogáin, 1990).

As Crystal (2000: 154) claims 'Languages need communities in order to live. So, only a community can save an endangered language'. Apart from a small number of language networks, Irish language communities do not currently exist outside of the Gaeltacht. The language ability possessed by all-Irish school pupils could be harnessed to form the nucleus of such a community. The 20-year strategy for Irish recognises the importance of the community in increasing the vitality of the language. Apart from language planning schemes that have commenced in the Gaeltacht, little action has taken place to date outside the Gaeltacht to foster the development of Irish language communities. The most encouraging efforts are located in NI where communities in the Falls Road, Belfast, and *An Carn* in County Derry, are working hard to create such communities. Another noteworthy example is that of *Na Gaeil Óga* in Dublin. This is a sports club where the members play Gaelic football, hurling and camogie through the medium of Irish, thus providing opportunities and a context for Irish use among its players. It is suggested by some (Edwards, 2017; Ó Giollagáin & Charlton, 2015) that such grass-root initiatives provide the best prospect for future language use in the case of minority languages. The Irish situation contrasts with the Basque Country, for example, where each school devises its own language plan with short- and long-term objectives under the *Ulibarri* programme and is supported by teacher support centres (Aldekoa & Gardner, 2002; Ó Duibhir *et al.*, 2015a). The purpose of the *Ulibarri* programme is to normalise the use of the Basque language throughout the school by funding a wide range of extra-curricular events (Zalbide & Cenoz, 2008). Despite these efforts, normalising the use of Basque in wider society is proving very challenging.

There is a great deal of teaching of Irish in schools in Ireland. All-Irish pupils learn Irish to a high standard (Harris *et al.*, 2006) and reap the rewards of this teaching in part due to the amount of contact they have with the language and the opportunities to use what they learn throughout the school day. Their Irish is not without grammatical errors as we have seen from the analysis of their spoken language presented in Chapter 5. Nonetheless, the pupils appear to accept that Irish is normalised within the class context. While over 50% of primary pupils make an effort to speak Irish outside of the class when they are at school, only one-quarter make that effort in post-primary school. The evidence regarding Irish use in the playground where pupils are not as closely monitored by teachers is that approximately 35% of primary and 70% of post-primary pupils speak more English than Irish. This may indicate that Irish is not normalised in the context of the playground when not monitored closely by authority figures. This finding is in keeping with the language behaviour of Gaeltacht teenagers who use Irish more often when authority figures are present (Ó Giollagáin *et al.*, 2007) and with the findings of research studies in other minority language contexts (Thomas *et al.*, 2014).

While the growth of a grass-roots all-Irish school movement may be one of the most positive advances in the effort to revitalise Irish, its impact so far appears to be confined to the domain of the school. It could be argued that the issue of language use outside the education context is the 'X' factor that has been missing from Irish revitalisation efforts. This pattern has prevailed since the foundation of the Irish Free State (Walsh, 2012). If all-Irish school pupils are to convert their ability in Irish to become new speakers of Irish in their communities, they will need greater opportunities to use Irish in out-of-school and post-school contexts than are currently available. A combined effort involving all-Irish school communities supported by state agencies would be required to establish the greatest prospect of achieving this. In the context of minority languages, the state has a role in terms of language planning to create the conditions where capacity, opportunity and desire are nurtured (Grin, 2003). Regrettably, there has been little or no evidence of such initiatives to date. Instead, the policy of the state has made unreasonable demands on the education system which operates in a vacuum. Parents who have the language competence to speak in Irish with their children, should be encouraged to maximise opportunities to speak Irish in the home.

Note

(1) The AMTB can be viewed in Appendix A. The categories offered to the pupils were: 'Irish only', 'mostly Irish', 'equal mix of Irish and English', 'mostly English', 'English only' and 'other language'.

8 Principal and Class Teacher Interviews to Explore Pupils' Proficiency in Spoken Irish or French

Introduction

The focus of this volume so far has been largely on all-Irish pupils and to a lesser extent their parents. In this chapter, the scope of the research widens to include an exploration of the views of immersion teachers within and beyond the Irish context about the proficiency in the target language of their pupils. The chapter is divided into four main sections. This first section describes the background and purpose of the interviews. The second section describes the study design including information regarding the participants and the research methods employed. An account of the main themes that arose from the teacher interviews is given in the third section. The chapter concludes with a discussion of the emergent themes.

The views of 32 Republic of Ireland (RoI), Northern Ireland (NI) and Canadian immersion teachers and principals regarding their pupils' proficiency in spoken Irish or French were sought. The teachers and principals were located in all-Irish schools in the RoI ($n = 12$) and NI ($n = 6$), and French immersion schools in Toronto/Ottawa (T/O) ($n = 14$). The aim of the study was to better understand the origins and possible causes of the distinctive characteristics and weaknesses in the syntactic and lexical features of immersion pupils' spoken Irish or French from the perspectives of class teachers and principals. As noted by Lapkin *et al.* (2006), very few studies have focused on the views of teachers in this area. The presentation of their views in this chapter focuses on issues that emerged from the interviews; in particular, how they perceived the grammatical inaccuracies of the pupils' spoken language.

The objectives of this phase of the study were:

- to ascertain the attitudes of school principals, sixth- (RoI)/seventh-class (NI) teachers in Ireland and Grade 3–8 teachers in T/O towards pupils' proficiency in Irish/French;
- to explore the teachers' views of the factors influencing pupils' grammatical accuracy;
- to explore the teachers' assessments of the nature and range of grammatical errors made by the pupils;

- to investigate the remedial strategies adopted by teachers when pupils made grammatical errors.

Design

Interviews of teachers

A phenomenological approach was deemed most suitable to adopt in interviewing the teachers. The objective of the interviews was to explore their views of the attainment of their pupils in the target language relative to curriculum objectives. The phenomenological design focused on the human experience of the teacher in the classroom and school (Cohen *et al.*, 2011). The possibility of teachers having different reactions to pupils' errors is suggested by Lyster (2007). Previous studies revealed significant differences in the manner in which teachers respond to pupils' errors (Lyster, 2007). Adopting a phenomenological approach opened up the possibility of gaining a greater understanding of teachers' views of 'immersion speech' in all its complexity within individual classrooms and schools. The semi-structured nature of the interviews in this study facilitated not just the exploration of what was happening in classrooms but also the teachers' understanding of why and how it was happening (Dörnyei, 2007). The inclusion of teachers in both Ireland and Canada opened up the possibility of exploring the reactions of teachers to similar phenomena in different immersion settings. A copy of the interview schedule can be found in Appendix B.

Participants

Table 8.1 outlines the backgrounds of the 32 teachers interviewed for the study. No distinction was made between teachers ($n = 20$) and principals ($n = 12$) in the analysis and discussion of the themes that emerged. For convenience, all are referred to as teachers and names were changed in order to maintain confidentiality. The teachers had varying degrees of teaching experience in an immersion school, ranging from less than 5 years to greater than 20 years. Eight of the 12 teachers in the RoI and six of the 14 in T/O were native speakers. The remainder had attained a near-native level of proficiency in the immersion language. The selection of teachers for interview in Ireland was determined by the purposive sample of schools invited to participate in the corpus studies reported in Chapter 5. The teachers in T/O were recruited through the Toronto District School Board (TDSB) and the Ottawa Carleton District School Board (OCDSB).

Interviews were conducted in 11 all-Irish primary schools on the same day I visited each school to conduct the stimulated recall activity with pupils (Chapter 6). I interviewed the French immersion teachers in T/O

Table 8.1 Background information on principals and class teachers selected for interview

Teacher pseudonym	Grade/class	Language background	No. of years teaching in immersion
Teachers in Irish immersion – Republic of Ireland			
Ciara	6	NS*	1–5
Seán	Principal teacher	NNS**	16–20
Ciarán	6	NS	6–10
Mairéad	Principal teacher	NS	11–15
Sinéad	6	NNS	1–5
Eoghan	Principal teacher	NS	6–10
Diarmaid	6	NNS	>20
Daithí	Principal teacher	NS	>20
Nóirín	Principal teacher	NS	11–15
Tomás	6	NS	6–10
Áine	Principal teacher	NS	6–10
Caitríona	Principal teacher	NNS	>20
Teachers in Irish immersion – Northern Ireland			
Ciara	7	NNS	11–14
Séamus	7	NNS	1–5
Máire	Principal teacher	NNS	11–14
Maeve	7	NNS	1–5
Sinéad	Principal teacher	NNS	11–14
Aoife	Principal and Year 7 teacher	NNS	>20
Teachers in French immersion – Toronto and Ottawa, Canada			
Julie	7	NS	16–20
Sophie	7	NS	16–20
Sharon	7	NNS	6–10
Rachel	7	NS	16–20
Cheryl	Former immersion teacher with alternative role	NNS	16–20
Denise	7	NNS	6–10
Annemarie	8	NS	6–10
Chantal	6	NS	11–15
Pauline	8	NS	6–10
Caroline	5	NS	11–15
Laurence	3	NNS	6–10
Christine	6	NNS	6–10
Tom	Former immersion teacher with alternative role	NNS	6–10

*NS = native speaker; **NNS = near-native speaker.

over a four-week period in the teachers' schools or at a mutually agreed location. The French immersion sample included teachers from dual-track primary and middle schools who taught classes ranging from Grades 3 to 8, as shown in Table 8.1. Semi-structured interviews were conducted with the teachers, to explore all dimensions of their experiences relating to their pupils' spoken Irish/French. Each interview lasted between 25 and 35 minutes and was audio-recorded with the agreement of the participants. The teachers in Ireland were interviewed in Irish whereas the teachers in T/O were interviewed in English.

Data analysis

Interviews were transcribed and imported into the NVivo software package for analysis using an interpretive phenomenological approach (Coolican, 2004). The transcripts were coded and grouped into categories from which themes emerged. The views of the teachers in the RoI and NI were translated into English. Representative quotations from the teachers are included in the account below and combined with the researcher's interpretation to produce an interpretive-descriptive account. My experience as a teacher and principal in an all-Irish school, and as a teacher educator, helped to inform this interpretation.

Results

Six main themes emerged from the analysis of the teacher interviews:

(1) teachers' satisfaction with their pupils' proficiency in Irish/French;
(2) features of pupils' spoken Irish/French identified by the teachers;
(3) influence of English;
(4) materials and resources;
(5) pupil willingness to speak Irish/French;
(6) school planning to address identified weaknesses.

While undertaking the analysis, I was struck by the similarities in the views of the teachers across contexts. Arising from this, I decided to present the teachers' responses side by side in a thematic fashion to enable comparison.

Teacher satisfaction with pupils' proficiency in Irish/French

Good fluency but need for improvement

In general, teachers across the three contexts felt that pupils were reasonably proficient in the immersion language but that the standard could be improved as expressed in the following statements.

RoI – Seán	NI – Maeve	T/O – Cheryl
I wouldn't be entirely satisfied with it to be honest.	They are able to say a great deal but they often say it incorrectly!	I think that it is satisfactory. There are a lot of gaps I think that it could be better in terms of their accuracy, their fluency, their vocabulary.

One of the strengths that all teachers identified was pupil fluency and ability to communicate ideas without any apparent difficulty.

RoI – Caitríona	NI – Séamus	T/O – Pauline
They are certainly fluent but I would like them to be more accurate. They become lazy as they become fluent.	There is a wide range of ability but they all definitely have at least a satisfactory level of fluency. They would not have native-like fluency, however.	Still some English patterns emerge in their French expressions but … it never, ever hinders their actual ability to get the meaning across.

The picture that emerged more generally from the teachers' comments was one of virtually all pupils having very good communicative ability in the immersion language. They were able to get their meaning across with relative ease but this was achieved in a way that lacked grammatical accuracy and did not conform to native speaker norms. Some teachers felt that this situation was as good as one could expect given the lack of support for Irish/French outside of school in the pupils' homes and wider community. Others were more critical and felt that it should be possible to improve the standard. Those with the latter view suggested that a different pedagogical approach may be required if the pupils' grammatical accuracy was to be improved. Recommendations in relation to an analytical approach in immersion education are made in Chapter 9. Overall, the views of the teachers were in keeping with the research literature in this area (Swain & Johnson, 1997; Tedick & Wesely, 2015).

Features of pupils' spoken Irish/French

The teachers identified the following as the most frequent errors made by pupils:

- the structure of the pupils' sentences in Irish and French was influenced by English syntax;

- in the case of Irish, the substantive verb was used incorrectly instead of the copula and the imperative form of verbs was used instead of the verbal noun;
- in the case of French, the inappropriate use of the verbs être (to be) and *avoir* (to have) and not knowing when to address someone with the *tu* or *vous* form of the verb.

The errors in Irish, identified by all-Irish teachers, were among the most common errors identified in the analysis of the all-Irish school corpus in Chapter 5 and they were also the subject of the stimulated recall sessions in Chapter 6. The errors identified by the French immersion teachers are similar to those reported by Knaus and Nadasdi (2001) and Mougeon *et al.* (2004). The teachers also reported that errors were a feature from an early stage, and in their experience, many errors persist over time and were difficult to eradicate.

RoI – Ciarán	NI – Aoife	T/O – Marion
Grammar is the most difficult thing for the children to learn, the grammar and the structure. They would have the words and if they thought about it, they would have them in the right order.	There is a lack of accuracy, and structures from the English language can be heard. The same errors are there and I assume that there must be deep linguistic reasons that the same errors emerge again and again.	Oh yeah, it's *J'ai sept ans*, not *Je suis sept ans*. So, they know if they pause to think about it. But the habit has been formed I guess and it doesn't matter enough because 'You understood that I meant that I was seven years old so who cares …'

So, while the errors were obviously different in each language, the pattern of the pupils not thinking about their utterances was a common theme. When the teachers were asked why they thought that the errors persist over time and are difficult to eradicate, many believed that while the pupils knew the correct form, they did not monitor their output in unplanned communication.

RoI – Caitríona	NI – Sinéad	T/O – Rachel
…they are not thinking. They assume that once they are fluent that there is no need for accuracy. They don't need to think about English grammar, it comes to them naturally. It is direct translation most of the time, but it is certainly laziness.	They understand the structures but patterns in the structure of English come more naturally to them. If they are asked to say the thing correctly, however, they succeed in doing so, for the most part.	The sentence structure sometimes would be English, but with French words. So, if I don't speak English, if I don't understand English at all, I listen to the kid speaking, I have no idea what he's saying.

In the stimulated recall sessions described in Chapter 6, pupils also acknowledged 'not thinking' about the form of their utterances when they were engaged in the playground design task. The strategic goal of pupils was to be able to produce an utterance that did not lead to a breakdown in communication. The question of the structure of the utterance and whether it conformed to target norms appeared secondary. To ascribe this phenomenon to laziness may be unfair to the pupils, however. The reason for them not monitoring their output may have been related to excessive demands on their processing power during the communicative task which required attentional resources (Skehan, 1998).

Influence of English on pupils' Irish/French

Another reason offered by the teachers for the persistence of errors was the influence of English on the pupils' Irish/French. Many teachers referred to translation from English and a lack of vocabulary as obstacles in the immersion language. This phenomenon is found in other immersion contexts (Thomas *et al.*, 2014) and noted as a feature of second language (L2) learners of Irish by Ó Baoill (1981).

RoI – Diarmaid	NI – Séamus	T/O – Pauline
… almost every one of them is from an English-speaking background, they speak English naturally at home and they translate very quickly and naturally and that is what emerges from them more than how would you say that correctly in Irish.	The structure of the English language is endemic throughout their Irish; a lack of vocabulary I would say is often the reason for this. Well that's what the children tell me anyway '…I don't know the Irish for it!'	They do translate from English to French and as a result they use idioms very inappropriately.

Strategies adopted by teachers to improve proficiency and to correct errors

Teachers were asked about the strategies they adopted when confronted with grammatical errors. All teachers used different strategies depending on the situation; ranging from humour, continuous correction, grammar lessons and peer correction. No teacher expressed the opinion that any particular strategy was better than another but that they had a battery of strategies which they drew on depending on the context in which the error occurred, the student who made the error and the focus of the lesson.

A number of teachers had a way of signalling to the pupils by means of a prompt that there was something not quite right about what they had just said, as the following excerpts illustrate.

RoI – Diarmaid	NI – Ciara	T/O – Sharon
'Excuse me, what is that again?' And then they would know that they have done something (incorrect), and most of the time they know it (correct form).	'What's that you said?' And then they would know that they have made a mistake in their speech and they generally correct themselves without difficulty.	I'll ask them, 'Are you sure?'

Corrective feedback of this type has been shown to be effective in drawing learners' attention to their errors and can lead to interlanguage development (Lyster *et al.*, 2013). Many teachers like Diarmaid and Pauline used humour:

RoI – Diarmaid	T/O – Pauline
I suppose I use humour more than anything else to encourage them. I would hate to damage in any way the natural enthusiasm that most of them have.	Humour. Lots of teachers, they make fun when a person says 'Je suis fini'. 'Oh you're dead'. So, humour I would definitely say.

These comments, and those of other teachers, demonstrated how they strived to maintain a balance between correction and ensuring that there is a positive atmosphere in the class in which the pupils were encouraged to speak the immersion language. The teachers indicated that they adopt approaches that are sensitive to the feelings of the students.

Some teachers discussed the complexity of the task for teachers in a classroom situation in endeavouring to teach curriculum content while focusing on the language needs of the student at the same time.

RoI – Caitríona	NI – Sinéad	T/O – Cheryl
If someone said something like 'He is man' in the middle of a history lesson I'd stop immediately and correct it – something very basic, but you couldn't correct every single error.	… teachers do not have enough time to correct everything and to encourage extended responses all of the time.	So, there is a lot of pressure, I see it now. To get the content across and so you don't always have the time to work on the language.

These comments are pertinent to the Cammarata and Tedick (2012) study of how immersion teachers balance language and content. They found that immersion teachers tend to see themselves as content teachers rather than language teachers. Mac Ardghail (2014) noted in his study the tension that exists for teachers in not wishing to continually interrupt the flow of content lessons with constant language error corrections. The teachers' comments in this study bring into focus the dual nature of the immersion teacher's role in being both a language and a content teacher. The challenge for teachers is to strike a balance between the two roles. The teachers in this study strived to achieve that balance in ways that were sensitive to the feelings of the pupils. Teachers claimed they do not ignore student language errors. In some instances, the errors were dealt with immediately and in other cases, later in a form-focussed lesson.

All teachers reported that they taught grammar formally. The errors that pupils made were often noted and 'focus on formS'-type lessons were taught in an attempt to correct them. In some all-Irish schools, there was a whole-school focus on particular phrases that cause difficulties for the pupils, as explained by Áine and Sinéad below. Many of the French immersion teachers such as Sophie reported using dictation as a way to focus on particularly challenging structures in French.

RoI – Áine	NI – Sinéad	T/O – Sophie
… the phrase of the week is sent around every Monday and we concentrate on the correct form being sought.	… we have a 'structure of the week' system in operation in our school. We compiled a list of the most frequent inaccuracies and difficulties in the pupils' speech and, as part of a whole-school initiative, attention is paid to one structure each week.	Sometimes I would take words or structures from their writing and prepare the *dictée* [dictation] with it … Sometimes I could take a *dictée* from the History text.

Teaching materials and resources

An issue that most teachers commented on was that of limited teaching materials. This theme emerged in the Ó Duibhir *et al.* (2015c) study also. In general, teachers acknowledged that there had been a considerable improvement in recent years, but that more resources were needed.

RoI – Seán	NI – Maeve	T/O – Laurence
But there are a lot of problems as well regarding resources for the senior classes. It is very difficult to source interesting reading materials in particular.	There is still a great shortage of Irish-medium resources. Everything is available in English and I use quite a few of these resources. I still have to write and create my own teaching resources because they simply aren't available in Irish.	So, if you compare it to the English language market, the materials that we have don't tend to be as widely available. If you compare it to what we had in the past to what we have now, there are always efforts being made to bring more materials in.

Limited resources made it difficult for teachers and schools to plan a structured programme for all classes. Lack of suitable attractive teaching and learning materials presented challenges in improving the pupils' standard of Irish/French.

Exposure to Irish/French outside the school context

Many teachers raised concerns about the lack of exposure to the immersion language outside of the school and the challenges that this posed for teachers and schools trying to increase the pupils use of Irish/French socially.

RoI – Eoghan	NI – Sinéad	T/O – Tom
They speak it (Irish) in the classroom, out in the yard for the most part. The place where we fail is the language outside of school. Not a word is spoken outside of school and I don't know if we can have an influence there.	The children have a lack of contact with Irish outside of the school. We try to organise social events through the medium of Irish but it can be difficult to find staff to help with these events.	Beyond the walls of the school it becomes even harder to build any kind of immersion environment because you can't use it in the community. There simply wouldn't be places where they can go and use French.

While the teacher, Tom, quoted above teaches in Toronto, it should be noted that the sociolinguistic background of pupils in Ottawa differs from that of pupils in Toronto and indeed all-Irish pupils in Ireland as exposure to the target language in the community in Ottawa is inevitable. Some teachers in Ottawa reported that pupils required a reasonable ability in spoken French in order to secure a part-time job. Speaking about the issue of exposure to French in the community, Julie said that 'it's very easy, probably their neighbour speaks French. Even someone in their family, their grandparents often will only speak to them in French'. She believed that such exposure to French outside of school had a positive impact on pupil's proficiency in French 'because their French is not only a school language'.

Despite this increased exposure to French in Ottawa compared to Toronto, the teachers in the Ottawa schools still believed that their students' proficiency could be better and that it contained many errors. A corpus study comparing the Toronto and Ottawa pupils might shed light on possible differences in proficiency. Overall, greater exposure to Irish/French outside of school as occurs in Ottawa would be desirable for all immersion contexts. Irish immersion pupils cited out-of-school activities in Irish as factors that motivated them to speak Irish outside school (Ó Cathalláin, 2011; Ó Duibhir *et al.*, 2015c). Some Irish immersion teachers expressed the desire for more support from parents in this regard and wished that the Irish language skills of parents could be improved and utilised. Many all-Irish schools organised trips to the Gaeltacht and participated in events and activities for Irish-medium schools. Parents in Toronto can take their children on holiday to Québec where they have opportunities to use their French. These activities and visits appeared to have a positive effect on the pupils' attitudes to speaking Irish/French, as reported by the teachers, and in many cases demonstrated to the pupils that Irish/French is a language that is alive outside of school. It is difficult, nonetheless, to ascertain to what extent exposure to the L2 results in an improvement in pupils' accuracy. The pupils in the stimulated recall activity cited lack of exposure to Irish outside of school as influencing their code-mixing behaviour and general accuracy in Irish in the recall sessions.

Pupil willingness to speak Irish/French

General encouragement of pupils and inculcating a positive attitude

It was evident from the responses of the Irish immersion teachers that immense time and effort is expended in maintaining Irish during all school activities. The effort required to maintain this drive to promote Irish requires persistent and constant vigilance on the part of the teacher. The sheer demands of maintaining an Irish language environment may partly explain why grammatical inaccuracy and the influence of English are relegated to second place. All the teachers were questioned about their pupils' willingness to speak Irish/French and this elicited a variety of responses, some positive and some negative depending on the school.

The French immersion teachers reported that the students, by and large, do not speak French to one another outside of the classroom nor did they think that it was a realistic expectation. Within the classroom, teachers reported different levels of willingness on the students' part to speak French to their peers. Most teachers reported that it was a struggle to encourage students to converse in French among themselves when they were preparing a presentation for example.

The following comments give a flavour of the Irish and French contexts.

RoI – Ciara	NI – Aoife	T/O – Caroline
I always have to encourage them (to speak Irish) even though they are in an all-Irish school, they lose it and they revert to English again when you are not listening to them or looking at them … it's very difficult to motivate them especially in the senior classes.	I believe that they have a very positive attitude to Irish and there is no doubt that they enjoy Irish. By the time they reach Year 7, however, they want to be 'cool' and don't want to look like the teacher's pet.	Amongst themselves usually when they're doing it for a project they'll be usually in English. I have to really encourage them 'Can we try and do this for half an hour in French today?'

In the Kavanagh and Hickey (2012) study, pupils were reluctant to speak Irish to their parents when the parents tried to initiate conversations in Irish. Combined with the responses of the teachers above, this may indicate that the immersion language, when not encountered outside of the education context, is not normalised in the lives of the pupils. This further highlights the sociocultural dimension of language learning for these pupils. The norm of speaking Irish had some acceptance among all-Irish pupils in their speech community in the classroom. The French immersion pupils were less compliant in the classroom, as were the all-Irish pupils in the playground. These findings are similar to those of Welsh-medium pupils (Thomas et al., 2014) where the presence of the teacher had a positive impact on compliance.

Incentives and sanctions

Virtually all teachers reported that they used incentives to encourage pupils to speak the immersion language, particularly in the junior classes. The type of incentive varied from school to school. Many Irish immersion schools operated a system where each class teacher chooses the 'Irish speaker of the week', i.e. the pupil who makes the greatest effort to speak Irish each week.

RoI – Ciara	NI – Séamus	T/O – Caroline
They have a 'speaking card' and they get a signature at the end of the day if they have been heard speaking Irish that day and when they reach 18 there is a small prize and at 25 there will be a bigger prize to motivate them.	We put a great emphasis on 'Irish speaker of the month' in our school and all of the children understand that it is a whole school system and that they will receive recognition throughout the whole school for this great achievement.	... all teachers have got incentives. They send badges [home] to get them to speak French in the classroom. And even that, you know, we cannot make them and that's always the difficulty.

Some of the French immersion teachers in particular felt that incentives were inappropriate and that pupils should be encouraged to be internally motivated. Others expressed the view that if the teacher had high expectations, this influenced student behaviour. In some dual-track schools such as Annemarie's, the French immersion teachers only teach through the medium of French so that students immediately associate that teacher with French. She explained that 'French immersion teachers always try and put themselves in a position where you don't speak English to them (the pupils). You never teach them in English because otherwise they start mixing both languages that they hear you speak ... It's a real conditioning system'. Subjects taught through the medium of English in these schools are taught by other teachers. A French immersion teacher might teach more than one class in this situation. In the case of the Irish immersion teachers, they teach all subjects including English language arts so the contexts differ from this perspective.

While many schools had a system of sanctions in conjunction with the incentives, the emphasis was on encouraging the pupils to speak the immersion language rather than on punishing them for using English. Teachers were reluctant to adopt the role of 'language police' as Denise (T/O) described it: 'When you're perceived as being the language police it can sometimes backfire so I try to make it as pleasant as possible for them'. In all-Irish schools where sanctions were imposed, many operated a system where the principal was informed if a pupil was repeatedly speaking English. A note might follow to the pupil's parents informing them of the problem if persistent. Many teachers were continually seeking new and improved ways to motivate their pupils to speak Irish.

In general, the all-Irish teachers were satisfied with the willingness of their pupils to speak Irish, but reported that they had to continually promote and attend to pursuing this objective. This applied in particular to pupils' compliance with speaking Irish at break-time in the playground. It was also evident that the teachers expend a good deal of time and energy in devising incentive schemes and in implementing policy in this area. The teachers recognise that the vast majority of the pupils live their lives outside of school through English, and that as a result, it is easier for them to speak English. There appeared to be a delicate balance to be struck between the imposition of rules to speak Irish, and inculcating a positive attitude towards speaking Irish. Many teachers were reluctant to overcorrect pupils in case they undermined the pupils' confidence in their ability to speak Irish or turned them against the language.

The French immersion teachers echoed many of these views. The school context was different, however, in that the French immersion schools were dual-track schools. For this reason, many teachers did not believe that it was possible to impose the speaking of French outside of the classroom. Indeed, many would have been happy if their pupils conversed with one another in French in the classroom during group work and other collaborative activity. Many teachers like Chantal (T/O) expressed frustration with their inability to get students to converse in French with one another: 'I would say it's my biggest frustration as a French immersion teacher – the children will not speak French to each other in a social environment. They'll speak French to me but if they can help it they'll start off in English'. I sensed that this challenge was wearing down some French immersion teachers as they were not achieving the standards that they expected or in some cases, had achieved in the past.

The ease or difficulty of learning through Irish was raised by a number of all-Irish teachers. They recognised the artificiality of the immersion context where the children are asked to suspend reality and speak and learn in their weaker language. As Diarmaid stated, 'I often ask them (the pupils) here what they think about Irish and learning through Irish ... and they understand that it is more difficult for them to learn through Irish and for us too, it is more difficult to teach through a second language'. The views of teachers echo those of the pupils in the stimulated recall sessions and in the responses to the AMTB which identified that extra effort was required to speak with accuracy and pupils do not always make that extra effort.

Teachers favour incentives over sanctions when encouraging pupils to use the L2. This seems like a wise approach given the extra demand that immersion education places on pupils. Pupils do have positive attitudes towards learning their L2 as demonstrated in the AMTB study in Chapter 7, but do not relish being pushed beyond their capabilities. As one pupil shared, 'I like to speak Irish but if I speak English I am in big trouble. Sometimes I think that it is only a language'.

School planning and staff meetings in relation to pupils' proficiency in Irish

All-Irish immersion teachers reported that their pupils' proficiency in Irish was regularly discussed at staff meetings. As Seamus (NI) stated: 'The pupils' competence in Irish is discussed regularly at staff meetings'; and Caitríona (RoI) commented: 'There are very few meetings where it is not discussed, as that is really the foundation stone of the school really'. Many all-Irish teachers reported having a school plan that monitored pupils' progress throughout the school and promoted improvement in the use of Irish. In Sinéad's (NI) school, she stated that: 'Regarding staff meetings, the use of Irish is discussed but accuracy in Irish is not discussed in much detail'. She believed accuracy should be considered and improved. Mairéad (RoI) focused on the area of language enrichment in her school's plan: 'The thing that I would be worried about is that there is not enough language enrichment from the middle to the senior classes that you are adding to the richness'.

The views of many of the French immersion teachers contrasted with the views of the Irish immersion teachers. Approximately half the French immersion teachers stated that they did not have opportunities to meet with other immersion teachers within their schools to discuss issues such as students' proficiency in French. It seemed to depend on the attitude of the principal whether time was set aside for immersion track meetings. As Christine (T/O) explained: 'I'm not sure if it depends on the principal or not. I kind of have the feeling that it does. My principal is fairly supportive and she encourages, definitely, whatever collaboration can happen she is happy for it to happen. So, she does kind of mandate it and she even gives us prep time'. In other cases, an immersion teacher took on a leadership role and ensured that meetings took place. This was the case in Chantal's (T/O) school: 'we meet as French immersion teachers and we meet as division teachers and I would say particularly in the primary (school)... there's a big support network for them'. Where meetings occurred, teachers found them beneficial but reported that there was generally insufficient time available to address pupils' proficiency.

In schools where these meetings did not take place, French immersion teachers would welcome them. The absence of such meetings led to a situation where as Pauline (T/O) stated: 'We feel very isolated'. Pauline also commented that for her a 'professional development opportunity would be the ability to just sit down as a team and plan ... just the opportunity to sit down with somebody else and brainstorm would be wonderful. We don't have that'. The reason that Rachel's (T/O) school didn't have such meetings was that, 'We don't tend to divide them [French and English tracks] that way, okay. So here we divide them as just, you know, grade level. Like junior, intermediate rather than French, English. You know we try not to make the differentiation that way'. Annemarie (T/O) offered this explanation: 'I think it's the dual-track that's preventing this'. It appears that structural issues within some of the dual-track schools prevented teachers meeting to jointly plan how they might address the quality of the pupils' French. Where this planning did take place, it was largely dependent on there being a supportive and understanding principal in the school. Similar structural issues arose in relation to Irish-medium units in Northern Ireland (Ó Duibhir *et al.*, 2015c), which are similar to the immersion tracks in Canada. Teachers there reported that they were greatly dependent on the attitude of the school principal as to whether their unit was supported with discrete time for planning.

While the non-target-like features of the pupils in teachers all-Irish schools were a persistent phenomenon, it was evident from the responses that these features were taken seriously and that all schools had plans in place to address these weaknesses. The pupils' spoken accuracy in Irish was prioritised by all schools and different strategies had been devised to enhance it. Many teachers stated that the work they do with their pupils in primary school is part of a process of enhancement, and that as long as the pupils continue with education through Irish, which the majority of them do (Ó Duibhir *et al.*, 2015c), then they will become more accurate over time. Many teachers witnessed this when past pupils return to visit the school or they meet them socially.

Discussion

The purpose of interviewing teachers was to ascertain their views in relation to the proficiency of their pupils spoken Irish/French and to explore with them the factors that influence this level of proficiency. The sample consisted of 20 class teachers and 12 principals across Irish and French immersion contexts. The results pertain to the teachers interviewed and may not represent the views of the wider body of immersion teachers.

Teachers in both French and Irish schools appear to be reasonably satisfied with their students' proficiency in Irish/French but would like it to improve. Some thought that pupil proficiency was probably as good as could be expected under the circumstances in which immersion schools operate where the pupils have little exposure to the immersion language outside of school. This view reflected the reasonable expectations exhorted by Swain and Johnson (1997) of a high, but not native speaker level of proficiency in the L2. Others thought that this standard could be improved upon. Many mentioned that because the pupils live in an English-speaking world outside of school, it impacts on their language behaviour in school. While pupils acquired a good level of fluency in Irish/French, it was acknowledged that this needs to be built upon as they progress through school. These results were consistent with those of other studies of immersion pupils' target language attainment and use (Gathercole & Thomas, 2009; Hermanto et al., 2012; Tedick & Wesely, 2015).

The most common errors of the all-Irish pupils that emerged from the corpus analysis in Chapter 5 were the same as those identified by the teachers. The French immersion teachers also identified inaccuracies in the pupils' French which were consistent with the literature in this area (Nadasdi et al., 2005). Many teachers experienced frustration that some errors seem to recur despite the strategies adopted to correct them. All teachers adopted strategies for correcting their pupils when confronted with errors. In the main, these took the form of prompts that encouraged the pupil to pause and rephrase what had been uttered. The extent to which this happened, however, was hampered by the burden of implementing curricular content in all areas. Despite the teachers' best efforts, they felt that once their pupils could communicate with them and with one another, the pupils appeared to lack the motivation to do so in a way that was always grammatically accurate. This view is supported by the pupils' responses in the AMTB (see Chapter 7) and the opinions they expressed in the recall sessions. Day and Shapson (1987) found a similar pattern in their study of French immersion students in Canada.

Teachers were dissatisfied with the range of teaching materials at their disposal for teaching Irish/French while acknowledging that the situation had improved in recent years. Some teachers found it a continual challenge to encourage their pupils to speak Irish/French while others did not appear to experience the same level of difficulty. This finding was also reflected in the Irish immersion pupils' responses to the write-in items in the AMTB where some pupils disliked having to speak Irish at all times in school. The teachers acknowledged that it was easier for pupils to speak English and they had a range of incentives and sanctions to help them counteract this and to encourage them to speak Irish/French. The teachers spent a lot of time and effort to ensure that pupils complied with the school norm of speaking Irish/French and were innovative in this regard. Some teachers felt, however, that while incentives were necessary for younger pupils, a different approach may be required for senior pupils where intrinsic motivation should be encouraged. The responses of the pupils to the free text items in the AMTB highlighted the importance of the positive approach adopted by the teachers. There was evidence in the stimulated recall sessions of resistance to the school norm of no English from some pupils and an element of embarrassment when corrected in front of their peers.

The issue of pupils' proficiency in Irish was central to school planning in each of the all-Irish schools and time was allocated at most staff meetings to formally discuss and develop plans in this area. All-Irish teachers reported that there were school plans in place for improving pupils' proficiency in Irish. It appeared that the proactive strategies adopted for specifically addressing the errors consisted of formal grammar lessons. However, the review of research presented in Chapter 3 indicated that this approach may have limited success and a shift to a more analytical approach may yield better outcomes.

In the case of pupils' proficiency in French, the dual-track structure of the schools limited the opportunities for the pupils to speak French outside of the classroom. The teachers reported that the pupils were even reluctant to use French within the classroom when conversing with one another. School planning to address pupils' grammatical inaccuracies in French was also restricted by structural issues in half of the French immersion schools. In these instances, teachers reported not having opportunities to meet as a team of immersion teachers to address issues related to their specific context. Planning meetings in these schools dealt with issues common to the entire school and did not address immersion-specific issues.

Finally, the teachers reported that many pupils are reluctant to use the immersion language outside of the classroom and school context. This is in keeping with the investigation of all-Irish pupils and their parents' home use of Irish as reported in Chapter 7.

9 Discussion

In compiling this volume, I set out to establish the degree to which all-Irish primary schools were capable of producing competent Irish speakers. Based on the evidence presented in the previous chapters, we can conclude that pupils attain very good communicative competence in Irish but lack grammatical accuracy. This finding is very much in keeping with one-way immersion programmes elsewhere for minority languages where there is little exposure to the immersion language outside the school context.

A secondary question in this research was the extent to which competence in Irish might be converted to active bilingualism in society. The evidence base that I have presented for this latter question is less extensive and is based on the following factors:

- the home language practices of parents with their children, particularly those parents who attended an all-Irish school;
- the home language practices of pupils with their parents;
- the language behaviour of pupils within the school but outside the classroom.

Having analysed this evidence, we can tentatively conclude that the conversion rate of this potential is poor but that further longitudinal research is needed to be more definitive.

In reaching these conclusions, it is worth recapping the sources upon which they are based. The principal aim of this book was to bring together the results of a number of studies that investigated and evaluated the proficiency in Irish of pupils in all-Irish primary schools. The primary focus for assessing the pupils' competence was the corpus of speech samples recorded during a collaborative task in 13 all-Irish and 3 Gaeltacht schools for comparative purposes. The ability of the pupils to complete the task in Irish with fluency and communicative ease was very evident in the recordings. The analysis of their errors and an error rate of 30.2% in their utterances confirm that they do not reach native-like levels in spoken production after seven-plus years of immersion education. The disappointment that the pupils expressed in the stimulated recall activity about the level of their Irish confirmed the non-native-like features that are present.

We should not be overly critical of the pupils' Irish, however, given the limitations of the school context for language acquisition (Baker,

2003; Hermanto *et al.*, 2012; Thomas *et al.*, 2014). The pupils and the teachers are to be commended for doing so well and for generating such positive attitudes to Irish as expressed in the Attitude/Motivation Test Battery (AMTB). The pupils reported very positive attitudes to Irish and to learning Irish but, unfortunately, this positivity did not translate into out-of-classroom or out-of-school use of Irish for most of them.

Evidence of the pupils' use of Irish outside the classroom and parents' language use in the home was based on pupils' responses to an AMTB questionnaire and a matched sample parent questionnaire. Overall, neither parents nor pupils used the Irish they have acquired to the extent that they might. Without initiatives to normalise the use of Irish outside the school context, it is difficult to see this situation changing. A small number of parents (32) in our study, representing 9.6% of the sample, had attended all-Irish schools at primary and/or post-primary level. We found no correlation, however, between parental attendance at an all-Irish school and frequency of speaking Irish with their children at home. It would be interesting to see if this result would be replicated with a larger sample.

Teachers recognised the success that pupils attained in communicative competence in Irish. They would obviously like the pupils' Irish to be more accurate and in this endeavour, they make every effort to improve accuracy from an instructional perspective. Nonetheless, they recognise the limitations imposed by the dominance of English in the pupils' lives. This view was supported by their counterparts in Toronto and Ottawa.

While the body of studies presented in this volume was comprehensive in terms of its multi-method approach, it does have some limitations. The corpus of Irish-medium pupils' speech is based on a sample of 89 pupils in 13 all-Irish primary schools and 23 pupils in 3 Gaeltacht schools. While every effort was made to ensure that the schools chosen were representative of the different demographic and social variables present in schools, the results obtained may not be generalisable to the full spectrum of all-Irish primary schools. It must also be borne in mind that the pupils were in the main aged 11–12 years. Should they continue with Irish-medium education, they could be expected to improve the accuracy of their spoken Irish. A similar corpus of sixth-year/Year 14 (18-year-old) all-Irish pupils' Irish would be valuable for comparative purposes.

Another possible limitation is that the presence of the researcher in the classroom while the children were being recorded may have influenced the pupils' output. Similarly, during the stimulated recall sessions the presence of the researcher may have had a bearing on the opinions expressed by the pupils.

The corpus of pupils' speech compiled may be considered relatively small at almost 54,000 words when compared to corpora of world languages such as English or French. Nonetheless, it is the first Irish language corpus of primary school pupils' speech. It is based on oral data only, gathered in a relatively naturalistic setting. The speech samples gathered during a collaborative task may have been limited by the nature of the task itself. Future studies will determine how representative the corpus is of all-Irish and Gaeltacht pupil speech.

The remainder of this chapter presents some conclusions based on the findings of the research studies presented in this volume and discusses implications that arise for policy and practice in all-Irish schools and in immersion in general.

Conclusions

A number of findings emerge from this body of studies that increase the understanding of second language acquisition in Irish immersion education and in the wider immersion context more generally. It has been confirmed that all-Irish pupils speak a variety of Irish that resembles a code that contains non-target-like forms and is somewhat resistant to change. It may not be a code in the strictest sense, however, as there is inconsistency in the deviant forms that the pupils produce as evidenced in the analysis in Chapter 5. The variety of Irish is perfectly acceptable for peer-to-peer communication and the norm of 'minimal peer correction' is well established, despite the fact that the pupils realise that their output contains grammatical errors. All-Irish schools are very effective in promoting Irish as the communicative language of the school. This does not necessarily extend to the playground for all pupils, however. The effort and dedication required by teachers to maintain this context for authentic Irish use should not be underestimated and any recommendations in relation to improving pupil accuracy must bear this in mind.

A number of recommendations are made below in relation to practice and research in immersion education. If the ultimate goal of an immersion programme from a minority language perspective is to enable pupils to participate in the speech community and to extend the use of that language, then I would suggest a high level of competence in the language is a desirable outcome. While we have seen in the Darmody and Daly (2015) study that there is a correlation between competence in Irish and use, competence can be seen as necessary but not sufficient to guarantee that Irish will be spoken. Grin (2003) suggests that opportunities and the desire to use a minority language are also necessary. I contend that a level of proficiency approaching native speaker norms is important for the survival of Irish in order to integrate the entire Irish-speaking community which is perilously small. Others will disagree, believing that Irish has entered a post-traditional phase and that new speakers will emerge speaking a pidgin or simplified variety. The following recommendations are made in the context of that ultimate goal, bearing in mind that all-Irish primary pupils have many more years of formal education remaining in which to improve their Irish, provided they transfer to a post-primary all-Irish school. The current rate of transfer is approximately 40.2% (Ní Thuairisg & Ó Duibhir, 2016).

Pedagogical Practice

Analytical approach to language

Convincing arguments have been made in the research literature for a more analytical approach to second language learning in immersion to include form-focused instruction and corrective feedback (Lyster & Tedick, 2014). The findings of this body of studies suggest that the current, strongly experiential, approach does not lead to grammatical accuracy by the end of primary school. An analytical approach would shift attention from meaning to language form. As teachers identify emerging inaccurate features, these together with the features identified in Chapter 5 could be the forms to be focused on. While not advocating extensive explicit teaching of grammar, some explanation of grammatical elements adjusted to the maturity level of the pupils may be warranted. The type of explicit-inductive approach to grammar teaching in Ó Duibhir *et al.* (2016) and Ní Dhiorbháin and Ó Duibhir (2017) offer one potential approach to address the pupils' grammatical inaccuracies. Instructional materials have been produced for Irish immersion teachers to guide them in such an explicit-inductive approach (Ní Dhiorbháin, 2014).

Reconceptualise school norm to include the accurate use of Irish

The stimulated recall activity showed that all-Irish pupils interpret the school norm of speaking Irish as 'not using English words'. This interpretation may be sufficient in the early years of immersion until pupils gain basic interpersonal communication skills in Irish. Once this has been achieved, the emphasis needs to shift to affirming pupils, not only for speaking Irish, but also for the quality of their Irish. Reconceptualising the school norm as speaking Irish in a more target-like way may involve sacrificing a degree of fluency initially, but may be worthwhile in the context of achieving greater accuracy in the longer term. To continue with the current policy is to give pupils practice that is making 'permanent' rather than 'perfect' (Hammerly, 1991). By not addressing particular features at the appropriate time, there is a danger that the inaccurate forms will be stored in long-term memory and becoming automatised (Skehan, 1998). These forms are then less susceptible to change. A monitored pilot longitudinal intervention programme in a number of schools could help identify challenges, explore the approaches discussed here and develop strategies to improve outcomes at all stages of development.

Another area worthy of investigation in this context is that of empowering pupils explicitly to take greater responsibility for improving the quality of their own Irish. The AMTB revealed that motivational factors play a role in pupils' accurate use of Irish. Motivational factors combined with peer norms may operate counter to the efforts of the teacher and school in promoting accurate use of the target language. This underscores the situated nature of learning in an immersion context where there is a high level of target language input but no guarantee of uptake. While the extrinsic motivation of rewards and sanctions may be effective in junior classes, enabling pupils in senior classes to become more autonomous learners might be more fruitful (Little, 2007). In the explicit-inductive approach adopted in Ó Duibhir et al. (2016), focus group interviews with the pupils revealed that they welcomed the ownership of the learning process that this approach granted them. The pupils stated that they believed the approach would lead to longer-term learning because they had to work out the grammatical rules for themselves (Ní Dhiorbháin & Ó Duibhir, 2017).

The use of recordings of pupils engaged in language use

An important finding of the research was that the all-Irish pupils were unaware of the extent of their code-mixing behaviour. This highlighted the benefits of collaborating with pupils in exploring their use of Irish and using video recordings of the pupils engaged in real tasks as an object upon which to reflect. Short extracts of speech recordings could be transcribed by pupils to facilitate critical reflection. In the stimulated recall activity reported in this volume, pupils detected inaccurate forms most readily when the written transcripts were shown to them. Transcription of collaborative dialogues in other research studies has also shown that it facilitates pupils to engage in 'languaging' (Swain et al., 2011).

Provide opportunities for 'pushed output'

In the stimulated recall activity, the pupils revealed that they monitor their output more critically when they speak with the teacher than when they speak with their friends and this was reinforced in their responses in the AMTB. Similar findings were observed by Thomas et al. (2014) in the Welsh-medium context. This type of 'pushed output' has been shown to be effective in shifting learners from semantic to syntactic processing (Swain, 2005). Teachers should seek to maximise the opportunities for the production of 'pushed output' by setting tasks for pupils that involve the preparation of oral presentations and materials for real audiences. These tasks require pupils to reflect on what they want to say and teachers can assist them in choosing the most appropriate language forms. Tasks such as these also enable the teacher to integrate language and content objectives more effectively.

Whole-school approach to inaccurate features of pupils' Irish

In order to deal more effectively with the inaccurate features of all-Irish pupils' Irish, it is recommended that teachers monitor, on a whole-school basis, the emergence of these non-target forms, and to identify the optimum time to intervene. The input that pupils receive should also be monitored to ensure that the critical forms are salient. Where forms are not noticed, enhanced input will be required. A significant factor to emerge from the studies presented was the manner in which the Gaeltacht pupils used the copula with the demonstrative pronoun *sin* 'that'. This form of the copula needs to be explicitly taught to all-Irish pupils, as it is either a form that teachers do not use or it is not sufficiently salient in the input that pupils receive. Teachers should be alerted to this feature and encouraged to use this form if they do not do so already and to draw pupils' attention to it as an alternative.

Further Research

Corpus-based research

The features of all-Irish pupils' Irish that deviate from native speaker norms are acquired through a largely experiential approach with a certain amount of 'focus on formS'. The type of 'focus-on-formS' work appears, from the comments of the pupils and teachers, to emphasise the manipulation of forms rather than relating them to meaningful communication. Further corpus-based research with both younger and older all-Irish pupils would help to identify the developmental patterns associated with the acquisition of these features. It might indicate when the need for these forms emerges in the general instructional context or in discourse between pupils. Identifying developmental patterns would enable the explicit teaching of the correct forms to be embedded in authentic communicative contexts. It could also emerge that some of the deviant features are mastered when the pupils are older. The evidence from the small number of studies reviewed in this area suggests that many of the non-target-like features still remain at the end of post-primary education (Walsh, 2007).

Integration with Irish speaker networks

One of the aims of teaching Irish in schools is to produce competent bilinguals who could integrate into Irish-speaking networks in later life to become new speakers of Irish. The present studies have highlighted that the majority of opportunities that all-Irish pupils have for speaking Irish are with their peers in school. There is very little motivation for them to significantly increase their grammatical accuracy in this situation. The evidence of Irish language use by former students of all-Irish schools who are now parents of children in all-Irish schools is disappointing from the perspective of intergenerational transmission. This underlines Fishman's (2013) observation that the over-reliance on the education system in Ireland is a major weakness in language revitalisation efforts. Given the small sample of former all-Irish school parents reported in this volume, a larger study of the language behaviour of former pupils of all-Irish schools would help to inform policy initiatives in this area.

In the preface, I posed the following questions that motivated me to undertake this series of studies: Are all-Irish schools successful in educating pupils to become competent Irish speakers? If so, how might this language competence be converted to active bilingualism in the wider community beyond the school gates? It appears that all-Irish schools are very successful in what they set out to do, which is to enable pupils to acquire a very good level of communicative competence in Irish. As with immersion schools elsewhere, the pupils do not achieve native-like competence in their spoken production. Based on the evidence of language outcomes in other jurisdictions, e.g. Wales (Thomas & Roberts, 2011), it appears unreasonable to expect all-Irish schools to achieve much more. The education system and Irish immersion schools as part of that system cannot be solely responsible for pupils' mastery of Irish. It is for parents, communities and other agencies of the state, to take ownership of the challenge of converting the language competence of pupils into out-of-school use and meaningful participation in Irish-speaking networks. Without the social use of Irish, active individual bilingualism is unlikely to become a reality. The success of immersion education, therefore, is limited by the opportunities for language use in society. In the absence of a critical mass of peers who share similar opportunities, competence and desire to speak Irish, it is unlikely that all-Irish pupils will become new speakers of Irish on a large scale. Former all-Irish pupils will remain an untapped source to help reach the Irish government's very ambitious target of 250,000 daily speakers of Irish by 2030 (Government of Ireland, 2010).

References

Adiv, E. (1980) An analysis of second language performance in two types of immersion programs. *Bulletin of the Canadian Association of Applied Linguistics* 2 (2), 139–152.
Aldekoa, J. and Gardner, N. (2002) Turning knowledge of Basque into use: Normalisation plans for schools. *International Journal of Bilingual Education and Bilingualism* 5 (6), 339–354. doi: 10.1080/13670050208667766
Allen, P., Swain, M., Harley, B. and Cummins, J. (1990) Aspects of classroom treatment: Toward a more comprehensive view of second language education. In B. Harley, P. Allen, J. Cummins and M. Swain (eds) *The Development of Second Language Proficiency* (pp. 57–81). New York: Cambridge University Press.
An Coimisinéir Teanga (2013) *Tuarascáil bhliantúil* [*Annual Report*]. An Spidéal: An Coimisinéir Teanga. See http://www.coimisineir.ie/userfiles/files/Tuarascail_Bhliantuil_2013_teasc_amhain.pdf (accessed 14 July 2014).
Andersen, G. (2001) *Pragmatic Markers and Sociolinguistic Variation: A Relevance-Theoretic Approach to the Language of Adolescents*. Amsterdam: John Benjamins.
Baetens Beardsmore, H. and Swain, M. (1985) Designing bilingual education: Aspects of immersion and 'European school' models. *Journal of Multilingual and Multicultural Development* 6 (1), 1–15.
Baker, C. (2001) *Foundations of Bilingual Education and Bilingualism* (3rd edn). Clevedon: Multilingual Matters.
Baker, C. (2003) Education as a site of language contact. *Annual Review of Applied Linguistics* 23, 95–112. doi: 10.1017/S0267190503000217
Baker, C. (2006) *Foundations of Bilingual Education and Bilingualism* (4th edn). Clevedon: Multilingual Matters.
Baker, C. and Wright, W.E. (2017) *Foundations of Bilingual Education and Bilingualism* (6th edn). Bristol: Multilingual Matters.
Bellin, W. (1996) *Evaluation of the Assessment of Key Stage 3 Mathematics through the Medium of Welsh in 1996*. Cardiff: Curriculum and Assessment Authority for Wales.
Bibeau, G. (1984) No easy road to bilingualism. *Language and Society* 12, 44–47.
Björklund, S., Mård-Miettinen, K. and Savijärvi, M. (2014) Swedish immersion in the early years in Finland. *International Journal of Bilingual Education and Bilingualism* 17 (2), 197–214. doi: 10.1080/13670050.2013.866628
Bloch-Trojnar, M. (2006) *Polyfunctionality in Morphology: A Study of Verbal Nouns in Modern Irish*. Lublin: Wydawnictwo Folium.
Bournot-Trites, M. and Reeder, K. (2001) Interdependence revisited: Mathematics achievement in an intensified French immersion program. *The Canadian Modern Language Review* 58 (1), 27–43.
Bournot-Trites, M. and Tellowitz, U. (2002) *Report of Current Research on the Effects of Second Language Learning on First Language Literacy Skills*. Halifax, NS: The Atlantic Provinces Educational Foundation.
Buss, M. (2002) *Verb i språkbadselevers lexikon: En sociolingvistisk studie i andraspråket* [*Verbs in the vocabulary of immersion pupils: A sociolinguistic study of their second language*]. Acta Wasaensia 105. Vaasa: University of Vaasa.

Cammarata, L. and Tedick, D.J. (2012) Balancing content and language in instruction: The experience of immersion teachers. *The Modern Language Journal* 96 (2), 251–269. doi: 10.1111/j.1540-4781.2012.01330.x

CCEA (2009) The Northern Ireland Curriculum: Primary (Irish Medium) See http://www.nicurriculum.org.uk/docs/irish_medium/foundation/IrishMedium PrimaryCurriculum.pdf (accessed 29 October 2013).

Cenoz, J. and Gorter, D. (2017) Minority languages and sustainable translanguaging: Threat or opportunity? *Journal of Multilingual and Multicultural Development* 1–12. doi: 10.1080/01434632.2017.1284855

Central Statistics Office (CSO) (1932) *Census of Population 1926: Volume 8: Irish Language.* Dublin: Stationery Office.

Central Statistics Office (CSO) (2017) *Census 2016 Summary Results Part 1.* Dublin: Stationery Office.

Chaudron, C. (2003) Data collection in SLA research. In C. Doughty and M.H. Long (eds) *The Handbook of Second Language Acquisition* (pp. 762–828). Oxford: Blackwell.

Coady, M.R. and Ó Laoire, M. (2002) Mismatches in language policy and practice in education: The case of gaelscoileanna in the Republic of Ireland. *Language Policy* 1, 143–158.

Cohen, L., Manion, L. and Morrison, K. (2011) *Research Methods in Education* (7th edn). London: Routledge.

Coolahan, J. (1973) *A Study of Curricular Policy for the Primary and Secondary Schools of Ireland, 1900–1935, with Special Reference to the Irish Language and Irish History.* PhD thesis, Trinity College Dublin.

Coolahan, J. (1981) *Irish Education: Its History and Structure.* Dublin: Institute of Public Administration.

Coolican, H. (2004) *Research Methods and Statistics in Psychology* (4th edn). London: Hodder & Stoughton.

Corcoran, T. (1925) The Irish language in the Irish schools. *Studies: An Irish Quarterly Review* 14 (55), 377–388.

Council of Europe (2008) *Language Education Policy Profile: Ireland.* Strasbourg: Language Policy Division.

Crystal, D. (2000) *Language Death.* Cambridge: Cambridge University Press.

Cummins, J. (1977) Immersion education in Ireland: A critical review of Macnamara's findings. *Working Papers on Bilingualism* 13, 121–127.

Cummins, J. (1981) The role of primary language development in promoting educational success for language minority students. In California State Department of Education (edn) *Schooling and Language Minority Students: A Theoretical Framework* (pp. 3–49). Los Angeles, CA: Evaluation, Dissemination and Assessment Center, California State University.

Cummins, J. (1982) Reading achievement in Irish and English medium schools. *Oideas* 26, 21–26.

Cummins, J. (1999) Immersion education for the millennium: What we have learned from 30 years of research on second language immersion. See http://www.iteachilearn.com/cummins/immersion2000.html (accessed 3 September 2004).

Cummins, J. (2000) *Language, Power and Pedagogy: Bilingual Children in the Crossfire.* Clevedon: Multilingual Matters.

Dalton-Puffer, C. (2007) *Discourse in Content and Language Integrated Learning (CLIL) Classrooms.* Amsterdam: John Benjamins.

Darmody, M. and Daly, T. (2015) *Attitudes Towards the Irish Language on the Island of Ireland.* Dublin: Economic and Social Research Institute.

Day, E.M. and Shapson, S.M. (1987) Assessment of oral communicative skills in early French immersion programmes. *Journal of Multilingual and Multicultural Development* 8 (3), 237–260.
Day, E.M. and Shapson, S.M. (1996) *Studies in Immersion Education*. Clevedon: Multilingual Matters.
DeKeyser, R. (2000) The robustness of critical period effects in second language acquisition. *Studies in Second Language Acquisition* 22 (4), 499–533.
DeKeyser, R. (2003) Implicit and explicit learning. In C. Doughty and M.H. Long (eds) *The Handbook of Second Language Acquisition* (pp. 313–348). Oxford: Blackwell.
Department of Education and Science (1999) *Primary School Curriculum*. Dublin: Stationery Office.
Department of Education and Skills (2016) *Policy on Gaeltacht Education: 2017–2022*. Dublin: Department of Education and Skills.
Dörnyei, Z. (2005) *The Psychology of The Language Learner: Individual Differences in Second Language Acquisition*. Mahwah, NJ: Lawrence Erlbaum Associates.
Dörnyei, Z. (2007) *Research Methods in Applied Linguistics*. Oxford: Oxford University Press.
Dörnyei, Z. (2009) Individual differences: Interplay of learner characteristics and learning environment. *Language Learning* 59, 230–248. doi: 10.1111/j.1467-9922.2009.00542.x
Dörnyei, Z. and Csizér, K. (2002) Some dynamics of language attitudes and motivation: Results of a longitudinal nationwide survey. *Applied Linguistics* 23 (4), 421–462. doi: 10.1093/applin/23.4.421
Dörnyei, Z. and Skehan, P. (2003) Individual differences in second language learning. In C. Doughty and M.H. Long (eds) *The Handbook of Second Language Acquisition* (pp. 589–630). Oxford: Blackwell.
Dörnyei, Z. and Ushioda, E. (2009) *Motivation, Language Identity and the L2 Self*. Bristol: Multilingual Matters.
Doughty, C. (2003) Instructed SLA: Constraints, compensation, and enhancement. In C. Doughty and M.H. Long (eds) *The Handbook of Second Language Acquisition* (pp. 256–310). Oxford: Blackwell.
Doughty, C. and Williams, J. (1998) Pedagogical choices in focus on form. In C. Doughty and J. Williams (eds) *Focus on Form in Classroom Second Language Acquisition* (pp. 197–285). Cambridge: Cambridge University Press.
Doyle, A. (2015) *A History of The Irish Language: From the Norman Invasion to Independence*. Oxford: Oxford University Press.
Edwards, J. (2017) Celtic languages and sociolinguistics: A very brief overview of pertinent issues. *Language, Culture and Curriculum* 30 (1), 13–31. doi: 10.1080/07908318.2016.1230618
Ellis, R. (1994) *The Study of Second Language Acquisition*. Oxford: Oxford University Press.
Ellis, R. (2003) *Task-Based Language Learning and Teaching*. Oxford: Oxford University Press.
Ellis, R. (2005) Principles of instructed language learning. *System* 33 (2), 209–224. doi: 10.1016/j.system.2004.12.006
Ellis, R. (2008) *The Study of Second Language Acquisition* (2nd edn). Oxford: Oxford University Press.
Ellis, R. and Barkhuizen, G. (2005) *Analysing Learner Language*. Oxford: Oxford University Press.
Ellis, R. and Shintani, N. (2014) *Exploring Language Pedagogy Through Second Language Acquisition Research*. London: Routledge.
Ellis, R., Loewen, S. and Erlam, R. (2006) Implicit and explicit corrective feedback and the acquisition of L2 grammar. *Studies in Second Language Acquisition* 28, 339–368.

Firth, A. and Wagner, J. (1997) On discourse, communication, and (some) fundamental concepts in SLA research. *The Modern Language Journal* 81 (3), 285–300. doi: 10.1111/j.1540-4781.1997.tb05480.x

Firth, A. and Wagner, J. (2007) Second/foreign language learning as a social accomplishment: Elaborations on a reconceptualized SLA. *The Modern Language Journal* 91, 800–819. doi: 10.1111/j.1540-4781.2007.00670.x

Fishman, J.A. (1991) *Reversing Language Shift*. Clevedon: Multilingual Matters.

Fishman, J.A. (2013) Language maintenance, language shift, and reversing language shift. In T.K. Bhatia and W.C. Ritchie (eds) *Handbook of Bilingualism and Multilingualism* (pp. 466–494). Somerset, NJ: Wiley.

Fortune, T.W. and Tedick, D.J. (2008) One-way, two-way and indigenous immersion: A call for cross-fertilization. In T.W. Fortune and D.J. Tedick (eds) *Pathways to Multilingualism: Evolving Perspectives on Immersion Education* (pp. 3–21). Clevedon: Multilingual Matters.

Gardner, R.C. (1985) *Social Psychology and Second Language Learning: The Role of Attitudes and Motivation*. London: Edward Arnold.

Gardner, R.C. and MacIntyre, P. (1992) A student's contributions to second-language learning. Part I: Cognitive variables. *Language Teaching* 25, 211–220.

Gardner, R.C. and MacIntyre, P. (1993) A student's contributions to second-language learning. Part II: Affective variables. *Language Teaching* 26, 1–11.

García, O. (2009) *Bilingual Education in the 21st Century: A Global Perspective*. Oxford: Wiley-Blackwell.

García, O. and Wei, L. (2013) *Translanguaging: Language, Bilingualism and Education*. Basingstoke: Palgrave Macmillan.

Gass, S.M. and Mackey, A. (2000) *Stimulated Recall Methodology in Second Language Research*. Mahwah, NJ: Lawrence Erlbaum Associates.

Gass, S.M. and Mackey, A. (2006) Input, interaction and output. *AILA Review* 19, 3–17.

Gass, S.M. and Selinker, L. (2008) *Second Language Acquisition: An Introductory Course* (3rd edn). London: Routledge.

Gathercole, V.C.M. and Thomas, E.M. (2009) Bilingual first-language development: Dominant language takeover, threatened minority language take-up. *Bilingualism: Language and Cognition* 12 (2), 213–237.

Genesee, F. (1987) *Learning Through Two Languages: Studies of Immersion and Bilingual Education*. Cambridge, MA: Newbury House.

Genesee, F. (1998) French immersion in Canada. In J. Edwards (ed.) *Language in Canada* (pp. 305–325). Cambridge: Cambridge University Press.

Genesee, F. (2008) Dual language in the global village. In T.W. Fortune and D.J. Tedick (eds) *Pathways to Multilingualism: Evolving Perspectives on Immersion Education* (pp. 22–45). Clevedon: Multilingual Matters.

Genesee, F., Holobow, N.E., Lambert, W.E. and Chartrand, L. (1989) Three elementary school alternatives for learning through a second language. *The Modern Language Journal* 73 (3), 250–263.

Genesee, F., Lindholm-Leary, K., Saunders, W.M. and Christian, D. (2006) *Educating English Language Learners: A Synthesis of Research Evidence*. New York: Cambridge University Press.

Grin, F. (2003) *Language Policy Evaluation and the European Charter for Regional or Minority Languages*. Basingstoke: Palgrave Macmillan.

Government of Ireland (2010) *20-Year Strategy for the Irish Language 2010–2030*. Dublin: Stationery Office.

Granger, S. (2002) A bird's-eye view of learner corpora research. In S. Granger, J. Hung and S. Petch-Tyson (eds) *Computer Learner Corpora, Second Language Acquisition and Foreign Language Teaching* (pp. 3–33). Amsterdam: John Benjamins.

Hammerly, H. (1989) Toward fluency and accuracy: A response to Allen, Cummins, Harley, Lapkin and Swain. *The Canadian Modern Language Review* 45 (4), 776–783.
Hammerly, H. (1991) *Fluency and Accuracy: Toward Balance in Language Teaching and Learning*. Clevedon: Multilingual Matters.
Harley, B. (1987) *The Development of Second Language Proficiency. Final Report. Volume II: Classroom Treatment*. Toronto: Modern Language Centre, Ontario Institute for Studies in Education.
Harley, B. (1991) Directions in immersion research. *Journal of Multilingual and Multicultural Development* 12 (1&2), 9–19.
Harley, B. (1993) Instructional strategies and SLA in early French Immersion. *Studies in Second Language Acquisition* 15, 245–259.
Harley, B. and Hart, D. (1997) Language aptitude and second language proficiency in classroom learners of different starting ages. *Studies in Second Language Acquisition* 19 (3), 379–400.
Harley, B., Cummins, J., Swain, M. and Allen, P. (1990) The nature of language proficiency. In B. Harley, P. Allen, J. Cummins and M. Swain (eds) *The Development of Second Language Proficiency* (pp. 7–25). Cambridge: Cambridge University Press.
Harley, B., Howard, J. and Hart, D. (1998) Grammar in Grade 2: An instructional experiment in primary French immersion. In S. Lapkin (ed.) *French Second-Language Education in Canada: Empirical Studies* (pp. 177–193). Toronto: University of Toronto Press.
Harrington, S. (2006) Early error in lesser used languages: Perception and categorisation. In A. Gallagher and M. Ó Laoire (eds) *Language Education in Ireland: Current Practice and Future Needs* (pp. 193–203). Dublin: Irish Association for Applied Linguistics.
Harris, J. (1982) Achievement in spoken Irish at the end of primary school. *Irish Journal of Education* 16 (2), 85–116.
Harris, J. (1984) *Spoken Irish in Primary Schools: An Analysis of Achievement*. Dublin: Linguistics Institute of Ireland.
Harris, J. (2002) Research, innovation and policy change: Lessons from the ITÉ evaluation of the Irish programme at primary level. In J.M. Kirk and D. Ó Baoill (eds) *Language Planning and Education: Linguistic Issues in Northern Ireland, the Republic of Ireland, and Scotland* (pp. 82–99). Belfast: Queens University Press.
Harris, J. (2007) Bilingual education and bilingualism in Ireland north and south. *The International Journal of Bilingual Education and Bilingualism* 10 (4), 359–368.
Harris, J. and Murtagh, L. (1987) Irish and English in Gaeltacht primary schools. In G. Mac Eoin, A. Ahlqvist and D. Ó hAodha (eds) *Third International Conference on Minority Languages: Celtic Papers. Multilingual Matters* 32 (pp. 104–124). Clevedon: Multilingual Matters.
Harris, J. and Murtagh, L. (1988) National assessment of Irish-language speaking and listening skills in primary-school children: Research issues in the evaluation of school-based heritage-language programmes. *Language Culture and Curriculum* 1 (2), 85–130.
Harris, J. and Murtagh, L. (1999) *Teaching and Learning Irish in Primary School: A Review of Research and Development*. Dublin: Linguistics Institute of Ireland.
Harris, J. and Conway, M. (2002) *Modern Languages in Irish Primary Schools: An Evaluation of the National Pilot Project*. Dublin: Linguistics Institute of Ireland.
Harris, J., Forde, P., Archer, P., Nic Fhearaile, S. and O'Gorman, M. (2006) *Irish in Primary Schools: Long-Term National Trends in Achievement*. Dublin: Department of Education and Science.
Henry, A. and Tangney, D. (1999) Functional categories and parameter settings in the second-language acquisition of Irish in early childhood. In M. DeGraff (ed.) *Language Creation and Language Change: Creolization, Diachrony and Development* (pp. 239–253). Cambridge, MA: MIT.

Henry, A., Andrews, Á. and Ó Cainín, P. (2002) *Developing Linguistic Accuracy in Irish-Medium Primary Schools*. Bangor: Department of Education.

Hermanto, N., Moreno, S. and Bialystok, E. (2012) Linguistic and metalinguistic outcomes of intense immersion education: How bilingual? *International Journal of Bilingual Education and Bilingualism* 15 (2), 131–145. doi: 10.1080/13670050.2011.652591

Hickey, T. (1997) *An Luath-Thumadh in Éirinn: Na Naíonraí [Early Immersion Education in Ireland: Na Naíonraí]*. Dublin: Linguistics Institute of Ireland.

Hickey, T. (2009) Code-switching and borrowing in Irish. *Journal of Sociolinguistics* 13 (5), 670–688. doi: 10.1111/j.1467-9841.2009.00429.x

Hickey, T.M. and Stenson, N. (2016) One step forward and two steps back in teaching an endangered language? Revisiting L2 reading in Irish. *Language, Culture and Curriculum* 29 (3), 302–318. doi: 10.1080/07908318.2016.1231200

Hornsby, M. (2017) Finding an ideological niche for new speakers in a minoritised language community. *Language, Culture and Curriculum* 30 (1), 91–104. doi: 10.1080/07908318.2016.1230622

Irish National Teachers' Organisation (1941) *Report of the Committee of Inquiry into the Use of Irish as a Teaching Medium to Children whose Home Language is English*. Dublin: INTO.

Johnstone, R., Harlen, W., MacNeil, M., Stradling, B. and Thorpe, G. (1999) *The Attainments of Pupils Receiving Gaelic-Medium Primary Education in Scotland*. Stirling: Scottish Centre for Information on Language Teaching.

Jones, D. (1996) Assessment of communicative competence of children in Welsh immersion programmes. In J. Arnau and J. Artigal (eds) *Els Programes d'immersió: una Perspectiva Europea [Immersion Programs: A European Perspective]* (pp. 594–608). Barcelona: Universitat de Barcelona. See http://eric.ed.gov/ERICWebPortal/Home.portal?_nfpb=true&_pageLabel=RecordDetails&ERICExtSearch_SearchValue_0=ED400686&ERICExtSearch_SearchType_0=eric_accno&objectId=0900000b80127de8.

Jones, V.A. (2006) *A Gaelic Experiment: The Preparatory System 1926–1961 and Coláiste Mobhí*. Dublin: Woodfield Press.

Kavanagh, L. and Hickey, T.M. (2012) 'You're looking at this different language and it freezes you out straight away': Identifying challenges to parental involvement among immersion parents. *Language and Education* 27 (5) 432–450. doi: 10.1080/09500782.2012.714388

Kennedy, I.A. (2012) Irish Medium Education: Cognitive Skills, Linguistic Skills, and Attitudes Towards Irish. PhD thesis, Bangor University.

Knaus, V. and Nadasdi, T. (2001) Être ou ne pas être in Immersion French. *The Canadian Modern Language Review* 58 (2), 287–306.

Kowal, M. and Swain, M. (1997) From semantic to syntactic processing: How can we promote it in the immersion classroom? In R.K. Johnson and M. Swain (eds) *Immersion Education: International Perspectives* (pp. 284–309). Cambridge: Cambridge University Press.

Krashen, S.D. (1985) *The Input Hypothesis: Issues and Implications*. London: Longman.

Lantolf, J.P. and Thorne, S.L. (2006) *Sociocultural Theory and the Genesis of Second Language Development*. Oxford: Oxford University Press.

Lapkin, S. and Swain, M. (2004) What underlies immersion students' production: The case of avoir besoin de. *Foreign Language Annals* 37 (3), 349–355.

Lapkin, S., Swain, M. and Shapson, S. (1990) French immersion research agenda for the 90s. *The Canadian Modern Language Review* 46 (4), 638–674.

Lapkin, S., MacFarlane, A. and Vandergrift, L. (2006) *Teaching French as a Second Language in Canada: Teachers' Perspectives*. Ottawa: Canadian Association of Second Language Teachers, Canadian Association of Immersion Teachers and The Canadian Teachers' Federation.

Lewis, G., Jones, B. and Baker, C. (2012) Translanguaging: Origins and development from school to street and beyond. *Educational Research and Evaluation* 18 (7), 641–654. doi: 10.1080/13803611.2012.718488

Little, D. (1991) *Learner Autonomy 1: Definitions, Issues and Problems*. Dublin: Authentik.

Little, D. (2007) Language learner autonomy: Some fundamental considerations revisited. *Innovation in Language Learning and Teaching* 1 (1), 14–29. doi: 10.2167/illt040.0

Long, M. (1991) A design feature in language teaching methodology. In K. de Bot, R.B. Ginsberg and C. Kramsch (eds) *Foreign Language Research in Cross-Cultural Perspective* (pp. 39–52). Amsterdam: Benjamins.

Long, M.H. (1996) The role of the linguistic environment in second language acquisition. In W.C. Ritchie and T.K. Bhatia (eds) *Handbook of Second Language Acquisition* (pp. 413–468). San Diego, CA: Academic Press.

Long, M.H. and Robinson, P. (1998) Focus on form: Theory, research, and practice. In C. Doughty and J. Williams (eds) *Focus on Form in Classroom Second Language Acquisition* (pp. 15–41). Cambridge: Cambridge University Press.

Lynch, T. (2001) Seeing what they meant: Transcribing as a route to noticing. *ELT J* 55 (2), 124–132. doi: 10.1093/elt/55.2.124

Lyster, R. (1987) Speaking immersion. *The Canadian Modern Language Review* 43 (4), 701–717.

Lyster, R. (1998a) Diffusing dichotomies: Using the multidimensional curriculum model for developing analytic teaching materials in immersion. In S. Lapkin (ed.) *French Second-Language Education in Canada: Empirical Studies* (pp. 197–218). Toronto: University of Toronto Press.

Lyster, R. (1998b) Immersion pedagogy and implications for language teaching. In J. Cenoz and F. Genesee (eds) *Beyond Bilingualism: Multilingualism and Multilingual Education* (pp. 64–95). Clevedon: Multilingual Matters.

Lyster, R. (2004) Differential effects of prompts and recasts in form-focused instruction. *Studies in Second Language Acquisition* 26 (3), 399–432.

Lyster, R. (2007) *Learning and Teaching Languages Through Content: A Counterbalanced Approach* (Vol. 28). Amsterdam: John Benjamins.

Lyster, R. (2011) Content-based second language teaching. In E. Hinkel (ed.) *Handbook of Research in Second Language Teaching and Learning. Volume II* (pp. 611–630). New York: Routledge.

Lyster, R. and Rannta, L. (1997) Corrective feedback and learner uptake: Negotiation of form in communicative classrooms. *Studies in Second Language Acquisition* 19 (1), 37–66.

Lyster, R. and Mori, H. (2006) Interactional feedback and instructional counterbalance. *Studies in Second Language Acquisition* 28 (2), 269–300.

Lyster, R. and Mori, H. (2008) Instructional counterbalance in immersion pedagogy. In T.W. Fortune and D.J. Tedick (eds) *Pathways to Multilingualism: Evolving Perspectives on Immersion Education* (pp. 133–151). Clevedon: Multilingual Matters.

Lyster, R. and Tedick, D.J. (2014) Research perspectives on immersion pedagogy: Looking back and looking forward. *Journal of Immersion and Content-Based Language Education* 2 (2), 210–224. doi: 10.1075/jicb.2.2.04lys

Lyster, R., Saito, K. and Sato, M. (2013) Oral corrective feedback in second language classrooms. *Language Teaching* 46 (1), 1–40. doi: 10.1017/S0261444812000365

Mac Aogáin, E. (1990) *Teaching Irish in the Schools: Towards a Policy for 1992*. Dublin: Linguistics Institute of Ireland.

Mac Ardghail, B. (2014) Integrating content and language learning in all-Irish primary schools: A case study on opportunities for second language acquisition in a sixth-class classroom. Unpublished MPhil thesis, Trinity College Dublin.

Mac Cóil, L. (2003) Irish: One of the languages of the world. In M. Cronin and C. Ó Cuilleanáin (eds) *The Languages of Ireland* (pp. 127–147). Dublin: Four Courts Press.

Mac Congáil, N. (2004) *Irish Grammar Book*. Indreabhán: Cló Iar-Chonnachta.
Mac Corraidh, S. (2008) *Ar thóir an dea-chleachtais: The Quest for Best Practice in Irish-Medium Primary Schools in Belfast*. Belfast: Queens University Press.
Mac Corraidh, S. (2013) Sealbhú agus foglaim na Gaeilge san oideachas lán-Ghaeilge. *Éigse Loch Lao* 2, 51–62.
Mac Donnacha, S., Ní Chualáin, F., Ní Shéaghdha, A. and Ní Mhainín, T. (2005) *Staid Reatha Na Scoileanna Gaeltachta: A Study of Gaeltacht Schools 2004 [The Curent State of Gaeltacht Schools 2004]*. Dublin: An Chomhairle um Oideachas Gaeltachta agus Gaelscolaíochta.
Mac Gréil, M. and Rhatigan, F. (2009) *The Irish Language and the Irish People*. Maynooth: Department of Sociology, Maynooth University.
Mac Mathúna, L. (1997) Ar thóir an fhocail chruinn: Polasaí agus cur chuige lucht iriseoireachta, téarmaíocht agus oideachais [In seach of the accurate word: The policy and approach of journalists, terminology and education]. In M. Nic Eoin and L. Mac Mathúna (eds) *Ar thóir an fhocail chruinn [In Search of the Accurate Word]* (pp. 55–62). Dublin: Coiscéim.
Mac Mathúna, L. (2008) Linguistic change and standardization. In C. Nic Pháidín and S. Ó Cearnaigh (eds) *A New View of The Irish Language* (pp. 76–92). Dublin: Cois Life.
Mac Murchaidh, C. (2013) *Cruinnscríobh na Gaeilge* (Eag 5) *[The Accurate Writing of Irish* (5th edn)]. Dublin: Cois Life.
Mac Síomóin, T. (2014) *The Broken Harp: Identity and Language in Modern Ireland*. Dublin: Nua-Scéalta.
Macnamara, J. (1966) *Bilingualism and Primary Education: A Study of Irish Experience*. Edinburgh: Edinburgh University Press.
Maguire, G. (1991) *Our Own Language: An Irish Initiative*. Clevedon: Multilingual Matters.
May, S. (2001) *Language and Minority Rights: Ethnicity, Nationalism and The Politics of Language*. Harlow: Longman.
May, S. and Hill, R. (2005) Māori-medium education: Current issues and challenges. *The International Journal of Bilingual Education and Bilingualism* 8 (5), 377–403.
Maybin, J. (2006) *Children's Voices: Talk, Knowledge, and Identity*. Basingstoke: Palgrave Macmillan.
McAdory, S.E. and Janmaat, J.G. (2015) Trends in Irish-medium education in the Republic of Ireland and Northern Ireland since 1920: Shifting agents and explanations. *Journal of Multilingual and Multicultural Development* 36 (5), 528–543. doi: 10.1080/01434632.2014.969273
McCloskey, J. (2001) *Guthanna in Éag: An Mairfidh an Ghaeilge Beo? [Dying Voices: Will Irish Survive]*. Dublin: Cois Life.
Mhic Mhathúna, M. (2008) Supporting children's participation in second-language stories in an Irish-language preschool. *Early Years: Journal of International Research and Development* 28 (3), 299–309.
Mitchell, R., Myles, F. and Marsden, E. (2013) *Second Language Learning Theories* (3rd edn). London: Routledge.
Mougeon, R., Rehner, K. and Nadasdi, T. (2004) The learning of spoken French variation by immersion students from Toronto, Canada. *Journal of Sociolinguistics* 8 (3), 408–432.
Muñoz, C. and Singleton, D. (2011) A critical review of age-related research on L2 ultimate attainment. *Language Teaching* 44 (1), 1–35. doi: 10.1017/S0261444810000327
Murtagh, L. (2003) Retention of Irish skills: A longitudinal study of general and communicative proficiency in Irish among second level school leavers and the influence of instructional background, language use and attitude/motivation variables. Unpublished PhD thesis, Rijksuniversiteit Groningen.
Murtagh, L. (2006) Attitude/motivation, extra-school use of Irish, and achievement in Irish among final-year secondary school (Leaving Certificate) students. In A. Gallagher and

M. Ó Laoire (eds) *Language Education in Ireland: Current Practice and Future Needs* (pp. 34–59). Dublin: Irish Association for Applied Linguistics.

Murtagh, L. (2007) Out-of-school use of Irish: Motivation and proficiency in immersion and subject only post-primary programmes. *The International Journal of Bilingual Education and Bilingualism* 10 (4), 428–453.

Murtagh, L. (2009) The role of motivation in learning and using Irish among primary and secondary level students: A review of the evidence. In S. Drudy (ed.) *Education in Ireland: Challenge and Change* (Chapter 9). Dublin: Gillmacmillan.

Myers-Scotton, C. (2006) *Multiple Voices: An Introduction to Bilingualism*. Oxford: Blackwell Publishing.

Myles, F. (2005) Interlanguage corpora and second language acquisition research. *Second Language Research* 21 (4), 373–391. doi: 10.1191/0267658305sr252oa

Nadasdi, T., Mougeon, R. and Rehner, K. (2005) Learning to speak everyday (Canadian) French. *The Canadian Modern Language Review* 61 (4), 543–563.

Nassaji, H. and Fotos, S. (2007) Issues in form-focused instruction and teacher education. In S. Fotos and H. Nassaji (eds) *Form-Focused Instruction and Teacher Education: Studies in Honour of Rod Ellis* (pp. 7–15). Oxford: Oxford University Press.

National Council for Curriculum and Assessment (2006) *Language and Literacy in Irish-Medium Primary Schools: Descriptions of Practice*. Dublin: National Council for Curriculum and Assessment.

National Council for Curriculum and Assessment (2015) Primary Language Curriculum: Irish-Medium Schools. See http://www.curriculumonline.ie/Primary/Curriculum-Areas/Language-New-Junior-infants-2nd-class (accessed 29 January 2016).

National Programme Conference (1922) *National Programme of Primary Instruction*. Dublin: Browne and Nolan.

Ní Dhiorbháin, A. (2014) Bain súp as! Treoir nua maidir le múineadh na gramadaí [Enjoy! New guide to grammar teaching]. See http://www.cogg.ie/wp-content/uploads/inneacs.pdf (accessed 8 July 2015).

Ní Dhiorbháin, A. (2017) *Oideolaíochtaí um theagasc an léireolais do bhunmhúinteoirí faoi oiliúint*. EdD thesis, Dublin City University, Dublin.

Ní Dhiorbháin, A. and Ó Duibhir, P. (2017) An explicit-inductive approach to grammar in Irish-medium immersion schools. *Language Awareness* 26 (1), 3–24. doi: 10.1080/09658416.2016.1261870

Nic Eoin, M. (2005) *Trén bhfearann breac: An Díláithriú Cultúir agus Nualitríocht na Gaeilge [Through the Speckled Land: The Dislocaiton of Culture and Modern Literature in Irish]*. Dublin: Cois Life.

Nic Fhlannchadha, S. and Hickey, T.M. (2016) Minority language ownership and authority: Perspectives of native speakers and new speakers. *International Journal of Bilingual Education and Bilingualism* 1–16. doi: 10.1080/13670050.2015.1127888

Nic Pháidín, C. (2003) 'Cén fáth nach?' – Ó Chanúint go Críól ['Why not?' From dialect to creole]. In R. Ní Mhianáin (ed.) *Idir Lúibíní: Aistí ar an Léitheoireacht agus ar an Litearthacht [Between Brackets: Essays on Reading and Literature]* (pp. 113–130). Dublin: Cois Life.

Ní Thuairisg, L. (2014) Léargas ar thaithí mhúinteoirí iar-bhunscoileanna na Gaeltachta: Dúshláin ghairmiúla agus riachtanais oiliúna. Unpublished PhD thesis, Dublin City University.

Ní Thuairisg, L. and Ó Duibhir, P. (2016) An leanúnachas ón mbunscoil go dtí an iar-bhunscoil lán-Ghaeilge i bPoblacht na hÉireann [Continuity from primary to post-primary all-Irish school in the Republic of Ireland]. See http://www.gaelscoileanna.ie/files/An-Lean--nachas-on-mbunscoil-go-dt---an-iar-bhunscoil-l--n-Ghaeilge-_MF-2016.pdf.

Norris, J.M. and Ortega, L. (2000) Effectiveness of L2 instruction: A research synthesis and quantitative meta-analysis. *Language Learning* 50 (3), 417–528.
Northern Ireland Statistics and Research Agency (2012) Census 2011: Key statistics for Northern Ireland. See http://www.nisra.gov.uk/Census/key_report_2011.pdf (accesssed 14 May 2015).
Norton, B. (2013) *Identity and Language Learning: Extending the Conversation* (2nd edn). Bristol: Multilingual Matters.
Ó Baoill, D. (1981) *Earráidí Scríofa Gaeilge Cuid 3: Réamhfhocail agus Comhréir* [*Written Errors in Irish Part 3: Prepositions and Syntax*]. Dublin: Linguistics Institute of Ireland.
Ó Broin, B. (2014) New urban Irish: Pidgin, creole, or bona fide dialect? The phonetics and morphology of city and Gaeltacht speakers systematically compared. *Journal of Celtic Linguistics* 15 (1), 69–91.
Ó Buachalla, S. (1984) Educational policy and the role of the Irish language from 1831 to 1981. *European Journal of Education* 19 (1), 75–92.
Ó Catháin, B. (2001) Dearcadh an teangeolaí ar chomharthaí sóirt Ghaeilge an lae inniu. In R. Ó hUiginn (ed.) *Léachtaí Cholm Cille XXXI* [*Colmcille Lectures XXXI*] (pp. 128–149). Maynooth: An Sagart.
Ó Cathalláin, S. (2011) Early Literacy in All-Irish Immersion Primary Schools: A Micro-Ethnographic Case Study of Storybook Reading Events in Irish and English. PhD thesis, University of Stirling.
Ó Ceallaigh, T.J. (2013) Form-Focused Instruction in Irish-Medium Immersion Education: A Critical Examination of Teachers' Perspectives and Practices. A Small-Scale Qualitative Case Study. PhD thesis, University College Cork.
Ó Cíobháin, P. (1999) Cathair ghríobháin na samhlaíochta [The Labyrinth of the imagination]. In M. Ó Cearúil (ed.) *An Aimsir Óg: Scéalta, Aistí, Dánta* [*Young Times: Stories, Essays, Poems*] (pp. 105–111). Dublin: Coiscéim.
Ó Conchubhair, S. (2003) Féidearthachtaí nua i dteagasc agus i bhfoghlaim na copaile sa Ghaeilge [New possibilities in teaching the copula in Irish]. *Teagasc na Gaeilge* [*Teaching of Irish*] 8, 127–143.
O'Connell, T.J. (1968) *History of the Irish National Teachers' Organisation, 1868–1968*. Dublin: Irish National Teachers' Organisation.
O'Connor, M. (2010) *The Development of Infant Education in Ireland, 1838–1948: Epochs and Eras*. Bern: Peter Lang.
Ó Cuirreáin, S. (2014) 'Bíonn an fhírinne garbh' [The truth is harsh]. *Comhar* 74 (2), 10–12.
Ó Curnáin, B. (2007) *The Irish of Iorras Aithneach, County Galway*. Volumes I–IV. Dublin: Dublin Institute for Advanced Studies.
Ó Domhnalláin, T. and Ó Baoill, D. (1978) *Earráidí Scríofa Gaeilge Cuid 1: Earráidí Briathra* [*Written Errors in Irish Part 1: Verbal Errors*]. Dublin: Linguistics Institute of Ireland.
Ó Domhnalláin, T. and Ó Baoill, D. (1979) *Earráidí Scríofa Gaeilge Cuid 2: Ainmfhocail, Cáilíochtaí, Forainmneacha, Cónaisc agus Míreanna* [*Written Errors in Irish Part 2: Nouns, Qualifiers, Pronouns, Connectors and Affixes*]. Dublin: Linguistics Institute of Ireland.
Ó Dónaill, É. (2000) 'Tá sé suas duit féin': Impleachtaí Mheath na Gaeilge do mhúineadh na teanga ['It is up to you': The implications of the decline of Irish for the teaching of the language]. In L. Mac Mathúna, C. Mac Murchaidh and M. Nic Eoin (eds) *Teanga, Pobal Agus Réigiún: Aistí ar Chultúr na Gaeltachta Inniu* [*Language, Community and Region: Essays on the Culture of the Gaeltacht Today*] (pp. 48–63). Dublin: Coiscéim.
Ó Duibhir, P. (2009) The spoken Irish of sixth-class pupils in Irish immersion schools. Unpublished PhD thesis, Trinity College Dublin.
Ó Duibhir, P. (2010) 'It's only a language': The attitudes and motivation of Irish-medium education students to the Irish language. In W. Hutchinson and C. Ní Ríordáin (eds) *Language Issues: Ireland, France, Spain* (pp. 121–138). Brussels: Peter Lang.

Ó Duibhir, P. (2012) Cúrsaí oideachais agus Straitéis 20 Bliain don Ghaeilge [Education matters and the 20-year Strategy for Irish]. In C. Lenoach, C. Ó Giollagáin and B. Ó Curnáin (eds) *An chonair chaoch: An mionteangachas sa dátheangachas* [*The Blind Path: Minority Linguistics in Bilingualism*] (pp. 269–283). Gaillimh: Leabhar Breac.

Ó Duibhir, P. and Cummins, J. (2012) *Towards an Integrated Language Curriculum in Early Childhood and Primary Education (3–12 years)*. Dublin: NCCA.

Ó Duibhir, P., Ní Chuaig, N., Ní Thuairisg, L. and Ó Brolcháin, C. (2015a) *Educational Provision Through Minority Languages: Review of International Research*. Dublin: Department of Education and Skills.

Ó Duibhir, P., Ní Thuairisg, L., NigUidhir, G. and Ó Cathalláin, S. (2015b) *Tionchar na Scoileanna Lán-Ghaeilge ar Chruthú Nuachainteoirí Gníomhacha Gaeilge* [The Impact of Irish-medium Schools on The Creation of Active New Speakers of Irish]. Paper presented at the All-Island Conference on Immersion Education: Immersion Education Easy or Challenging?, Mary Immaculate College, University of Limerick.

Ó Duibhir, P., Ó Cathalláin, S., NigUidhir, G., Ní Thuairisg, L. and Cosgrove, J. (2015c) *Anailís ar Mhúnlaí Soláthair Gaelscolaíochta* [*Analysis of Models of Irish-Medium School Provision*]. Dublin: The North/South Standing Commmittee on Irish-Medium Education.

Ó Duibhir, P., Ní Dhiorbháin, A. and Cosgrove, J. (2016) An inductive approach to grammar teaching in Grade 5 & 6 Irish immersion classes. *Journal of Immersion and Content-Based Language Education* 4 (1), 33–58. Doi: 10.1075/jicb.4.1.02dui

Ó Giollagáin, C. (2014) Unfirm ground: A re-assessment of language policy in Ireland since independence. *Language Problems and Language Planning* 38 (1), 19–41. doi: 10.1075/lplp.38.1.02gio

Ó Giollagáin, C. and Mac Donnacha, S. (2008) The Gaeltacht today. In C. Nic Pháidín and S. Ó Cearnaigh (eds) *A New View of the Irish Language* (pp. 108–120). Dublin: Cois Life.

Ó Giollagáin, C. and Charlton, M. (2015) *Nuashonrú ar an Staidéar Cuimsitheach Teangeolaíoch ar Úsáid aa Gaeilge sa Ghaeltacht: 2006–2011* [*Update of the Comprehensive Linguistic Survey of the Use of Irish in The Gaeltacht: 2006–2011*]. Galway: Údarás na Gaeltachta.

Ó Giollagáin, C. and Pétervárÿ, T. (2016) An pobal Gaelach sa Stát Éireannach: Forbairt agus éigeandáil [The Irish language community in the Irish State: Development and emergency]. In C. Ó Giollagáin and B. Ó Curnáin (eds) *Beartas úr na nGael* [*A New Plan for Irish People*] (pp. 15–58). Galway: Leabhar Breac.

Ó Giollagáin, C., Mac Donnacha, S., Ní Chualáin, F., Ní Shéaghdha, A. and O'Brien, M. (2007) *Comprehensive Linguistic Study of the Use of Irish in The Gaeltacht*. Dublin: Department of Community, Rural and Gaeltacht Affairs.

Ó hÉallaithe, D. (2010) Gaeilge ag 30% de pháistí na Gaeltachta [30% of Gaeltacht children have Irish]. *Gaelscéal* (Irish language newspaper). See http://www.gaelport.com/nuacht?NewsItemID=4955 (accessed 18 October 2013).

Ó Gairbhí, S.T. (2017) Dia idir sin agus Duolingo [God between us and Duolingo]. *Comhar* 77 (4), 4.

Ó hIfearnáin, T. (2007) Raising children to be bilingual in the Gaeltacht: Language preference and practice. *The International Journal of Bilingual Education and Bilingualism* 10 (4), 510–528.

Ó hUiginn, R. (1994) Gaeilge Chonnacht [Connaught Irish]. In K. McCone, D. McManus, C. Ó hÁinle, N. Williams and L. Breatnach (eds) *Stair na Gaeilge: In Ómós do Pádraig Ó Fiannachta* [*The History of Irish: In Honour of Pádraig Ó Fiannachta*] (pp. 539–609). Maynooth: Roinn na Sean-Ghaeilge Coláiste Phádraig.

O'Keefe, A., McCarthy, M. and Carter, R. (2007) *From Corpus to Classroom: Language Use and Language Teaching*. Cambridge: Cambridge University Press.

Ó Laoire, M. (2000) Learning Irish for participation in the Irish language speech community outside the Gaeltacht. *Journal of Celtic Language Learning* 5, 20–33.
Ó Laoire, M. (2004) *Siollabais chumarsáide na Gaeilge* [A Communicative Syllabus for Irish]. Dublin: Coiscéim.
Ó Laoire, M. (2006) Múineadh na Gaeilge agus na Nuatheangacha eile: Polasaí agus Pleanáil Teanga [The teaching of Irish and the other modern languages: Policy and language planning]. In A. Gallagher and M. Ó Laoire (eds) *Language Education in Ireland: Current Practice and Future Needs* (pp. 1–23). Dublin: Irish Association for Applied Linguistics.
Oliver, R. (2002) The patterns of negotiation for meaning in child interactions. *The Modern Language Journal* 86 (1), 97–111.
Oliver, R. and Mackey, A. (2003) Interactional context and feedback in child ESL classrooms. *The Modern Language Journal* 87 (4), 519–533.
Olsen, R. and Kagan, S. (1992) About cooperative learning. In C. Kessler (ed.) *Cooperative Language Learning* (pp. 1–30). Englewood Cliffs, NJ: Prentice-Hall.
O'Malley Madec, M. (2001) English discourse markers in the speech of native speakers of Irish. In B. Ó Catháin and R. Ó hUiginn (eds) *Béalra: Aistí ar theangeolaíocht na Gaeilge* (pp. 260–273). Maigh Nuad: An Sagart.
O'Malley Madec, M. (2007) How one word borrows another: The process of language-contact in two Irish-speaking communities. *International Journal of Bilingual Education and Bilingualism* 10 (4), 494–509.
Ó Murchadha, N.P. and Migge, B. (2017) Support, transmission, education and target varieties in the Celtic languages: An overview. *Language, Culture and Curriculum* 30 (1), 1–12. doi: 10.1080/07908318.2016.1230621
Ó Riagáin, P. (1997) *Language Policy and Social Reproduction: Ireland, 1893–1993*. Oxford: Clarendon.
Ó Riagáin, P. (2000) Irish language production and reproduction 1981–1996. In J.A. Fishman (ed.) *Can Threatened Languages be Saved? Reversing Language Shift, Revisited: A 21st Century Perspective* (pp. 195–214). Clevedon: Multilingual Matters.
Ó Riagáin, P. (2007) Relationships between attitudes to Irish, social class, religion and national identity in the Republic of Ireland and Northern Ireland. *The International Journal of Bilingual Education and Bilingualism* 10 (4), 369–393.
Ó Riagáin, P. (2008) Irish-language policy 1922–2007: Balancing maintenance and revival. In C. Nic Pháidín and S. Ó Cearnaigh (eds) *A New View of the Irish Language* (pp. 55–65). Dublin: Cois Life.
Ó Riagáin, P. and Ó Gliasáin, M. (1979) *All-Irish Primary Schools in the Dublin Area*. Dublin: Linguistics Institute of Ireland.
Ó Riagáin, P., Williams, G. and Vila i Moreno, F.X. (2007) *Young People and Minority Languages: Language Use Outside the Classroom*. Dublin: Centre for Language and Communication Studies, TCD.
O'Rourke, B., and Walsh, J. (2015) New speakers of Irish: Shifting boundaries across time and space. *International Journal of the Sociology of Language*, 231, 63–83.
Ó Tuathaigh, G. (2008) The state and the Irish language: An historical perspective. In C. Nic Pháidín and S. Ó Cearnaigh (eds) *A New View of the Irish Language* (pp. 26–41). Dublin: Cois Life.
Parsons, C. and Lyddy, F. (2009) The sequencing of formal reading instruction: Reading development in bilingual and English-medium schools in Ireland. *International Journal of Bilingual Education and Bilingualism* 12 (5), 493–512.
Pellerin, M. and Hammerly, H. (1986) L'expression orale après treize ans d'immersion française. *The Canadian Modern Language Review* 42, 592–606.
Péterváry, T., Ó Curnáin, B., Ó Giollagáin, C. and Sheahan, J. (2014) *Iniúchadh ar an gCumas Dátheangach: An Sealbhú Teanga i measc Ghlúin Óg na Gaeltachta* [An

Investigation of Bilingual Competence: Langauge Acquisition by the Young Gaeltacht Generation]. Dublin: An Chomhairle um Oideachas Gaeltachta agus Gaelscolaíochta.

Philp, J., Mackey, A. and Oliver, R. (2008) Child's play? Second language acquisition and the younger learner in context. In J. Philp, R. Oliver and A. Mackey (eds) *Second Language Acquisition and the Younger Learner: Child's Play?* (pp. 3–23). Amsterdam: John Benjamins.

Pinter, A. (2011) *Children Learning Second Languages.* London: Palgrave Macmillan.

Pinter, A. (2014) Child participant roles in applied linguistics research. *Applied Linguistics* 35 (2), 168–183. doi: 10.1093/applin/amt008

Polio, C., Gass, S. and Chapin, L. (2006) Using stimulated recall to investigate nativenonnative speaker interaction. *Studies in Second Language Acquisition* 28 (2), 237–267.

Pujolar, J. and Gonzàlez, I. (2013) Linguistic 'mudes' and the de-ethnicization of language choice in Catalonia. *International Journal of Bilingual Education and Bilingualism* 16 (2), 138–152. doi: 10.1080/13670050.2012.720664

Rannóg an Aistriúcháin (2012) *Gramadach na Gaeilge: An Caighdeán Oifigiúil, Caighdeán Athbhreithnithe* [*Irish Grammar: The Official Standard, A Revised Standard*]. Dublin: Stationery Office.

Rannóg an Aistriúcháin (2016) *Gramadach na Gaeilge: An caighdeán oifigiúil* [*Irish Grammar: The Official Standard*]. Dublin: Seirbhís Thithe an Oireachtais [Houses of the Oireachtas Service].

Rannta, L. and Lyster, R. (2007) A cognitive approach to improving immersion students' oral language abilities: The awareness-practice-feedback sequence. In R. DeKeyser (ed.) *Practice in a Second Language: Perspectives from Applied Linguistics and Cognitive Psychology* (pp. 141–160). Cambridge: Cambridge University Press.

Ritchie, W.C. and Bhatia, T.K. (2006) Social and psychological factors in language mixing. In T.K. Bhatia and W.C. Ritchie (eds) *The Handbook of Bilingualism* (pp. 336–352). Oxford: Blackwell.

Romaine, S. (2006) Planning for the survival of linguistic diversity. *Language Policy* 5 (4), 441–473.

Rule, S. (2004) French interlanguage oral corpora: Recent developments. *Journal of French Language Studies* 14 (3), 343–356.

Sato, M. and Lyster, R. (2007) Modified output of Japanese EFL learners: Variable effects of interlocutor versus feedback types. In A. Mackey (ed.) *Conversational Interaction in Second Language Acquisition* (pp. 123–142). Oxford: Oxford University Press.

Schmidt, R.W. (2001) Attention. In P. Robinson (ed.) *Cognition and Second Language Instruction* (pp. 3–32). Cambridge: Cambridge University Press.

Scott, M. (2004) *WordSmith (Version 4).* Oxford: Oxford University Press.

Scott, M. and Tribble, C. (2006) *Textual Patterns: Key Words and Corpus Analysis in Language Education.* Amsterdam: John Benjamins.

Seedhouse, P. (2004) *The Interactional Architecture of the Language Classroom: A Conversation Analysis Perspective.* Oxford: Blackwell.

Sharwood Smith, M. (1993) Input enhancement in instructed SLA: Theoretical bases. *Studies in Second Language Acquisition* 15 (2), 165–179. doi: 10.1017/S0272263100011943

Shehadeh, A. (2002) Comprehensible output, from occurrence to acquisition: An agenda for acquisitional research. *Language Learning* 52 (3), 597–647.

Shiel, G., Gilleece, L., Clerkin, A. and Millar, D. (2011) *The 2010 National Assessments of English Reading and Mathematics in Irish-Medium Schools: Summary Report.* Dublin: Education Research Centre.

Skehan, P. (1994) Second language acquisition strategies, interlanguage development and task-based learning. In M. Bygate (ed.) *Grammar and the Language Teacher* (pp. 175–199). Hemel Hempstead: Prentice-Hall.

Skehan, P. (1996) A framework for the implementation of task-based instruction. *Applied Linguistics* 17 (1), 38–62. doi: 10.1093/applin/17.1.38

Skehan, P. (1998) *A Cognitive Approach to Language Learning*. Oxford: Oxford University Press.

Smith-Christmas, C. (2017) 'Is it really for talking?': The implications of associating a minority language with the school. *Language, Culture and Curriculum* 30 (1), 32–47. doi: 10.1080/07908318.2016.1230619

Smyth, E., and Darmody, M. (2016) *Attitudes to Irish as a school subject among 13-year-olds: Working Paper no. 525*. Dublin: Economic and Social Research Institute.

Spielman-Davidson, S. (2000) Collaborative dialogues in the zone of proximal development, grade eight French immersion students learning the conditional tense. Unpublished PhD thesis, Ontario Institute for Studies in Education, University of Toronto.

Spilka, I. (1976) Assessment of second-language performance in immersion programs. *The Canadian Modern Language Review* 32, 543–561.

Spolsky, B. (2012) Family language policy – the critical domain. *Journal of Multilingual and Multicultural Development* 33 (1), 3–11. doi: 10.1080/01434632.2011.638072

Stern, H.H. (1990) Analysis and experience as variables in second language pedagogy. In B. Harley, P. Allen, J. Cummins and M. Swain (eds) *The Development of Second Language Proficiency* (pp. 93–109). Cambridge: Cambridge University Press.

Stern, H.H. (1992) *Issues and Options in Language Teaching*. Oxford: Oxford University Press.

Swain, M. (1993) The output hypothesis: Just speaking and writing aren't enough. *The Canadian Modern Language Review* 50, 158–164.

Swain, M. (1998) Focus on form through conscious reflection. In C. Doughty and J. Williams (eds) *Focus on Form in Classroom Second Language Acquisition* (pp. 64–81). Cambridge: Cambridge University Press.

Swain, M. (2000) The output hypothesis and beyond: Mediating acquisition through collaborative dialogue. In J.P. Lantolf (ed.) *Sociocultural Theory and Second Language Learning* (pp. 97–114). Oxford: Oxford University Press.

Swain, M. (2005) The output hypothesis: Theory and research. In E. Hinkel (ed.) *Handbook of Research in Second Language Teaching and Learning* (pp. 471–483). Mahwah, NJ: Lawrence Erlbaum Associates.

Swain, M. (2006) Languaging, agency and collaboration in advanced second language proficiency. In H. Byrnes (ed.) *Advanced Language Learning: The Contribution of Halliday and Vygotsky* (pp. 95–108). London: Continuum.

Swain, M. (2013) The inseparability of cognition and emotion in second language learning. *Language Teaching* 46 (2), 195–207. doi: 10.1017/s0261444811000486

Swain, M. and Lapkin, S. (1982) *Evaluating Bilingual Education: A Canadian Case Study*. Clevedon: Multilingual Matters.

Swain, M. and Johnson, R.K. (1997) Immersion education: A category within bilingual education. In R.K. Johnson and M. Swain (eds) *Immersion Education: International Perspectives* (pp. 1–18). Cambridge: Cambridge University Press.

Swain, M. and Lapkin, S. (1998) Interaction and second language learning: Two adolescent French immersion learners working together. *The Modern Language Journal* 82 (3), 320–337.

Swain, M. and Lapkin, S. (2001) Focus on form through collaborative dialogue: Exploring task effects. In M. Bygate, P. Skehan and M. Swain (eds) *Researching Pedagogic Tasks: Second Language Learning, Teaching and Testing* (pp. 99–118). Harlow: Longman.

Swain, M. and Lapkin, S. (2005) The evolving sociopolitical context of immersion education in Canada: Some implications for program development. *International Journal of Applied Linguistics* 15 (2), 169–186. doi: 10.1111/j.1473-4192.2005.00086.x

Swain, M. and Lapkin, S. (2008) Lexical learning through a multitask activity: The role of repetition. In T.W. Fortune and D.J. Tedick (eds) *Pathways to Multilingualism: Evolving Perspectives on Immersion Education* (pp. 119–132). Clevedon: Multilingual Matters.

Swain, M., Kinnear, P. and Steinman, L. (2011) *Sociocultural Theory in Second Language Education*. Bristol: Multilingual Matters.

Tarone, E. and Swain, M. (1995) A sociolinguistic perspective on second language use in immersion classrooms. *The Modern Language Journal* 79 (2), 166–178.

Tedick, D.J. and Wesely, P.M. (2015) A review of research on content-based foreign/second language education in US K-12 contexts. *Language, Culture and Curriculum* 28 (1), 25–40. doi: 10.1080/07908318.2014.1000923

Thomas, E.M. and Gathercole, V.C.M. (2007) Children's productive command of grammatical gender and mutation in Welsh: An alternative to rule-based learning. *First Language* 27 (3), 251–278.

Thomas, E.M. and Roberts, D.B. (2011) Exploring bilinguals' social use of language inside and out of the minority language classroom. *Language and Education* 25 (2), 89–108. doi: 10.1080/09500782.2010.544743

Thomas, E.M., Apolloni, D. and Lewis, G. (2014) The learner's voice: Exploring bilingual children's selective language use and perceptions of minority language competence. *Language and Education* 28 (4), 340–361. doi: 10.1080/09500782.2013.870195

Thordardottir, E. (2011) The relationship between bilingual exposure and vocabulary development. *International Journal of Bilingualism* 15 (4), 426–445. doi: 10.1177/1367006911403202

Tocalli-Beller, A., and Swain, M. (2005) Reformulation: The cognitive conflict and L2 learning it generates. *International Journal of Applied Linguistics*, 15 (1), 5–28.

Turnbull, M. (2002) Cooperative learning in second language classes: Two techniques to consider. In M. Turnbull, J. Bell and S. Lapkin (eds) *From the Classroom: Grounded Activities for Language Learning* (pp. 150–157). Toronto: Canadian Modern Language Review.

Turnbull, M., Lapkin, S. and Hart, D. (2001) Grade 3 immersion students' performance in literacy and mathematics: Province-wide results from Ontario (1998–99). *The Canadian Modern Language Review* 58 (1), 9–26.

Ushioda, E. (2011a) Why autonomy? Insights from motivation theory and research. *Innovation in Language Learning and Teaching* 5 (2), 221–232. doi: 10.1080/17501229.2011.577536

Ushioda, E. (2011b) Language learning motivation, self and identity: Current theoretical perspectives. *Computer Assisted Language Learning* 24 (3), 199–210. doi: 10.1080/09588221.2010.538701

Van den Branden, K. (1997) Effects of negotiation on language learners' output. *Language Learning* 47 (4), 589–636.

Van Lier, L. (2007) Action-based teaching, autonomy and identity. *Innovation in Language Learning and Teaching* 1 (1), 46–65.

VanPatten, B. (1996) *Input Processing and Grammar Instruction in Second Language Acquisition*. Norwood, NJ: Ablex.

VanPatten, B. (2002) Processing instruction: An update. *Language Learning* 52 (4), 755–803.

VanPatten, B. (2016) Why explicit knowledge cannot become implicit knowledge. *Foreign Language Annals* 49 (4), 650–657. doi: 10.1111/flan.12226

VanPatten, B. and Jegerski, J. (2010) *Research in Second Language Processing and Parsing*. Amsterdam: John Benjamins.

Vygotsky, L.S. (1978) *Mind in Society: The Development of Higher Psychological Processes* (M. Cole, V. John-Steiner, S. Scribner and E. Souberman [eds]; A.R. Luria, M. Lopez-Morillas and M. Cole, with J.V. Wertsch [trans.]). Cambridge, MA: Harvard University Press. (Original manuscripts [ca. 1930–1934].)

Walsh, C. (2007) *Cruinneas na Gaeilge Scríofa sna hIar-Bhunscoileanna lán-Ghaeilge i mBaile Átha Cliath* [*The Accuracy of Written Irish in Post-Primary All-Irish Schools in Dublin*]. Dublin: An Chomhairle um Oideachas Gaeltachta agus Gaelscolaíochta.

Walsh, J. and O'Rourke, B. (2015) Mudes teangeolaíocha agus nuachainteoirí na Gaeilge [Linguistic mudes and new speakers of Irish]. *COMHARTaighde, 1* [Internet]. See http://www.comhartaighde.com/eagrain/1/walsh-orourke/walsh-orourke2015.pdf (accessed 26 November 2015). doi:10.18669/ct.2015.09

Walsh, T. (2012) *Primary Education in Ireland, 1897–1990: Curriculum and Context.* Oxford: Peter Lang.

Wang, Y. and Jenkins, J. (2016) 'Nativeness' and intelligibility: Impacts of intercultural experience through English as a lingua franca on Chinese speakers' language attitudes. *Chinese Journal of Applied Linguistics* 39 (1), 38. doi: 10.1515/cjal-2016-0003

Wajnryb, R. (1990) *Grammar Dictation.* Oxford: Oxford University Press.

Wolf, N.M. (2014) *An Irish-Speaking Island: State, Religion, Community, and the Linguistic Landscape in Ireland, 1770–1870.* Madison, WI: The University of Wisconsin Press.

Wolfram, W. (2006) Variation and language: Overview. In K. Brown (ed.) *Encyclopedia of Languages and Linguistics II* (pp. 333–340). Oxford: Elsevier.

Zalbide, M. and Cenoz, J. (2008) Bilingual education in the Basque Autonomous Community: Achievements and challenges. *Language, Culture and Curriculum* 21 (1), 5–20. doi: 10.2167/lcc339.0

Appendix A: Pupil Questionnaire – Attitude/Motivation Test Battery (AMTB)

The questionnaire was administered in Irish – translation provided here.

Ceistneoir an dalta (Pupil questionnaire)

Scoil (school)

(i) Cén rang ina bhfuil tú? What class are you in?	Rang 5 (fifth class) (ROI) ○	Rang 7 (seventh class) (NI) ○	Bliain 4 (fourth year) (ROI) ○	GCSE (NI) ○	
(ii) An buachaill nó cailín tú? Are you a boy or a girl?	Buachaill (Boy) ○	Cailín (Girl) ○			
(iii) Cén aois thú How old are you?	10 ○	11 ○	12 ○	15 ○	16 ○	17 ○
(iv) Cad é an gnáth-theanga a labhraíonn tú sa bhaile? What is your usual home language?	Gaeilge amháin (Irish only) ○	Gaeilge der chuid is mó (mostly Irish) ○	Meascán cothrom de Ghaeilge agus Bhéarla (equal mix of Irish and English) ○	Béarla den chuid is mó (mostly English) ○	Béarla amháin (English only) ○	Teanga eile (language other than Irish or English) ○

Ceisteanna cleachta (Practice questions)

	1: Easaontaím go mór (strongly disagree)	2: Easaontaím beagáinín (disagree)	3: Neodrach (neutral)	4: Aontaím beagáinín (agree)	5: Aontaím go mór (strongly agree)
(A) Is fearr liom banana ná úll. (I prefer bananas to apples.)	○	○	○	○	○
(B) Is fuath liom sceallóga. (I hate chips.)	○	○	○	○	○
(C) Tá laethanta saoire an tsamhraidh ró-fhada. (Summer holidays are too long.)	○	○	○	○	○

Fonn foghlama Gaeilge (Desire to learn Irish) (6 mhír/*items*)

(11)	Dá mbeadh seans agam Gaeilge a labhairt tar éis am scoile, ba mhaith liom iarracht a dhéanamh í a labhairt.	o	o	o	o	o	If there was a chance to speak Irish outside school, I would like to try to speak it.
(26)	Ba mhaith liom freastal ar Chúrsa Samhraidh Ghaeilge.	o	o	o	o	o	I would like to go to a summer course in Irish.
(16)	I gcomparáid le hábhair scoile eile mar an Mhatamaitic agus léitheoireacht an Bhéarla, ní maith liom an Ghaeilge mórán.	o	o	o	o	o	Compared to subjects like maths and English reading, I don't like Irish very much.
(21)	Dá mbeadh teaghlaigh ina labhraítear Gaeilge ina gcónaí in aice liomsa, ba mhaith liom labhairt leo i nGaeilge.	o	o	o	o	o	If there were Irish-speaking families living near me, I would like to speak Irish to them.
(30)	Ba mhaith liom a bheith in ann Gaeilge a labhairt cosúil le cainteoir dúchais.	o	o	o	o	o	I would like to be able to speak Irish like a native speaker.
(8)	Ba mhaith liom níos lú ama a chaitheamh ag foghlaim na Gaeilge ar scoil.	o	o	o	o	o	I would like to spend less time learning Irish at school.

Dearcadh i leith foghlaim na Gaeilge (Attitude to learning Irish) (7 mhír/*items*)

(4)	Is cur amú ama é a bheith ag déanamh staidéir ar an nGaeilge ar scoil.	o	o	o	o	o	Learning Irish in school is a waste of time.
(7)	Nuair a fhágfaidh mé an scoil, éireoidh mé as a bheith ag déanamh staidéir ar an nGaeilge ar fad toisc nach bhfuil aon suim agam inti.	o	o	o	o	o	When I leave school, I will give up learning Irish completely because I am not interested in it.
(11)	Bainim an-taitneamh ar fad as a bheith ag déanamh staidéir ar an nGaeilge ar scoil.	o	o	o	o	o	I really enjoy learning Irish.
(17)	Is ábhar scoile tábhachtach í an Ghaeilge.	o	o	o	o	o	Irish is an important school subject.
(24)	Is fuath liom a bheith ag foghlaim na Gaeilge ar scoil.	o	o	o	o	o	I hate learning Irish at school.
(31)	Tá foghlaim na Gaeilge tábhachtach ach tá foghlaim an Bhéarla níos tábhachtaí.	o	o	o	o	o	Learning Irish is important but learning English is more important.
(2)	Ba mhaith liom an oiread Gaeilge agus is féidir liom a fhoghlaim.	o	o	o	o	o	I would like to learn as much Irish as possible.

Spreagadh ó thuismitheoirí (Parental encouragement) (5 mhír/*items*)

(1)	Déanann mo thuismitheoirí (chaomhnóirí) iarracht cabhair a thabhairt dom le mo chuid Gaeilge.	o	o	o	o	My parents try to help me with my Irish.
(5)	Ceapann mo thuismitheoirí gur chóir dom an Ghaeilge a fhoghlaim, toisc go bhfuil cónaí orainn in Éirinn.	o	o	o	o	My parents feel that because we live in Ireland, I should study Irish.
(15)	Is minic a deir mo thuismitheoirí liom a thábhachtaí is a bheidh an Ghaeilge dom nuair a fhágfaidh mé an scoil.	o	o	o	o	My parents often tell me how important Irish will be for me when I leave school.
(20)	Molann mo thuismitheoirí go mór dom oibriú go dian ar an nGaeilge.	o	o	o	o	My parents really encourage me to work hard at my Irish.
(27)	Spreagann mo thuismitheoirí mé mo chuid Gaeilge a chleachtadh an oiread agus is féidir.	o	o	o	o	My parents encourage me to improve my Irish as much as possible.

Féinchoincheap ar chumas sa Ghaeilge (Irish-ability self-concept) (6 mhír/*items*)

(18)	Dá dtabharfainn cuairt ar an nGaeltacht, bheinn ábalta treoir a lorg agus a leanúint i nGaeilge chun mo bhealach a dhéanamh.	o	o	o	o	If I visited the Gaeltacht I would be able to look for and follow directions to make my way.
(28)	Tá sé deacair an Ghaeilge a labhairt an t-am go léir ar scoil.	o	o	o	o	It is difficult to speak Irish all the time at school.
(6)	Cheapfadh cainteoir dúchais go raibh Gaeilge an-mhaith agam.	o	o	o	o	A native Irish speaker would think that my Irish was very good.
(22)	Spreagann múinteoirí na scoile mé le Gaeilge a labhairt i gcónaí is mé ar scoil.	o	o	o	o	My teachers encourage me to speak Irish always when I am at school.
(23)	Tuigim cainteoirí dúchais gan aon fhadhb nuair a bhíonn siad ag caint as Gaeilge.	o	o	o	o	I understand native speakers without difficulty when they are speaking Irish.
(14)	Labhraím Gaeilge cosúil le cainteoir dúchais.	o	o	o	o	I speak Irish like a native speaker.

Úsáid na Gaeilge (Use of Irish) (13 mhír/items)

(3)	Léim leabhair i nGaeilge uaireanta nach leabhair scoile iad.	o o o o	I sometimes read books in Irish that are not schoolbooks.		
(35)	Le bheith fírinneach, ní dhéanaim mórán iarrachta an Ghaeilge a labhairt lasmuigh den rang nuair a bhím ar scoil.	o o o o	To be honest, I don't really try very hard to learn Irish at school.		
(32)	Is rud tábhachtach dom é Gaeilge a labhairt i gcónaí nuair a bhím ag caint le mo chairde ar scoil.	o o o o	It is important for me to always speak Irish when I am speaking with my friends at school.		
(33)	Labhraím níos mó Béarla ná Gaeilge i gclós na scoile.	o o o o	I speak more English than Irish in the school playground.		
(34)	Tá sé i bhfad níos deacra orm Gaeilge a labhairt ná Béarla.	o o o o	It is much more difficult for me to speak Irish than English.		
(29)	Bheinn míchompordach ag labhairt Gaeilge le mo chairde scoile taobh amuigh d'am agus d'imeachtaí scoile.	o o o o	I would be uncomfortable speaking Irish to my school friends outside of school and school activities.		
(9)	Tuigim go ndéanaim botúin uaireanta nuair a bhím ag labhairt Gaeilge ach bheadh an iomarca trioblóide ann iad a cheartú.	o o o o	I know that I make mistakes when I am speaking Irish but it would be too much trouble to correct them.		
(12)	Bím míchompordach nuair a labhraítear liom as Gaeilge taobh amuigh den scoil.	o o o o	I am uncomfortable when Irish is spoken to me outside of school.		
(13)	Is fearr liom Gaeilge ná Béarla a labhairt le mo chairde ag am sosa.	o o o o	I prefer to speak Irish rather than English to my friends at break-time.		
(19)	B'fhearr liom Matamaitic a fhoghlaim trí Bhéarla seachas trí Ghaeilge.	o o o o	I would prefer to learn maths through English than through Irish.		
(25)	Labhraím Gaeilge go minic lasmuigh d'am agus d'imeachtaí scoile.	o o o o	I often speak Irish outside of school and school activities.		
(36)	Is fuath liom é nuair a labhraíonn nó nuair a dhéanann mo thuismitheoir iarracht Gaeilge a labhairt liom sa bhaile.	o o o o	I hate it when my parent speaks to me or try to speak to me in Irish at home.		
(37)	Níl aon leabhar ar fáil as Gaeilge atá suimiúil le léamh.	o o o o	There are no interesting books available to read in Irish.		

Appendix B: Interview Schedule for Irish/French Immersion Teachers

(1) How many years teaching experience do you have in immersion education?

1–5 years ☐ 6–10 years ☐ 11–14 years ☐ 15–20 years ☐ >20 years ☐

How many years' experience teaching Grades 6/7?

1–5 years ☐ 6–10 years ☐ 11–14 years ☐ 15–20 years ☐ >20 years ☐

(2) What is your own language background?

(3) Pre-service and post-graduate education.

(4) Could you describe the programme for immersion education in your school? (e.g. total early, late, partial, immersion stream within English-medium school, etc.)

(5) When does the teaching of English commence?

(6) What percentage of time is spent teaching through the medium of English in this grade?

(7) What teaching and learning materials are available to support teaching the curriculum through the medium of Irish/French? How adequate are they in your opinion?

(8) What provisions are there for language arts lessons in Irish/French?

(9) I would like to ask you some questions now in relation to the children's proficiency in Irish/French.

   (a) How satisfactory in your opinion is the children's proficiency in Irish/French at the end of Grades 6/7? How would it compare to native speakers of a similar age? Is it a cause for concern?

   (b) How would you describe their fluency?

   (c) Do any issues arise in relation to the accuracy of the pupil's Irish/French? What are the most common errors?

    (d) Can you tell me about the strategies that you adopt when children make grammatical errors in Irish/French?

    (e) What strategies, if any, do you adopt to encourage the children to speak Irish/French?

    (f) Could you describe, to the best of your ability, the exposure the children have to French outside of school? (e.g. opportunities to speak Irish/French, contact with native speakers of French)

    (g) How would you describe the children's attitudes towards learning Irish/French?

(10) Can you tell me about issues discussed at staff meetings in relation to the pupils' proficiency in Irish/French? What is the school policy in this area?

(11) Can you identify any professional development needs that you may have regarding the pupils' proficiency in Irish/French?

(12) Have you any further comments that you would like to make in relation to your pupils' proficiency in Irish/French?

Index

activity 7–8, 34, 68, 110, 115–116, 138, 166
adjective 62, 87, 90, 110
affective filter hypothesis 31
Allen, P. 27, 36, 55
all-Irish school, see also Irish-medium school vii, 1, 6–8, 24, 51, 62–64, 68–69, 76, 81–82, 84, 86, 93–95, 98, 101, 105, 107, 110–113, 135, 147, 150, 171
analytical approach 27, 33, 45, 55–56, 66, 113–114, 157, 170, 174
attainment 5, 16, 52–54, 59, 66, 154, 169
attentional resources 28–30, 65, 159
attitude 4, 20, 38–39, 41, 60–61, 74–76, 142–144, 146, 163, 166–168
Attitude/Motivation Test Battery (AMTB) 39, 41, 74–76, 128, 142–144, 152, 166, 169, 175, 194–199

Baker, C. 3, 37, 41, 53, 139, 149, 171
Basque 3, 111, 139, 151
Béarla, see English
bilingualism 1–2, 7, 11, 13, 16, 26, 46, 70, 82, 139, 141, 171, 177
   additive 47–49, 51

Cammarata, L. 55, 161
Canada 2, 8, 19, 24, 38–39, 46–47, 49, 51, 67, 108, 154, 168
census of population 21–22, 139–140
clause
   infinitival 87, 100
   verbal noun 62, 63, 87–88, 97–107, 112–114, 122–124, 136
code-switching 22–23, 77, 82–86, 111, 113, 136
code-mixing 7, 8, 73, 77, 82–86, 109, 111, 113, 124–126, 135–136, 163, 175
cognitive 28–31, 33–34, 38, 40, 83, 115, 137
collaborative task 7–8, 32, 71, 115, 171
common underlying proficiency 53
communication 24, 29, 38, 41, 49, 56, 65, 72, 86, 158, 173
community language 2, 10, 20, 40
comprehension 27, 49, 51, 57

concord 27, 46, 77–78, 113
content and language integrated learning (CLIL) 136
controlled processing/practice 29–31
Coolahan, J. 13, 14
copula "*is*" 7, 61–64, 83, 88–96, 111–114, 120–122, 136
corpus
   compilation of 4, 7, 46, 67–76, 139, 172, 176
   corpus analysis 5, 77–86, 91, 96, 98, 108–114, 169
corrective feedback 32–33, 42–43, 56, 137, 174
   clarification requests 43, 56
   elicitation 43, 56
   prompts 43, 56, 137, 169
   recasts 43–44, 56
counterbalance hypothesis 56
critical period hypothesis 27, 33
culture 39, 47
Cummins, J. ix, 16, 44, 52, 53
curriculum 5, 9–11, 18, 32, 34, 37, 47, 53–54, 58–59, 154, 162

Darmody, M. 3, 17, 20, 32, 74, 140, 150, 173
Day, E. 38, 70, 111, 169
declarative knowledge 29, 30, 53
design of study 67, 72, 142, 154
Dörnyei, Z. 38, 39, 40, 41, 142, 154
dual-coding 29, 30
dyads 31, 42

early immersion 2, 26–27, 45, 49–51, 56, 65, 69
Ellis, R. 32–33, 35, 37, 38, 41, 44, 72, 134
English
   attainment 52–53, 70
   Béarla 24, 85, 86, 113, 125, 127, 129, 132, 135
   discourse markers 22–23, 82–84, 110–111, 113, 135
   dominant language 22, 35, 41, 51, 113, 135, 140, 146, 166, 168, 172

medium school 1–2, 16, 17, 24, 54, 58, 60, 62, 66, 74, 89
syntax 23, 30, 87–88, 90, 100, 108, 110, 131, 137, 158
translation from 62, 64, 106, 108–109, 131–133, 156–159, 163
use of 22–23, 84, 86, 111, 118, 124–130, 134–136, 146–148, 164, 174
experiential 55, 66, 133, 176
explicit 32–33, 43–45, 114, 134, 138, 174–176
exposure to target language 4, 7, 13, 18, 23, 36–38, 47, 50–51, 70, 134–138, 162–163, 171

focus on form 44–46
 attention 5, 27, 28, 30, 32, 43–45, 56, 65, 90, 112, 118, 120–124, 136–137, 174
 form-meaning connections 28
focus on formS 133–134
formulaic language 29, 57–58, 137
fossilization 50, 114
French immersion 3, 8, 31, 43, 45, 49, 70, 110, 153–170

Gaeilge, see Irish
Gaelscoil, see all-Irish school and Irish-medium school
Gaeltacht
 heartland areas 10, 20–24, 41, 64, 140, 147, 151
 schools 2, 7, 17, 20, 51, 57–58, 68–70, 77–110, 172
Gardner, R.C. 39, 40, 60, 151
Genesee, F. 18, 19, 47, 49–51, 53, 88
genitive case 62, 134
gloss 84
government policy 1, 9–15, 18, 20, 22, 139, 152, 177
 20-Year Strategy for Irish 3, 20, 22, 139, 140, 150, 151
grammar
 accuracy 4–6, 23–24, 36, 49, 55, 72–75, 103, 107, 111–116, 133–134, 115, 157–159, 163, 171–174
 errors 24, 42–44, 61–63, 81–82, 86, 114, 115–116, 120, 131, 136–138, 157–158, 160–161, 169–171
Grin, F. 3, 140, 142, 152, 173

Harley, B. 26, 27, 30, 36, 43, 45, 48, 49, 55, 79

Harris, J. 1, 3, 19, 51, 58–61, 75, 142, 150, 151
Hickey, T. 23, 57, 74, 83, 149, 164
high coverage items 49, 79
hypothesis testing 31, 42, 86

identity 6, 12, 37, 38–41, 60, 66, 68, 141
imagined community 40
immersion, total early 5, 13, 18–19, 27, 47, 50, 69
imperative mood 36, 99, 101, 158
implicit 27, 32–33, 36, 45, 55, 134, 137–138
initial mutation (lenition and eclipsis) 86–88
input
 hypothesis 31, 49
 language 26–33, 41, 44–45, 54, 57, 63, 65, 83, 96, 137, 175–176
 processing 28–29, 31, 33, 44, 65
interaction hypothesis 31
interactionist approach 6, 30, 31–32, 41
interface hypothesis 31–32
interlanguage 7, 24, 27–30, 32, 37–38, 46, 50, 54, 56, 65–66, 131, 137–138, 160
Irish language 3–4, 11–23, 58, 60–61, 139, 151
 network 3, 22, 24, 140, 151, 176–177
 new speaker 3–4, 8, 21–23, 139, 141, 173, 177
 speaking 3, 10, 13, 24, 40, 64, 70, 141, 176
 use in society 5, 6, 18, 20, 33, 37, 149–150, 171, 177
 variety 3–4, 6, 22–24, 64, 67, 130–133, 141, 173
Irish-medium school 2, 8, 10–11, 15–21, 163
Irish verbs 7, 19, 36, 51, 61–64, 83, 87–103, 111–113, 121–122, 133, 158
 déan 88–90, 98, 102–103, 106, 112
 faigh 89–90, 98, 101–103, 112
 copula "*is*" 7, 61–64, 83, 88–96, 111–114, 120–122, 136
 cuir 88, 98–100, 102–103, 112

language maintenance 3, 15
language-related episodes 85–86, 111
languaging 34, 65, 175
Lapkin, S. ix, 27, 31, 44, 47, 48, 53, 86, 108, 138, 153
learner autonomy 35, 40, 45, 65
learner involvement 35–36, 65

linguistic features 7–8, 26–28, 62–66, 70–72, 86–105, 113–116, 126–135, 157–159, 176
Little, D. 35, 36, 175
Long, M. 31, 38, 44, 45
long-term memory 29, 137, 151
Lyster, R. 3, 5, 24, 27, 30, 32, 36, 42, 43, 55, 56, 72, 110, 114, 137, 154, 174

meaning-focused 38, 44, 113,
memory-based system 29–30, 137
metalinguistic clues 56
metalinguistic feedback 43
metalinguistic function 32
minority language viii, 5, 8, 11, 15–16, 26, 37, 40, 52, 66, 137, 141–142, 150–152, 171, 173
mistakes, see errors
morphology (of verbs) 7, 19, 51, 59, 86–90, 98, 100, 102–103, 113, 136
motivation 4, 8, 22, 37, 38–41, 50, 60–62, 74–75, 111, 142, 169, 175, 177
Murtagh, L. 2, 3, 51, 58, 60, 75, 140

Naíonra 16, 56–58
National Council for Curriculum and Assessment (NCCA) 1, 7, 18
native speaker 1, 3–4, 6–7, 13, 21, 23–24, 33, 68, 70, 81, 84, 103, 111, 114, 137–138, 141, 168, 176
native-like 6, 18, 35–36, 38, 51, 133, 171, 177
negotiation for meaning 31, 41, 55, 86
new speaker, see Irish language
Ní Dhiorbháin, A. 56, 103, 114, 174, 175
NigUidhir, G. (Maguire) 4, 37, 64
Ní Thuairisg, L. 10, 48, 60, 76, 142, 174
non-target-like 1, 4, 24, 49, 65–67, 71, 96, 114, 116, 173, 176
Northern Ireland 1, 4, 6, 9–11, 17, 21, 24, 63–64, 67, 153, 168
Noticing 27–28, 31–32, 38, 65, 118–121, 129, 134–138, 176
Noun 45, 62, 87, 90, 95, 105–106, 108, 113
numbers in Irish 94–95, 112–113

Ó Cathalláin, S. 4, 140, 163
Ó Duibhir, P. 17, 18, 35, 37, 44, 48, 53, 56, 60, 74, 76, 112, 114, 139, 140, 142, 143, 151, 162, 168, 174, 175
Ó Giollagáin, C. 2, 11, 15, 20, 23, 51, 65, 69, 139, 146, 147, 151
Ó Laoire, M. 3, 59, 60, 139, 140

Ontario ix, 74
opportunities to use target language 20, 140, 152, 163, 200
Ottawa ix, 4, 8, 53, 67, 153–155, 163, 172
output 31, 32, 34, 42, 50, 65, 72, 114, 136, 166, 175

parents 6, 16, 26, 46, 51, 60, 76, 140–143, 147–152, 163, 171–172
pedagogical practices 4, 25, 28, 47, 122, 157, 174–176
peer correction 160, 173
post-primary school 4, 13, 16, 17, 21, 23, 61, 74–75, 89, 112, 142–151, 174, 176
preposition 62, 88, 103
present tense 36, 61, 63, 92, 96–97, 101
primary school 1, 4, 5, 7, 16, 19, 37, 57–58, 69, 74, 141 143, 168, 173, 174
procedural knowledge 29, 30, 53
production 5, 8, 29, 36, 46, 49, 56, 57, 73, 84, 90, 96, 110, 171, 177
proficiency 1, 3–5, 7–8, 23–24, 38, 47–51, 64, 74, 110, 153–171
pronoun 7, 63, 80, 87, 89–90, 92–94, 103–108, 111–113, 121–122, 176

quality of language 27, 82, 115–118, 126, 168, 174, 175
questionnaire 8, 76, 143, 145, 172, 194–198

recasts 43–44, 56
reflection 8, 31, 35–36, 50, 56, 65–66, 72–73, 115–138, 175
repetition 43, 56
Republic of Ireland 1, 9, 17, 58, 62, 67, 139, 153, 155
revitalization 2, 3, 7, 11–12, 14–15, 20–23, 140

salience 28, 36, 45
scaffolding 34, 65
school principals 155–170
Scotland 2, 24, 52, 54, 139
second language acquisition (SLA) 5, 19, 23–24, 26–28, 32–37, 54–57, 63–65, 114, 138, 171, 174
semantic processing 45, 65, 175
sentences 63, 82, 87, 108, 128, 157, 159
short-term memory 28–29, 32
Skehan, P. 28–30, 39, 49, 134, 137, 159, 174
sociocultural 6, 33–46, 65, 72, 138, 164
standardised type token ratio 77–78

stimulated-recall activity 7, 68, 72–73, 76, 114–138, 154, 159, 163, 169, 174, 175
substantive verb, see Irish verbs
SVO (subject verb object) 87
Swain, M. 24, 27, 31–40, 44–50, 53, 72, 86, 108, 115, 136, 157, 175
syntactic processing 35, 45, 175
syntax 5, 7, 23, 28, 48, 50, 59, 63–64, 87, 90, 106, 108–110, 113, 133, 157

teacher education 46, 103, 137
teacher interviews 153–170
Tedick, D. 48, 52, 55, 157, 161, 169, 174
Thomas, E. 3, 23, 37, 70, 128, 130, 146, 151, 159, 164, 169, 172, 175, 177
Toronto 4, 8, 53, 67, 74, 153–155, 163, 172
translanguaging 132, 137
translation, see English

universal grammar (UG) 6, 26, 137

VanPatten, B. 28, 134, 137
vernacular 6, 12, 37, 141
vocabulary 23, 27, 48, 54, 59, 70, 77, 84, 110, 157, 159
VSO (verb subject object) 63, 87, 90, 108

Wales
　Welsh medium 23, 54, 128, 146, 164, 175
　Welsh language 3, 23
Walsh, C. 61–62, 89, 112, 114, 176
whole-school 17, 161, 165, 176
willingness to speak target language 8, 140, 149, 163–166
WordSmith 71, 77, 78, 113

young learners and speakers 23–24, 27, 29–30, 33, 40–41, 45, 50, 84, 169, 176

zone of proximal development (ZPD) 34–35, 50, 65

For Product Safety Concerns and Information please contact our EU Authorised Representative:

Easy Access System Europe

Mustamäe tee 50

10621 Tallinn

Estonia

gpsr.requests@easproject.com

www.ingramcontent.com/pod-product-compliance
Lightning Source LLC
Chambersburg PA
CBHW070608300426
44113CB00010B/1450